The Protection Roles of UN Human Rights Special Procedures

Nijhoff Law Specials

VOLUME 74

The Protection Roles of UN Human Rights Special Procedures

By

Dr. Bertrand G. Ramcharan, Ll.B. (Hons.) (Lon.), Ll.M, Ph.D. (LSE)
Barrister-at-Law (Lincoln's Inn)
Professor of International Human Rights Law, the Graduate Institute, Geneva
Chancellor of the University of Guyana

MARTINUS NIJHOFF PUBLISHERS

LEIDEN • BOSTON
2009

This book is printed on acid-free paper.

Library of Congress Cataloging-in-Publication Data

Ramcharan, B. G.
The protection roles of UN human rights special procedures / by Bertrand G. Ramcharan.
p. cm.
Includes bibliographical references and index.
ISBN 978-90-04-17147-3 (pbk. : alk. paper) 1. Human rights monitoring. 2. United Nations. 3. Human rights—International cooperation. I. Title.
K3240.R36 2008
341.4'8—dc22

2008045762

ISSN 0924-4549
ISBN 978 90 04 17147 3

PRINTED IN THE NETHERLANDS

CONTENTS

The General Assembly …"Approves the methods of work employed by the Special Rapporteur, in particular as regards urgent appeals, reiterates his need to be able to respond effectively to credible and reliable information that comes before him, invites him to continue to seek the views and comments of all concerned, including Member States, in the elaboration of his report, and expresses its appreciation of the continuing discrete and independent way in which he carries out his work."[1]

1 A/RES/51/86 of February 7, 1997, para. 7. The General Assembly was considering the work of the Special Rapporteur against torture.

FOREWORD

The United Nations is in the process of modernizing and updating its human rights machinery in the hope of raising the level of international protection of human rights. That is the fundamental goal, consistent with the General Assembly's affirmation of its commitment to the responsibility to protect. The Human Rights Council, which began functioning in 2006, is meant to spearhead efforts to implement the responsibility to protect, and its human rights special procedures – its fact-finding rapporteurs and working groups – are its first-line agents in the quest for international protection.

The Human Rights Council has reaffirmed that special procedures mandate-holders are independent United Nations experts charged with acting in an independent capacity and with exercising their functions in accordance with their mandates, through a professional, impartial assessment of facts based on internationally recognized standards, and free from any kind of extraneous influence, incitement, pressure, threat or interference, either direct or indirect, on the part of any party. The Council has urged all States to cooperate with, and assist, the special procedures in the performance of their tasks and to provide all information in a timely manner, as well as respond to communications transmitted to them by the special procedures without undue delay.

As the system of human rights special procedures goes forward to deal with the continuing and new challenges of human rights protection it is of great value to record and recall the considerable body of practice and precedents they have developed for the protection of human rights since the first special procedure was established in the mid 1960s. That is the particular merit of this path-breaking book, which brings out the following:

- Special procedures have insisted that it is for the United Nations to determine the means and methods of responding to situations of gross violations of human rights.
- Special procedures have established that no State may opt out of their obligations under the United Nations Charter and international human rights and humanitarian law.
- Special procedures have consistently affirmed that their methods of work must be influenced by the needs for protection in each situation.
- Special procedures have worked on the basis of state, individual, corporate, and international responsibility for gross violations of human rights.

- Special procedures have provided early warning of threatened gross violations of human rights and have called on the international community to contribute to preventive human rights strategies.
- Special procedures have issued public appeals, sent urgent letters to Governments, and acted in various ways to provide preventive and remedial protection for those at risk.
- Special procedures have visited countries and undertaken different measures to help mitigate and stop gross violations of human rights.
- Special procedures have sought to serve as channels of remedies, redress, and compensation for gross violations of human rights.
- Special procedures have examined and investigated the protection challenges thrown up by an evolving international community of new risks and challenges.
- Special procedures have engaged in brilliant advocacy on behalf of human rights protection, especially in dealing with the challenges of poverty and the implementation of basic economic, social, and cultural rights.

The author of this work, who was one of the pioneers in the establishment and operation of the system of special procedures, tells in this book the story of the establishment, history, operations, successes and challenges of the special procedures through the lens of efforts for international protection. In the introduction he summarises their protection roles, which he sets out further in the substantive chapters. In the conclusion he provides an assessment of their protection roles. He notes that while they contribute greatly, the challenges of international protection are still many, and the author invites the international community to a higher level of protection.

For these efforts, and for his own contribution to the international protection of human rights over the years, we are truly appreciative.

Peter Maurer
Ambassador and Permanent Representative of Switzerland
United Nations, New York
27 April, 2008

THE PROTECTION ROLE OF SPECIAL PROCEDURES

"Special procedures contribute to the protection of human rights by responding in a timely manner to situations of actual or threatened violations of human rights by contributing to the identification of threats to population groups and individuals, by undertaking visits to trouble spots, by making recommendations on law, policy, practice and corrective measures to governments and to the Human Rights Council, by calling for the wide dissemination of their findings, and by calling upon the governments and peoples of the UN to act effectively for the protection of human rights in discharge of the UN Charter's mandate on the universal protection of human rights.

"UN human rights special procedures mobilize the global community to protect the rights of actual and potential victims. The information and analysis from their reports and related recommendations help to empower groups and individuals in protecting their rights. They also alert the international community to urgent human rights situations which require effective measures to protect human rights.

"Visits by special procedures to victims, key locations and places where situations of concern manifest themselves such as situations where the right of self-determination is involved, prisons and places of detention, situations of displacement and locations where people are threatened with evictions and displacement, are, among others, an important part of the protection activities they engage in.

EARLY WARNING AND URGENT ACTION

"Urgent actions are an essential part of the work of special procedures. They concern actual and impending threats which need to be responded to expeditiously and effectively. It is crucial to identify governmental focal points which can address such actions in a timely and responsive manner.

...

"Special procedures help to activate the world community as an early warning mechanism and form an intrinsic part of the efforts of the UN and the international community to give effect to the responsibility to protect human rights and to maintain a global watch over human security. Non-response to early warnings from special procedures could have, and have had, devastating human rights consequences and call into question the credibility of the UN and the international community. The General Assembly and the Security Council's commitment to act on the responsibility to protect, particularly as regards genocide, ethnic cleansing, war crimes, and crimes against humanity, needs to be noted in this regard."

The Lund Statement to the UN Human Rights Council
on the Human Rights Special Procedures[2]

2 See UN document HRC/5/18 0f 13 June, 2007, paras. 23-25 and 33-34. The Lund Statement was drafted by a group of human rights experts. The author chaired the drafting sessions that produced the statement. See, generally, L.S. Sunga, "Introduction to the Lund Statement to the United Nations Human Rights Council on the Human Rights Special Procedures", 76 Nordic Journal of International Law (2007), pp 1-20.

INTRODUCTION

The Special Rapporteurs, representatives, envoys, working groups and similar 'special procedures' of the Human Rights Council are among the most important human rights protection actors of the United Nations in the world today. They deal with issues of civil and political rights, economic and social rights, and invoke international human rights law as well as international humanitarian law, as pertinent to the situations or issues they deal with. They focus on thematic issues or on country situations, as decided upon by the Human Rights Council.[3]

In the days of the Cold War, some powerful countries of the Eastern bloc viewed with disfavour the idea that the UN would engage in 'fact-finding' into situations where gross violations of human rights were alleged to be taking place. The United Nations Secretariat therefore decided to designate the team servicing these fact-finding bodies, successively, the 'Special Procedures' unit/section/branch/Division. A restructuring of the Office of High Commissioner for Human Rights in 1997 abolished the Special Procedures Branch but it was re-established in 2003/2004.[4]

In their initial conception, 'special procedures' were meant to perform one or more of four crucial functions: studies and analyses of situations, fact-finding and reporting, urgent action to protect those at risk, and advice to government(s) directly concerned, as well as to the then Commission on Human Rights, now the Human Rights Council. Although these four functions are at the heart of the concept, over the years the tasks assigned to them have expanded.[5] The special procedures in existence perform one or more of the following protection functions:

- They contribute to protection through studies, analyses, recommendations and the development of norms.
- They contribute to protection in providing channels and fora for the victims of human rights violations to publicize their plight.
- They contribute to protection through fact-finding.
- They contribute to protection through advocacy.
- They contribute to protection through their efforts for the prevention of

---

3 See the Bibliography at the end of this work.

4 The author, as the then High Commissioner for Human Rights a.i. re-established the Branch.

5 See, generally, B.G. Ramcharan, The Quest for Protection: A Human Rights Journey at the United Nations. Geneva, The Human Rights Observatory, 2005.

violations, including urgent action and appeals.

- They contribute to containment and mitigation through their transmittals of complaints to Governments and through visits on the spot.
- They contribute to protection through their efforts for justice and reconciliation.
- They contribute to protection through their efforts to promote and in some instances provide redress and remedies .
- They contribute to protection through their follow-up activities.
- They are pioneering new approaches to the protection of economic, social and cultural rights. This is being done by mandate holders on food, health, shelter, extreme poverty, development, and international solidarity.

The then Commission on Human Rights appointed the first investigative rapporteur in 1967 to deal with the situation of human rights in *apartheid* South Africa and later with the situation in occupied Palestine after the 1967 Arab-Israeli war. The first fact-finding working group, to look into the human rights consequences of the apartheid regime in South Africa, was established by the Commission in 1968. In 1969 the General Assembly established a Special Committee to look into the situation of human rights in the Arab Occupied Territories. It is still in existence and has been the subject of vehement objections by Israel. The second working group of the Commission on Human Rights was established in 1975 to deal with the situation of human rights in Chile after General Augusto Pinochet's overthrow of the democratically elected government of President Salvador Allende.

The use of such human rights investigators was brought into broader use in the second half of the 1970s at the suggestion of the then Director of the Human Rights Division of the United Nations Secretariat, Dr. Theodoor van Boven.[6] He first suggested the appointment of a Special Rapporteur on the situation in Chile to take over from a labour-extensive five-person working group that had initially investigated allegations of human rights violations in that country. Then, when it proved difficult to obtain the appointment of a Special Rapporteur to deal with disappearances in Argentina, he worked with partners on the establishment, instead, of a thematic working group, the Working Group on Enforced and Involuntary Disappearances.[7] He also canvassed the designation of the first thematic rapporteur, on arbitrary and summary executions, to use the terminology of the period.[8]

6 See, generally, Theodoor C. Van Boven, People Matter. 1982, Meulenhoff.

7 See, generally, D.Livermore and B.G. Ramcharan, "Enforced and Involuntary Disappearances. An Evaluation of a Decade of United Nations Action, Canadian Human Rights Yearbook, 1989-1990, pp. 217-230.

8 See Chapter II below.

The emphasis at the time was on studies, analyses, and fact-finding and it took some effort to secure that the rapporteur/working group could engage in urgent action where violations of human rights appeared imminent. This is now a standard feature of the operations of special procedures. The number of special procedures, and their functions, have grown immensely since those early years and nowadays there are over three dozen special procedures[9].

Although there is no other group of United Nations human rights actors playing a more important direct protection role at the present time, the scope of that protection role has, thirty years later, hardly been brought to the fore with a view to highlighting their protection practices and helping steer the special procedures towards stronger protection roles in the future. That is the aim of this work: to focus on the protection role of the special procedures with a view to the identification of options for enhanced human rights protection in the future.

Human rights protection can be classified into preventive, mitigatory, and remedial protection.[10] This volume will try to look at the role of the special procedures through these three lens. The evidence suggests that up to now the special procedures engage mainly in post – violations fact-finding, mostly mitigatory efforts, a modest amount of remedial or compensatory work, and incipient preventive action. It will be suggested that in the future greater emphasis should be placed on preventive strategies. As a matter of theory, practicality and justice, protection strategies should emphasize the prevention of gross violations of human rights.[11]

An opening chapter first presents challenges of international protection in our times, followed by chapters on the origins and essence of the special procedures and on the foundations of human rights fact-finding, the protection roles of country mandates, the protection roles of thematic mandates, prevention, urgent action, mitigation through the transmittal of communications and visits on the spot, fact-finding, remedies and advocacy. Some general conclusions are offered at the end.

It will be submitted that notwithstanding the obstacles placed in their way, the special procedures are sorely needed to document and draw the attention of the international community to gross violations of human rights, to draw the attention of the world to situations where urgent action is needed, and to help

9 For a list of the contemporary special procedures, see the website of the Office of High Commissioner for Human Rights, www.ohchr.org.

10 See B.G. Ramcharan, *The Concept of Protection in the International Law of Human Rights*. Martinus Nijhoff, 1988.

11 See B.G.Ramcharan (Ed.), *Conflict Prevention in Practice*. Martinus Nijhoff, 2005. B.G. Ramcharan, "Contemporary Challenges of Human Rights Protection: A Call for Preventive Strategies in 37 *Rutgers Law Review*, No,2, Winter 2006, pp 495 – 516. L-A Alexander (Ed.), *The Prevention of Gross Violations of Human Rights*. Martinus Nijhoff, 2000.

the United Nations perform and strengthen its contribution to the protection of human rights across the globe. The special procedures are first-line actors in the discharge of the international community's responsibility to protect.

We shall suggest at the end that there is need to designate a Special Rapporteur on the promotion and protection of democratic governance to fill a gap in an area of structural importance for the future of human rights in the world.

Chapter I

CONTEMPORARY CHALLENGES OF INTERNATIONAL PROTECTION

INTRODUCTION

The need for international protection of human rights has never been greater. The delivery of international protection remains limited. The challenges of international protection are many in a world of poverty, conflicts, terrorism, state and non-state violence on their own population, inequality and poor governance in many societies. The United Nations General Assembly has endorsed the concept of the responsibility to protect but this has so far not been translated into practical action. This is one of the great challenges before the human rights movement.

The human rights treaty bodies are still, for the most part, engaged in exercises of persuasion, although the views they render on individual petitions have helped generate a significant international jurisprudence in favour of protection. The newly established Human Rights Council places the accent on dialogue and cooperation even in the face of gross violations of human rights. In the General Assembly and the Human Rights Council the majority of the membership of the UN is against 'confrontational' approaches – even when faced with conscience-shocking situations.

The Security Council is a political body responsible for the maintenance of international peace and security and, while contributing to human rights protection to the extent it can, places a premium on political approaches. The International Court of Justice deals with specific cases or requests for advisory opinions. The Secretary-General of the UN has overarching responsibilities and contributes occasionally, leaving the field to the Human Rights Council and the High Commissioner for Human Rights. The High Commissioner wears moral, political and administrative hats and is subject to different kinds of pressures as she tries to fulfil her responsibilities. She has placed the accent on national capacity-building and field activities, and uses her voice from time to time. The *ad hoc* international criminal tribunals have broken new ground in international justice but are facing financial challenges and the International Criminal Court has only just begun its journey of protection – in the face of stiff opposition by the world's pre-eminent power. In specialized agencies such as the ILO there seems to be more emphasis these days on cooperative approaches rather than the historical approach of measuring compliance and providing redress.

In this chapter we shall endeavour to assess some of the contemporary challenges of international protection with a view to seeing how the quest for protection might be taken forward in the coming years. It is appropriate that we begin with the political phenomena affecting the delivery of international protection

I. THE POLITICAL DIMENSIONS OF INTERNATIONAL PROTECTION

Gross violations of human rights are rampant throughout the world. The annual reports of Amnesty International, Human Rights Watch and other human rights organizations have convincing evidence of this. So do the reports of human rights 'special procedures', the experts of the Human Rights Council dealing with country situations and thematic global problems. The reports of the UN High Commissioner for Human Rights also bear witness to this. But how to respond to these violations is highly problematic because of the following political phenomena:

- Governments accused of gross violations of human rights rally political support among the majority of UN members who band together for a variety of reasons: they are afraid of interference by outside powers into their internal affairs; they provide mutual support for their own self-protection or for the defence of their particular interests; and they simply do not wish to be subjected to international criticism, whatever is taking place inside their own countries. In politics the majority rules and the result, for human rights is defensiveness on the part of the majority. The international protection of human rights suffers as a result.
- In the aftermath of the terrorist attacks in the United States on 11 September 2001 western powers, mainly, invaded Afghanistan and Iraq while a significant body of opinion in the international Islamic world appears to think that their brethren in Palestine are left to fend for themselves forty years after the commencement of foreign occupation. There is great distrust and dissension among countries of different philosophical or religious persuasions. The membership of the Islamic Conference, which consists of 57 UN member states, comes to the support of their brethren.
- As a 'war against terrorism' is pursued globally, even leading champions of human rights claim the right to act at variance with international human rights norms. Claims about torture, renditions, abductions and similar practices diminish their moral stature as defenders of human rights.

- There are shocking situations of political corruption in different parts of the world where rulers maintain themselves in power at all costs, even overriding the will of the electorate. Moral condemnation has been high in respect of some of these situations. But at the end of the day, regional and international leaders are left to pursue political methods of reconciliation and settlement as best they can. There is no international authority that can impose its writ. The result is that international good offices or mediation is often the best that can be tried.
- United Nations or regional peacekeepers are already deployed in over sixteen countries and the supply of such peace operation personnel is scarce. What's more, countries are, for the most part, rarely willing to place their own soldiers in harm's way in the quest for protection – and western countries provide fewer and fewer peacekeepers, even if they are main financers of peacekeeping operations.
- Principled stances against gross violations of human rights rarely receive the international backing needed to make them meaningful. Instead, the international actor, such as the special procedure or the UN High Commissioner, is often left to face withering assaults as the majority pleads the mantra of dialogue and cooperation instead of 'confrontation'
- As more and more people move across borders in search of better life-chances developed countries put up stronger walls against them and those who manage to get in face numerous problems of discrimination and inequality. Even developed countries that champion international human rights norms find it inconvenient when faced with norms for the protection of the basic human rights of migrant workers and their families.

The seven phenomena enumerated above are not likely to go away soon and the quest for international protection comes up against them. What do we find in practice? The contribution of the UN human rights special procedures is a good place to start because, in our submission, they are the first among the international protection actors – even if, overall, all the international protection actors are weak.

II. POLICIES AND PRACTICE OF UN HUMAN RIGHTS SPECIAL PROCEDURES: THE STRONGEST INTERNATIONAL PROTECTION ACTORS

The policies and practice of UN human rights special procedures may, in our submission, be presented as follows: mindful of their mandates, they pursue free choices of methods with the aim, usually, of assisting in the restoration of respect of human rights, preventing violations if possible, and protecting people at risk to the extent possible. They engage in dialogue and cooperation, humanitarian approaches, attempt to engage in facilitation, provide advice and technical assistance, engage in advocacy, undertake studies, promote standard-setting, perform early-warning functions, seek to help contain and mitigate violations, document violations for the record, denounce violators, seek to provide redress, and help support the quest for justice for victims. We discuss these different facets below keeping in mind that the fundamental rationale of human rights special procedures is to help protect people at risk and to serve the cause of justice.

i) **Implement the mandate:** The basic starting point, as the Human Rights Council has underlined in its code of conduct for special procedures, is that special procedures should respect their mandates. While doing this, however, there has been and continues to be considerable margin for the mandate holder to *interpret* the mandate in a sense that is favourable to the promotion and protection of human rights.

ii) **Choose the methods of implementation deemed most appropriate by the mandate-holder:** It is broadly accepted that, in pursuing the mandate established, special procedures mandate holders may choose the methods of implementation they consider most appropriate to the tasks before them. This provides considerable leeway, while at the same time, requiring respect for fundamental rules of due process.

iii) **Dialogue and cooperation:** The General Assembly and the Human Rights Council, in recent times, have placed a premium on dialogue and cooperation in the approach of mandate holders to the implementation of their responsibilities. It needs to be remembered always, however, that the purpose of dialogue and cooperation is to bring about effective protection and promotion of human rights.

iv) **Humanitarian/facilitatory approach:** From the outset of its mandate, the Working Group on Enforced and Involuntary Disappearances has pursued a humanitarian/facilitatory approach in seeking to help clarify the fate of 'disappeared persons'. It continues to hold to this line to this day. This author had cause recently to put to a recent Chairperson of the Working Group the submission of one of his students at the Geneva Graduate Institute of International and Development Studies that the Group should, in the circumstances of today, shift gear to a justice-oriented approach. The Chairperson was firm in his assessment that a facilitatory approach allowed the Group to deal with many situations that would be closed off to it by a justice-oriented approach.

v) **Assistance for the restoration of human rights:** All special procedures mandate holders endeavour to assist the process of restoring respect of human rights in the country (ies) covered by their mandate.

vi) **Efforts for early warning and prevention:** Some mandate-holders have provided early warning of potential problems through their studies, analyses, and advocacy. Some have provided early warning of potential atrocities in specific situations. The Special Rapporteur on extra-judicial, arbitrary and summary executions did this – alas to no avail – in alerting the international community to the dangers of a genocide in Rwanda in 1993.

vii) **Efforts for protection:** Different approaches have been pursued by mandate-holders in the effort to help protect people at risk. The dispatch of urgent telegrams or the issuance of public statements are cases in point. There is always a risk that the mandate-holder might not get the facts or the emphasis right. But there has to be latitude here because the aim is to help protect people from serious violations before they occur, if possible.

viii) **Mitigation and containment:** The visits on the spot or to neighbouring regions that mandate holders undertake can help mitigate or contain a situation.

ix) **Studies:** Both country-based and thematic mandate holders have carried out valuable studies that helped to identify groups at risk or to chart courses for protection in the future.

x) **Standard-setting:** Some mandate holders have contributed to the development of international standards needed for the prevention of gross violations and for the protection of people at risk. The Guiding Principles on Internal Displacement, the Declaration and then Convention on 'disappearances', and the 'deliberations' of the Working Group on Arbitrary Detention are examples of this.

xi) **Advocacy:** Some mandate-holders have engaged in strong advocacy for the better protection of human rights. This has been particularly the case with economic and social rights mandate-holders. The Special Rapporteurs on Violence Against Women have also had a good record of advocacy for the protection of the rights of women.

xii) **Documenting violations for the record:** A mandate-holder might come to the conclusion, especially where cooperation is lacking on the part of a government or governments, that the rationale for his or her existence is to document the violations for the record in the hope that future generations, nationally, regionally or internationally would be able to draw on the information in bringing perpetrators to justice or in drawing lessons for the prevention of similar violations in the future.

xiii) **Denouncing violators:** A mandate holder might conclude that the violations are so egregious and persistent that he or she has no choice but to denounce the violators and to continue doing so until there is change in the situation.

xiv) **Be a voice for the victims:** Some mandate holders have considered that they, and their activities and reports, should serve to give the victims a voice at the international level. The Special Rapporteur on Indigenous Peoples is an example of this.

xv) **Help provide redress:** The approach of the Working Group on Arbitrary Detention, from the outset, has been to consider allegations of arbitrary detention in a quasi-judicial procedure and to pronounce on whether the detention has in fact been arbitrary or not.

xvi) **Help support the quest for justice:** In some instances mandate-holders have identified specific individuals allegedly guilty of international crimes and have called for them to be brought to justice. The *Ad Hoc* Working Group on Human Rights in Southern Africa published the names of persons whom it accused of committing the crimes of genocide and apartheid.

Having identified the contribution of the special procedures to protection, we need to recognize that they are under considerable pressure from the membership of the UN to pursue lighter approaches. This pressure comes from western developed countries as well as from developing countries. The former find it inconvenient when the special procedures scrutinize them on, for example, their immigration practices or their anti-terrorism practices, while the latter object when they are exposed for gross violations of human rights. It is our assessment that on a scale of one to ten, the special procedures, while achieving the highest rating of any international entity, do not rise above three when it comes to actual protection.[12]

III. THE PROTECTION ROLE OF UN HUMAN RIGHTS TREATY BODIES

Human rights treaty bodies monitor the implementation of international human rights norms and make an important contribution to reinforcing the international protection framework. The Human Rights Committee which operates under the International Covenant on Civil and Political Rights, in its General Comment No. 6, declared that the right to life in Article 6 of the Covenant is the supreme right from which no derogation is permitted even in time of public emergency, and also, that it is the duty of States to prevent wars.

Furthermore, its General Comment No. 14 declared that nuclear weapons are among the greatest threats to the right to life that confront mankind today, and that the production, testing, possession, deployment and use of those

12 See on this, B.G. Ramcharan, Contemporary Human Rights Ideas. London, Routledge, 2008.

weapons should be prohibited and recognized as crimes against humanity.

Human rights treaty bodies consider and comment on reports, may consider and pronounce upon petitions, and may make visits to countries. In all three instances human rights treaty bodies contribute to the clarification and implementation of the protection concept.

Some human rights treaty bodies have established a practice according to which, in times of emergency, they request emergency reports from States parties. The Human Rights Committee has, since 1991, developed a procedure applicable to emergency situations. Under the procedure the Committee has requested urgent reports from more than a dozen states. In most cases the States parties were requested to submit the reports within three months. Reports thus submitted have been considered by the Committee as soon as possible, usually at the next scheduled session.

In 1995 a coalition of NGOs from one State party drew the attention of the Committee on Economic Social and Cultural Rights to imminent changes in the social welfare laws which might be construed as detrimental to implementation of the economic covenant in that country. The NGOs submitted written materials and sought and obtained the consent of the Committee to address it during the session set aside for NGO submissions. The Committee agreed that its chairperson would communicate the allegations to the government and solicit its views on the matter (E/C.12/1995/SR 4 and 5).

General Comment No. 31 adopted by the Human Rights Committee on 26 May 2004 is a superb example of the protection concept of the Committee. A State Party must respect and ensure the rights in the Covenant to anyone within its power or effective control. The obligations in the Covenant in general and under Article 2 in particular are binding on every State Party as a whole. All branches of government (executive, legislative and judicial), and other public or governmental authorities, at whatever level – national, regional or local – are in a position to engage the responsibility of the State Party.

States Parties must adopt legislative, judicial, administrative, educative and other appropriate measures in order to fulfil their legal obligations. It is important to raise levels of awareness about the Covenant not only among public officials and state agents but also among the population at large.

The positive obligations on States Parties to ensure Covenant rights will only be discharged if individuals are protected by the state not just against violations of Covenant rights by its agents, but also against acts committed by private persons or entities that would impair the enjoyment of Covenant rights in so far as they are amenable to application between private persons or entities. There may be circumstances in which a failure to ensure Covenant rights as required by article 2 would give rise to violations by States Parties of those rights as a result of States Parties' permitting or failing to take appropriate measures or to exercise due diligence to prevent, punish, investigate or redress the harm caused by such acts by private persons or entities. States parties have a duty to address the activities of private persons or entities such as the duty to ensure that private persons or entities do not inflict torture.

States parties are required to respect and to ensure the Covenant rights to all persons who may be within their territory and to all persons subject to their jurisdiction. This means that a State Party must respect and ensure the rights laid down in the Covenant to anyone within the power or effective control of that State Party, even if not situated within the territory of the State Party. The enjoyment of Covenant rights is not limited to citizens of States Parties, but must also be available to all individuals, regardless of nationality or statelessness, such as asylum seekers, refugees, migrant workers and other persons who may find themselves in the territory or subject to the jurisdiction of the State Party. This principle also applies to those within the power or effective control of the forces of a State Party acting outside its territory, regardless of the circumstances in which such power or effective control was obtained, such as forces constituting a national contingent of a State Party assigned to an international peace-keeping or peace-enforcement operation.

The Covenant applies also in situations of armed conflict to which the rules of international humanitarian law are applicable. While, in respect of certain Covenant rights, more specific rules of international humanitarian law may be specially relevant for the purposes of the interpretation of Covenant rights, both spheres of law are complementary, not mutually exclusive.

Article 2, paragraph 2 of the Covenant requires that States Parties take the necessary steps to give effect to the Covenant rights in the domestic order. It follows that, unless the Covenant's rights are already protected by their domestic law or practices, States Parties are required on ratification to make such changes to domestic laws and practices as are necessary to ensure their conformity with the Covenant. Where there are inconsistencies between domestic law and the Covenant, article 2 requires that the domestic law or practice be changed to meet the standards required by the Covenant's substantive guarantees.

Article 2 allows a State Party to pursue this in accordance with its own domestic constitutional structure and accordingly does not require that the Covenant be directly applicable in the courts by incorporation of the Covenant into national laws. The Committee takes the view, however, that Covenant guarantees may receive enhanced protection in those states where the Covenant is automatically or through specific incorporation part of the domestic legal order. The Committee invited those States Parties in which the Covenant did not form part of the domestic legal order to consider incorporation of the Covenant to render it part of domestic law to facilitate full realization of Covenant rights as required by article 2.

The requirement under Article 2, paragraph 2,to take steps to give effect to the Covenant rights is unqualified and of immediate effect. A failure to comply with this obligation cannot be justified by reference to political, social, cultural or economic considerations within the state.

Article 2.paragraph 3, requires that in addition to effective protection of Covenant rights States Parties must ensure that individuals also have accessible and effective remedies to vindicate those rights. Such remedies should be appropriately adapted so as to take account of the special vulnerability of certain categories of person, including in particular children. The Committee attaches importance to States Parties establishing appropriate judicial and administrative mechanisms for addressing claims of rights violations under domestic law.

Article 2, paragraph 3 of the Covenant requires that States Parties make reparation to individuals whose Covenant rights have been violated. Without reparation to individuals whose Covenant rights have been violated, the obligation to provide an effective remedy, which is central to the efficacy of Article 2, paragraph 3, is not discharged. In addition to the explicit reparation required by articles 9, paragraph 5, and Article 14, paragraph 6, the Committee considers that the Covenant generally, entails appropriate compensation. The Committee noted that, where appropriate, reparation can involve restitution, rehabilitation and measures of satisfaction, such as public apologies, public memorials, guarantees of non-repetition and changes in relevant laws and practices, as well as bringing to justice the perpetrators of human rights violations.

In general, the purposes of the Covenant would be defeated without an obligation integral to article 2 to take measures to prevent the recurrence of a violation of the Covenant. Accordingly, it has been a frequent practice of the Committee, in its consideration of individual petitions, to include in its Views the need for measures, beyond a victim-specific remedy, to be taken to avoid recurrence of the type of violation in question. Such measures may require changes in the State Party's laws or practices.

Where investigations reveal violations of certain Covenant rights, States Parties must ensure that those responsible are brought to justice. As with failure to investigate, failure to bring to justice perpetrators of such violations could in and of itself give rise to a separate breach of the Covenant. These obligations arise notably in respect of those violations recognized as criminal under either domestic or international law, such as torture and similar cruel, inhuman and degrading treatment (article 7), summary and arbitrary killing (article 6) and enforced disappearance (articles 7 and 9 and frequently 6). Indeed, the problem of impunity for these violations, a matter of sustained concern by the Committee, may well be an important contributing element in the recurrence of the violations. When committed as part of a widespread or systematic attack on a civilian population, these violations of the Covenant are crimes against humanity (Rome Statute of the ICC, Article 7).

Accordingly, where public officials or state agents have committed violations of the Covenant rights, the States Parties concerned may not relieve perpetrators from personal responsibility. Furthermore, no official status justifies persons who may be accused of responsibility for such violations being held immune from legal responsibility. Other impediments to the establishment of legal responsibility should also be removed, such as the defence of obedience to superior orders or unreasonably short periods of statutory limitation in cases where such limitations are applicable. States Parties should also assist each other to bring to justice persons suspected of having committee acts in violation of the Covenant that are punishable under domestic or international law.

The Committee further took the view that the right to an effective remedy may in certain circumstances require States Parties to provide for and implement provisional or interim measures to avoid continuing violations and to endeavor to repair at the earliest possible opportunity any harm that may have been caused by such violations.

In the preceding sections we considered the contribution to protection of the special procedures and the human rights treaty bodies. What does the newly-established Human Rights Council bring to protection? We consider this next.

IV. PROTECTION CHALLENGES OF THE HUMAN RIGHTS COUNCIL

The United Nations Human Rights Council, which began its existence on 19 June 2006, presents the international community with crucial questions of policy, law and judgment having a profound bearing on the future of the United Nations and its role in the protection of human rights.

A. The Legal Premises of the Human Rights Council

An opening issue for reflection is the extent to which international human rights law is applicable in the Human Rights Council. In international law, a state is obliged to respect the human rights of persons subject to its jurisdiction:

a) that it has undertaken to respect by international agreements;
b) that states generally are bound to respect as a matter of customary international law; and
c) that it is required to respect under general principles of law common to

the major legal systems of the world.[13]

A state violates international customary law if, as a matter of state policy, it practices, encourages, or condones: genocide, slavery or slave trade, ethnic cleansing, the murder or causing the disappearance of individuals, torture or other cruel, inhuman or degrading treatment or punishment, prolonged arbitrary detention, systematic racial discrimination, or a consistent pattern of gross violations of internationally recognized human rights.[14]

General Assembly resolution 60/251 establishing the Human Rights Council reaffirmed the essential foundations of international human rights law applicable to the work of the Council, including the Purposes and Principles of the United Nations Charter, the Universal Declaration of Human Rights, the Vienna Declaration and Programme of Action, the International Covenant on Civil and Political Rights and the International Covenant on Economic, Social and Cultural Rights.

The General Assembly reaffirmed that while the significance of national and regional particularities and various historical, cultural and religious backgrounds must be borne in mind, all States, regardless of their political, economic and cultural systems, have the duty to promote and protect all human rights and fundamental freedoms. The General Assembly emphasized the responsibility of all States, in conformity with the Charter, to respect human rights and fundamental freedoms for all, without distinction of any kind.

The General Assembly reiterated its commitment to strengthen the United Nations human rights machinery with the aim of ensuring effective enjoyment by all of all human rights – civil, political, economic, social and cultural rights, including the right to development and, to this end, resolved to create a Human Rights Council. There are thus good legal foundations for the work of the Human Rights Council along with the General Assembly's endorsement of the responsibility to protect, which we shall discuss below.

The General Assembly also laid down some significant policy premises for the Council that we look at next.

B. The Policy Premises of the Human Rights Council

The General Assembly affirmed the need for all States to continue international efforts to enhance dialogue and broaden understanding among civilizations, cultures and religions. It recognized that the promotion and protection of human rights should be based on the principles of cooperation and dialogue and aimed at strengthening the capacity of Member States to comply with their

---

13 Article 38 of the Statute of the International Court of Justice.

14 Second Restatement of the Foreign Relations Law of the USA, 1987,Articles 701. See also Article 702.

human rights obligations for the benefit of all human beings.

The core mandate given to the Human Rights Council was to promote universal respect for the protection of all human rights and fundamental freedoms for all, without distinction of any kind. The Council should address situations of violations of human rights, including gross and systematic violations, and make recommendations thereon. The Council is called upon to respond to 'human rights emergencies' and may hold special sessions in situations of need. The General Assembly decided that the work of the Council shall be guided by the principles of universality, impartiality, objectivity and non-selectivity, constructive international dialogue and cooperation with a view to the enhanced promotion and protection of all human rights.

The Council is further mandated to promote human rights education and learning as well as advisory services, technical assistance and capacity building, to be provided in consultation and with the consent of the Member States concerned; to serve as a forum for dialogue on thematic issues; to make recommendations to the General Assembly for the further development of international law in the field of human rights; to promote the full implementation of human rights obligations undertaken by States and the follow-up of the goals and commitments related to the promotion and protection of human rights emanating from United Nations conferences and summits; to contribute, through dialogue and cooperation, towards the prevention of human rights violations and respond promptly to human rights emergencies; to work in close cooperation in the field of human rights with governments, regional organizations, national human rights institutions, and civil society; to make recommendations with regard to the promotion and protection of human rights; and to undertake a universal periodic review of the fulfilment by each State of its human rights obligations and commitments.

The Human Rights Council must take forward the challenges of building a world on the foundations of justice. That will be its historic mission.

C. The Responsibility to Protect

In establishing the Council the General Assembly decided that it "should address situations of violations of human rights, including gross and systematic violations, and make recommendations thereon". The General Assembly also mandated the Council to "contribute, through dialogue and cooperation, towards the prevention of human rights violations and respond promptly to human rights emergencies". Furthermore, special sessions may be held in respect of situations of need. Earlier, the General Assembly had affirmed the responsibility to protect. How will the Council "address" situations of violations of human rights, prevent human rights violations, respond promptly to human rights emergencies, and discharge the responsibility to protect? For a start, it will need to be faithful to the policies and practice of the General Assembly on this matter.

The General Assembly, in its resolution 34/175, had pledged to act against mass and flagrant violations of human rights and had requested United Nations organs to do likewise. In establishing the Office of UN High Commissioner for Human Rights the General Assembly mandated the High Commissioner to protect as well as to promote human rights.

The report of the International Commission on Intervention and State Sovereignty launched the concept of the responsibility to protect. In the Commission's view, the responsibility to protect embraced three specific responsibilities: the responsibility to prevent, the responsibility to react; and the responsibility to protect[15].The United Nations summit of world leaders, meeting to mark the organizations 60th anniversary in 2005, endorsed the concept of the responsibility to protect.

D. Protection Instrumentalities of the Human Rights Council

The following protection instrumentalities of the Council may be identified: the plenary council, the universal periodic review process, its special procedures, its complaints procedure, its special sessions, the High Commissioner for Human Rights, the Secretary-General, the President of the Council, the Expanded Bureau of the Council, NGOs and civil society. We look at each of these in turn.

i) The Plenary Council and the Prevention of Gross Violations

The mandate of the Council requires it to contribute, through dialogue and cooperation, towards the prevention of human rights violations and respond promptly to human rights emergencies. The Council will need, eventually, to develop preventive policies and strategies. It could, once it has settled down: (a) Resolve to pursue a preventive approach, which will involve national, regional, and international efforts to prevent gross violations of human rights. (b) Inscribe an annual item on its agenda entitled "International Cooperation for the Prevention of Violations of Human Rights". (c) Discuss under the item on the prevention of violations of human rights, as it deems appropriate, situations of gross and systematic violations of human rights, and take decisions thereon on a case by case basis. (e) Decide, in its efforts to pursue preventive approaches and in dealing with situations of international concern, to endeavour through diplomatic contacts and other appropriate ways and means, to help

15 Report of the International Commission on Intervention and State Sovereignty. The International Development Research Centre, Ottawa, 2001.

the Government concerned to put an end to gross violations of human rights, to prevent their recurrence, and to provide relief and redress as required. (e) Decide to make appropriate recommendations to the General Assembly on a case by case basis on upholding the responsibility to protect.

ii) The Universal Periodic Review and the Prevention of Gross Violations of Human Rights.

The Council is mandated to undertake a universal periodic review, based on objective and reliable information, of the fulfilment by each State of its human rights obligations and commitments in a manner which ensures universality of coverage and equal treatment with respect to all States. The review is to be a cooperative mechanism, based on an interactive dialogue, with the full involvement of the country concerned, and with consideration given to its capacity-building needs. The Council, in conducting its review and dialogue with countries could express a special interest in their capacity building for the prevention of gross violations of human rights.

iii) The Special Procedures and the Prevention of Gross Violations of Human Rights

The Council inherited some 40 special procedures, thematic and country-based. The special procedures would need to gear their efforts more and more towards the prevention of gross violations of human rights and towards marshalling international action for the protection of actual and potential victims. The Council must be organized to act on urgent submissions of the special procedures in respect of human rights emergencies, gross and systematic violations of human rights, and situations of need.

iv) The President and the Bureau of the Council and the dispatch of special envoys

If there is a situation of gross and systematic violations occurring while the Council is in normal session it will be expected to marshal international protection efforts in respect of such situations. However, if the Council is not in session and there has been no request for a special session, the Council, in order to be faithful to its protection mandate, would need to be able to act promptly and effectively. The Council might receive submissions from one or more of its special procedures, the High Commissioner or the Secretary-General, or it might receive representations from Governments or non-governmental organizations. In cases of need, and in the judgment of the President or the Bureau, either may properly decide to issue a public statement or to dispatch a fact-finding envoy to the situation in question.

v) The UN Secretary-General

Under the rules of procedure of the General Assembly and its subsidiary bodies, the Secretary-General may submit reports or make statements to any of these bodies. The Secretary-General may thus refer to the Human Rights Council for its attention any situation of gross and systematic violations of human rights, any human rights emergency or any situation of need. This is equivalent to the competence of the Secretary-General under Article 99 of the Charter to refer to the Security Council any situation that he considers threatens or might threaten international peace and security.

vi) The UN High Commissioner for Human Rights

The UN High Commissioner for Human Rights might similarly submit reports or make statements to the Human Rights Council and, in the discharge of the protection functions of the High Commissioner, s would be expected to bring to the attention of the Council situations of gross and systematic violations of human rights, human rights emergencies, or situations of need.

vii) The Human Rights Treaty Bodies

In the course of their consideration of reports, complaints or petitions, the Human Rights treaty bodies would be free, if they consider it appropriate, to refer to the Human Rights Council for its attention any situation of gross and systematic violations of human rights, human rights emergency, or situation of need. The treaty bodies would also be free to send submissions to the Council when it is conducting its dialogue with a Member State under the periodic review system.

viii) NGOs and Civil Society

NGOs and civil society regularly make submissions to the Council on matters within its purview, including in respect of situations of gross and systematic violations of human rights, human rights emergencies, or situations of need. These may be handled under the complaints procedure of the Council. But in dire situations the Council must be equipped to respond to emergency submissions from NGOs and civil society. This could involve the responsibilities of the special procedures, the President and Bureau of the Council, the High Commissioner, the Secretary-General and Member Governments. One option available to Member Governments is to call for a Special Session of the Council.

ix) The Complaints Procedure of the Council and Human Rights Emergencies

The complaints procedure decided upon by the Council provides for its review organs to meet at least twice a year to sift through petitions submitted to the United Nations alleging gross violations of human rights. In situations of human rights emergencies the procedure must be able to act swiftly to activate the protection role of the Council.

x) Special Sessions of the Council

The Council may hold special sessions, when needed, at the request of a member of the Council with the support of one third of its membership. Members of the Council would have a duty to respond in good faith to submissions of special procedures, the Secretary-General, the High Commissioner, a human rights treaty body, the complaints procedure, or by NGOs. Where needed, members of the Council should be ready to call for and support special sessions for the purposes of protection.

ASSESSMENT

The Council is at the beginning of its work. It is proceeding along the lines of consensus and confidence-building, which are indeed commendable. At the same time it will need to be faithful to the responsibility to protect. The ideas presented above are meant to help in the process of reflection regarding the protection challenges of the Council.

The establishment of the Human Rights Council may be seen as part of a process to renew and modernize the human rights machinery of the United Nations. The task ahead is to help it realize its potential. In its first eight sessions so far the Human Rights Council has adopted decisions of long-range structural significance. High among these was a resolution adopted by the Council at its sixth session mandating the preparation of a declaration on human rights education. If this leads to a process in which greater attention is paid to spreading human rights education at the primary, secondary and tertiary levels, the Human Rights Council would have made a great contribution to reinforcing a universal culture of human rights.

The Council has also established important precedents when it comes to the development of a protection concept. The Council has discussed situations of gross violations of human rights. It has adopted resolutions expressing concern about some situations or deploring them. It has established urgent fact-finding missions and it has sought to pursue a dialogue with governments on situations of concern.

Admittedly, there are situations that the Council has not addressed and there are those who contend that the Council is not balanced in the way it addresses different situations. Be that as it may, what is significant is that the Council has established protection criteria and precedents that it can be called upon to follow in the future. From the point of view of fulfiling the promise and potential of the Council these precedents and criteria are important.

We turn next to the role of the Security Council.

V. THE SECURITY COUNCIL

THE COMPETENCES OF THE SECURITY COUNCIL UNDER THE UNITED NATIONS CHARTER

In order to ensure prompt and effective action by the UN, its Members confer on the Security Council primary responsibility for the maintenance of international peace and security and agree that in carrying out its duties under this responsibility the Security Council acts on their behalf. In discharging these duties the Ssecurity Council shall act in accordance with the Purposes and Principles of the United Nations. The Members of the Security Council agree to accept and carry out the decisions of the Council in accordance with the Charter. (Arts 24 and 25).

The Security Council is organized so as to be able to function continuously . (Art 28). It may hold meetings at other than the seat of the UN (Art. 28). It may establish such subsidiary organs as it deems necessary for the performance of its functions. (Art. 30).

Acting under Chapter VI of the Charter, which deals with the pacific settlement of disputes, the Security Council may investigate any dispute, or any situation which might lead to international friction or give rise to a dispute, in order to determine whether the continuance of the dispute or situation is likely to endanger the maintenance of international peace and security. (Art. 34) Any Member of the UN may bring any such dispute, or situation to the attention of the Security Council or the General Assembly. The Security Council may indicate appropriate procedures or methods of adjustment at any stage. (Art. 36) (Art. 37)

Acting under Chapter VII, the Security Council is vested with authority to determine if a situation threatens or breaches international peace and security (Art. 39). It may indicate provisional measures (Art. 40), or sanctions (Article 41). It may call upon military forces (Art. 42) In order to enable the UN to take urgent military measures, Members shall hold immediately available national air-force contingents for combined international enforcement action.

The Security Council thus has five key courses of action at its disposal: investigation, peace operations, sanctions, military enforcement, empowering partners. Luck has submitted that if the Security Council determines that a situation within a State could threaten the maintenance of international peace and security at some point, then it can take non-coercive action under Chapter VI or coercive steps under Chapter VII. He has also argued that the Council's investigations under Article 34, determinations under Article 39, and enforcement actions under Articles 41 and 42 need not be limited to the international level. However, his assessment is that the Security Council has displayed little consistency in applying humanitarian standards.[16]

In 2005 the Summit Outcome Document adopted by the General Assembly declared: "We are prepared to take collective action, in a timely and decisive manner, through the Security Council, in accordance with the Charter, including Chapter VII, on a case- by-case basis and in cooperation with relevant regional organizations, as appropriate, should peaceful means be inadequate and national authorities manifestly fail to protect their population from genocide, war crimes, ethnic cleansing and crimes against humanity."

While the Security Council remains a pre-eminently political organ, influenced by the political assessments and judgments of its membership, its practice with regard to human rights and related matters would nevertheless support the following propositions:

- The Security Council has acted on threats to the right to life and welfare of humanity as a whole. (e.g. climate change, HIV/AIDS)
- The Security Council has acted firmly on threats to the right to life and other human rights posed, e.g. by the risks of genocide and global terrorism.
- The Security Council has acted on human rights situations that threatened international peace and security.
- The Security Council has acted on human rights situations that breached international peace and security.
- The Security Council has acted on human rights situations that might lead to international friction or give rise to a dispute.
- The Security Council has acted on situations or issues of widespread international concern (e.g. protection of civilians, women and children in armed conflict) .
- The Security Council has used United Nations peacekeeping forces for protection purposes (e.g. UNPROFOR in Croatia and Bosnia)
- The Security Council has used United Nations peacekeeping forces for prevention purposes (UNPREDEP)
- The Security Council has encouraged the integration of human rights

16 E. C. Luck UN Security Council. Practice and Promise. London and New York, Routledge, 2006, pp. 82-83.

into processes of peacemaking, peacekeeping and peace-building.

- The Security Council has rallied behind the principle of democratic legitimacy, namely that it will not recognize military coups against democratically elected governments.
- The Security Council has authorized coalitions of Member States to act for the protection of human rights (e.g. aerial protection of populations in Iraq, protection of the independence and self-determination of Kuwait).
- The Security Council has established Commissions of Inquiry or Special Courts to try persons accused of international crimes.
- The Security Council has referred situations to the Prosecutor of the International Criminal Court.[17]

Prevention of Terrorism

Both the General Assembly and the Security Council have been prominent in the struggle against terrorism. The General Assembly has adopted numerous resolutions setting down policies and strategies and the Security Council, especially after September 11, 2001, has adopted a series of binding resolutions setting out policies and strategies for countering terrorism.

The Security Council for its part, in resolution 1269 (1999), called upon all States to cooperate with one another to prevent and suppress terrorist acts and to prevent and suppress in their territories, through all lawful means, the preparation and financing of any acts of terrorism. After the terrorist attack which took place in New York, Washington DC and Pennsylvania on 11 September 2001, the Security Council, acting under Chapter VII of the Charter of the United Nations, decided that all States shall take the necessary steps to prevent the Commission of terrorist acts including by provision of early warning to other States through the exchange of information. The Security Council also decided that all states shall prevent and suppress the financing of terrorist acts.

In the same resolution the Security Council decided to establish a committee consisting of all members of the Council to monitor implementation of its resolution with the assistance of appropriate expertise and called upon all States to report to the committee periodically on the steps take to implement it resolution. In resolution 1377 (2001) the Security Council recognized that many States would require assistance in implementing all the requirements of resolution 1373 (2001), and invited States to inform the Counter-Terrorism Committee of areas in which they required such support. In that context, the

17 See, generally, B.G. Ramcharan, The Security Council and the Protection of Human Rights, The Hague, Martinus Nijhoff, 2001.

Council invited the Counter-Terrorism Committee to explore ways in which States could be assisted, and in particular to explore with international, regional and sub-regional organizations:

- the promotion of best-practices in the areas covered by resolution 1373 (2001), including the preparation of model laws as appropriate,
- the availability of existing technical, financial, regulatory, legislative or other assistance programmes which might facilitate the implementation of resolution 1373 (2001),
- the promotion of possible synergies between these assistance programmes.

The Security Council continued to press the line of preventive action in its resolution 1624 adopted on 14 September, 2005. In that resolution the Council called upon States to adopt such measures as may be necessary and appropriate and in accordance with international law to prohibit by law incitement to commit a terrorist act or acts, to prevent such conduct, and to deny safe haven to any persons with respect to whom there is credible and relevant information giving serious reasons for considering that they have been guilty of such conduct.

The Security Council, as part of its preventive strategies, called upon States to continue international efforts to enhance dialogue and broaden understanding among civilizations, in an effort to prevent the indiscriminate targeting of different religions and cultures, and to take all measures as may be necessary and appropriate and in accordance with their obligations under international law to counter incitement of terrorist acts motivated by extremism and intolerance and to prevent the subversion of educational, cultural and religious institutions by terrorists and their supporters.

The Council called upon States to report to the Counter-Terrorism Committee, as part of their ongoing dialogue, on the steps they have taken to implement the resolution. The Council directed the Counter-Terrorism Committee to include in its dialogue with Member States their efforts to implement its resolution. The Council also directed the Counter-Terrorism Committee to work with Member States to help build capacity, including through spreading best legal practice and promoting exchange of information.

VI. THE GENERAL ASSEMBLY AND THE PROTECTION OF HUMAN RIGHTS

Under Article 13 of the UN Charter the General Assembly (GA) shall initiate studies and make recommendations for the development of international law and for promoting international cooperation in the economic, social, cultural, educational and health fields, and assisting in the realization of human rights and fundamental freedoms for all without distinction as to race, sex, language or religion.

Under Articles 55 and 56 of the Charter the UN shall promote universal respect for and observance of human rights and fundamental freedoms for all. Responsibility for the discharge of these functions of the Organization is vested in the GA and, under its authority, in the ECOSOC.

The GA has maintained from its early days that it would discuss, adopt resolutions and send fact-finding missions regarding situations of gross violations of human rights such as that of *apartheid*. In resolution 34/175, "*Effective Action Against Mass and Flagrant Violations of Human Rights*," the GA "Reaffirmed that mass and flagrant violations of human rights are of special concern to the United Nations," and urged the appropriate UN bodies, within their mandates to take timely and effective action in existing and future cases of mass and flagrant violations of human rights.

In establishing the Human Rights Council the GA mandated it to deal with situations of gross violations of human rights, human rights emergencies, and to act for the prevention of gross violations of human rights. The GA, as the parent body, has a role in relation to all of these issues.

The GA established the position of UN High Commissioner for Human Rights to act for the promotion and the protection of human rights.

In relation to threats to, or breaches of, international peace and security, the GA adopted the Uniting for Peace Resolution by which it decided that if the exercise of the veto by a permanent member of the Security Council prevented the Council from dealing with a situation it would be ready to take up such situations.

The standard-setting function of the GA has a protecting dimension. In the Millennium Declaration the GA set down values for the twenty-first century, including the value of freedom.

In acting to promote poverty reduction and to help achieve the right to development the GA is acting for the protection of economic social and cultural rights. The Millennium Development Goals represent the Assembly's latest efforts.

The GA has spearheaded efforts to combat discrimination on grounds of race and gender and these have important protecting dimensions. The GA recently adopted the UN Declaration on the Rights of Indigenous Peoples which has the purpose of extending protection to them.

There are many specific human rights items on the Agenda of the GA each year that deal with human rights. Most of these are discussed in the Social and Humanitarian Committee. Some are discussed in plenary. Some items discussed in the Economic Committee and the Legal Committee also deal with the promotion and protection of human rights.

Sometimes the GA adopts resolutions expressing concern regarding – or even condemning, gross violations of human rights in particular countries.

VII. ECOSOC

Chapter X of the Charter dealing with the Economic and Social Council is immediately preceded by Chapter IX with deals with International Economic and Social Cooperation. Article 55, falling within Chapter IX, provides that with a view to the creation of conditions of stability and well-being the United Nations shall promote: (a) higher standards of living, full employment, and conditions of economic and social progress and development; (b) solutions to international economic, social, health, and related problems and international cultural and educational cooperation; and (c) universal respect for, and observance of, human rights and fundamental freedoms for all without distinction as to race, sex, language, or religion. In article 56 all Members pledge themselves to take joint and separate action in cooperation with the Organization for the achievement of the purposes set forth in Article 55. Articles 57 and 58 deal with the relationship between the United Nations and the Specialized Agencies.

Article 60 makes it explicit that responsibility for the discharge of the functions set forth in Chapter IX shall be vested in the General Assembly and, under the authority of the General Assembly, in the Economic and Social Council. One could conclude from this that the scheme of the Charter was that the General Assembly was expected to have the assistance of the Economic and Social Council in carrying out the human rights functions enumerated in Articles 55 and 56. The fact that the Human Rights Council now reports directly to the General Assembly might require that special arrangements be made for the Economic and Social Council to make an input into the work of the Human Rights Council or to give the benefit of its views to the General Assembly on recommendations of the Human Rights Council.

The functions of the Economic and Social Council, as set out in Article 62 of the Charter, give it competence to initiate studies and reports with respect to international economic, social, cultural, educational, health, and related matters and to make recommendations with respect to any such matters to the General Assembly, to United Nations organs, and to the specialized agencies concerned. The Economic and Social Council may make recommendations for the purpose of promoting respect for, and observance of, human rights and fundamental freedoms for all. It may prepare draft conventions for submission to the General Assembly, with respect to matters falling within its competence. The Economic and Social Council may call international conferences on matters falling within its jurisdiction.

The Economic and Social Council may enter into arrangements with the specialized agencies and may seek reports from them. It may furnish information to the Security Council and shall assist the Security Council at its request.

Article 68 of the Charter specifically mandates the Economic and Social Council to set up commissions in economic and social fields and for the promotion of human rights. It was pursuant to this article that it had established the Commission on Human Rights.

The principal conclusion that may be drawn from this examination of the relevant Charter provisions is that a substantive contribution of the Economic and Social Council to the work of the Human Rights Council would require particular arrangements to be established with a view to ensuring that the insights of the Council, particularly drawn from its work on economic and social issues, and its interaction with the Specialized Agencies, could be brought to bear upon the work of the Human Rights Council.

Another issue that might be flagged is whether the General Assembly, with its wide-ranging responsibilities, would be able to integrate the economic and social dimensions into its deliberations on the work of the Human Rights Council. Furthermore, for the General Assembly to be able to do this, it would need to draw on the assistance of its Second (Economic) and Third (Social and Humanitarian Committees).

While the Commission on Human Rights remained in existence, the Economic and Social Council formally considered its annual report and authorized decisions proposed for approval by the Commission. There has been some substantive debate on the work of the Commission, but not much. The ECOSOC participants were mostly junior diplomats the majority of whom were interested in political rather than substantive questions. On occasions the ECOSOC might even have disagreed with the proposal of the Commission but this did not happen often.

To the extent that the ECOSOC engaged in substantive consideration of economic and social questions that was very much relevant to human rights issues such as the implementation of the right to development, the implementation of economic, social and cultural rights, and the interrelationship between the latter and civil and political rights. The ECOSOC has a Permanent Forum on Indigenous People, which was established on the recommendation of the Commission on Human Rights and all the work of the Commission and its Sub-Commission relating to indigenous people could be fed into the work of the Permanent Forum.

Under human rights-related Decades, such as the Decade against racism and racial discrimination, and the decade for indigenous people, ECOSOC received substantive reports from the Secretariat and sometimes there was good discussion of these issues in that body. On such thematic issues ECOSOC could provide the forum for bringing together the views of a wide cross-section of Governments, United Nations bodies and NGOs and the end result could be constructive.

Under some human rights treaties the annual reports of human rights bodies such as the Committee on Economic, Social and Cultural Rights are submitted to the General Assembly through the ECOSOC and there is the possibility of a discussion in ECOSOC with a view to the work of the treaty bodies cross-fertilizing with the work of other economic and social bodies and the specialized agencies. Formally, these treaty bodies will still be expected to report through the ECOSOC and so this role can continue. Under the International Covenant on Economic, Social and Cultural Rights the ECOSOC has functions that are distinctive to it.

ECOSOC is the organ that established the petition procedure laid down in its resolution 1503. Formally, it is ECOSOC that should take the authorising decisions required when, for example, it was decided to do a thorough study of the situation of human rights in a country of concern. With the General Assembly becoming the authorizing body in the future it should not be excluded that the majority in the Assembly might approach such decisions through political lens.

It must be admitted that the Economic and Social Council has not really played a substantive role on human rights issues for quite some time. This has been part of the overall problem of the lack of purpose and effectiveness in the Council for some time. In an address to the plenary of the Economic and Social Council in 2004 the then High Commissioner for Human Rights made a strong plea for the development of the human rights role of the ECOSOC[18] but it did not lead to any substantive development.

VIII. THE SECRETARY-GENERAL

Secretary-General Ban Ki-Moon, is in his second year in office and the broad lines of his approaches and policies as Secretary-General are still in the process of development. He took over as Secretary-General at a time when the organization was in deep controversy on several fronts: first, the aftermath of the Coalition invasion of Iraq; second, the oil for food scandals within the UN Secretariat; third, attacks on his predecessor for his leadership, administration and policy positions; fourth, deep dissatisfaction among the staff with the

18 See Address to the Economic and Social Council by B.G. Ramcharan, Acting High Commissioner for Human Rights, reproduced in B.G. Ramcharan, A UN High Commissioner in Defence of Human Rights, Martinus Nijhoff, 2005, p. 753.

way the Secretariat was being led; fifth, disquiet over the composition of the Security Council; and sixth, rising concerns in the wider world over the scale of poverty, the degradation of the environment, climate change and persistent conflicts in different parts of the world.

Secretary-General Ban, an avowed believer in discreet diplomacy, has sought to re-establish confidence in the United Nations and to demonstrate its relevance in tackling the key challenges facing humanity. He has thus far striven to be a harmonizer and a confidence builder. He has visited several of the major trouble spots and has sought to promote solutions to crises in places such as the Middle East, Africa and Asia.

Against this background, it is understandable that he has tried to be a steadying hand on issues of human rights. As a general summary of the first year and a half of Secretary-General Ban's handling of human rights matters one may say that he has so far taken a principled position on behalf of human rights seeing it within the UN triad of security, human rights and development. He has tried to be generally supportive and has for the most part been in holding pattern. He has not yet had occasion to place his own policy imprints on the human rights program but this will undoubtedly emerge as he continues in office. In what follows below we shall trace some broad outlines of his human rights imprint during his period in office.

Policy Commitment to Human Rights: The Triad of Security, Development and Human Rights

In his acceptance address as Secretary-General and on subsequent occasions, he has affirmed the centrality of human rights in the United Nations. Addressing the Economic and Social Council on 17 January 2007, he declared: "Development for all is central to the UN's mission. Together with security, and respect for human rights, it represents our core aspirations for a peaceful and better world."[19]

Support for International Human Rights Law

At his very first press conference, on 11 January 2007, dealing specifically with the issue of the death penalty, Secretary General Ban invoked the centrality of international human rights law as a general principle: "As Member States are taking their decision I expect they will comply with all aspects of international human rights law."

---

19 Secretary-General, Office of the Spokesperson, "Secretary-General's Remarks at the Ceremony for the Handover of the Presidency of the Economic and Social Council," 17 January, 2007.

Poverty Reduction and the Right to Development

Secretary-General Ban has pledged his firm commitment to work for the improvement of living conditions, education, water, sanitation and housing. On a visit to a Kenyan slum on 30 January 2007, he declared: "we must work together and generate political will to have a smooth implementation of the Millennium Development Goals (MDGs) and I will work very closely, and harder than before."[20] In an address to the African Union in Addis Abba, he drew on his own experiences as a child growing up in war-torn Korea in the 1950s:

> "I have seen the hardship and hunger, the degradation and disease that come with prolonged warfare. Elderly women scavenging for scraps, toddlers weak from malnutrition and unsafe drinking water, buildings dilapidated, corn fields rotting, and infrastructure on its knees."[21]

In a statement to the Group of 77 on 10 January 2007, Secretary-General Ban pointed to inequalities within the global economy that impeded development and said that success in tackling them hinged on building stronger, more effective international partnership. "More than anything else, a fair and equitable international trading regime can provide the basis for a true global partnership for development."[22]

In his first address to the ECOSOC as Secretary-General, Mr Ban recognized the centrality of development to the UN's mission: "Together with security and human rights, it represents our core aspirations for a peaceful and better world." He called for national governments to meet the MDGs.[23] National governments, he added, must be held accountable for meeting the MDGs. [24]

The Right to Life and the Death Penalty

During his first press conference on 11 January 2007 he stated:

> "...(M)any of you have been asking about my views on the death penalty. Today, let me answer that question in person.
>
> "I believe that life is precious and must be protected and respected, and

20 UN News Service, "At Kenyan Slum, Ban Ki-moon pledges to work harder to eradicate poverty," 30 January, 2007.

21 UN News Service, "Ban Ki-moon Calls for African Union Show, Unity of Purpose in Bringing Peace to Darfur," 29 January 2007.

22 UN News Service, "Secretary-General calls on 'Group of 77' Developing States to help him strengthen UN," 10 January 2007.

23 UN News Center, "Ban Ki-moon sets out vision for reinvigorated UN Economic and Social Council," 17 January 2007.

24 UN News Centre, "Secretary-General calls on 'Group of 77' developing States to help him strengthen UN", 10 January, 2007.

that all human beings have the right to live in dignity. International law affirms these values. I recognize the growing trend in international law and in national practice towards phasing out the death penalty. I encourage that trend. As Member States are taking their decisions, I expect they will comply with all aspects of international human rights law. As you know, I have also urged restraint by the Iraqi authorities in the execution of death sentences imposed by the Iraqi High Tribunal."[25]

Climate Change as a Security and Human Rights Issue

Secretary General Ban has taken on a distinct leadership role in calling upon the international community to address the threats of climate change. He has presented this as an issue of peace and security and as an issue of development. It is also a deep human rights issue touching as it does on the right to life of the inhabitants of the planet as a whole.

Addressing a student conference at the UN on 1 March 2007, he told them:

> "Today, war continues to threaten countless men, women and children across the globe. It is the source of untold suffering and loss. And the majority of the UN's work still focuses on preventing and ending conflict. But, the danger posed by war to all of humanity – and to our planet – is at least matched by the climate crisis and global warming."[26] He continued, "Global warming has profound implications for jobs, growth and poverty. It affects agricultural output, the spread of disease and migration patterns. It determines the ferocity and frequency of natural disasters. It can prompt water shortages, degrade land and lead to the loss of biodiversity. And, in coming decades, changes in our environment and the resulting upheavals – from droughts to inundated coastal areas to loss of arable lands – are likely to become a major driver of war and conflict."

The Holocaust

On 29 January 2007, on the international day of commemoration in memory of the victims of the holocaust, Secretary General Ban emphasized the importance of remembrance in tribute to those who perished and in global efforts to stem the tide of human cruelty:

> "It keeps us vigilant for new outbreaks of anti-Semitism and other forms of intolerance. And it is an essential response to those misguided individuals

25 Secretary-General, Office of the Spokesperson, "Secretary-General's Press Conference," 11 January 2007.

26 SG/SM/10893, ENV/DEV/914, 1 March 2007.

who claim that the Holocaust never happened, or has been exaggerated."[27]

Prevention of Genocide

Secretary-General Ban, has publicly declared the importance he attaches to UN efforts for the prevention of genocide and his support for the position of UN special adviser on the prevention of genocide.

Slavery and Slavery-like Practices

At an exhibition on the triumph over slavery, held in New York on 1 March 2007, Secretary-General Ban declared:

> "The story of the end of the slave trade deserves to be told here at the United Nations. Indeed *the defence of human rights is at the heart of this organization's global mission.* Our Charter proclaims equal rights. The Universal Declaration of Human Rights states that 'no one shall be held in slavery or servitude.'"[28]

> He continued,

> "We should remember that even today, many millions of our fellow human beings are being subjected to slavery-like practices. These include debt bondage and the use of children in armed conflict. The victims are typically too scared to speak out. For all that has been accomplished in our campaign for human rights, we still have much to do."[29]

The Rights of Women

On the occasion of the international day of women's rights Secretary-General Ban declared his firm support for the implementation of international norms on equal rights of women.

World Press Freedom

In a statement on World Press Freedom Day, in May, 2007, Secretary-General Ban registered the importance he attached to freedom of the press.

Responsibility to Protect

SG Ban Ki-moon has supported the General Assembly's Declaration on the

---

27 UN News Service, "UN Marks Holocause Day as Constant Reminder to Prevent Future Genocides," 29 January 2007.

28 Italics provided

29 SG/SM/10895, HQ/653, 2 March 2007.

Responsibility to Protect and he has announced that he has designated of a Special Adviser on the Responsibility to Protect.

The Human Rights Council

In a video message to the Opening meeting of the fourth session of the Human Rights Council on 12 March 2007, Secretary-General Ban told the Council that the world was watching to see if the Council would live up to its promise. He hoped that the Council members would work together to promote an objective and universal approach to human rights.[30]

Autonomy of the UN High Commissioner for Human Rights

In response to a question on 13 January 2007, SG Ban Ki Moon's spokeswoman affirmed that the Secretary-General would allow his High Commissioner for Human Rights to act independently, and would respect the High Commissioner's autonomy.[31]

Violations of Human Rights

Secretary-General Ban Ki-Moon has been ready to use the voice of the Secretary General in condemning human rights violations.

a. Darfur

Secretary General Ban has taken a personal interest in the situation in Darfur from the outset of his term. At a press conference on 11 January 2007, he drew attention to the human rights, humanitarian and security issues involved in that situation. Addressing the African Union in Addis Ababa on 29 January 2007, he declared:

> "Together we must work to end the violence and scorched-earth policies adopted by various parties, including militias, as well as the bombings which are still a terrifying feature of life in Darfur ... Life-saving humanitarian work must be allowed to resume, and civil society in Darfur must have a voice in the peace process. And we must persuade non-signatories to join, while building consensus for the urgent deployment of a UN-AU force on the ground."[32]

---

30 See highlights of the noon-briefing by the Spokesperson for the Secretary-General, 12 March 2007, p.2.

31 UN Daily Press conference 13 January 2007.

32 UN News Service, "Ban Ki-moon Calls on African Union Show Unity of Purpose in Bringing Peace to Darfur," 29 January 2007.

b. Call for shutting down of Guantanamo

At his first press conference on 11 January 2007, SG Ban called for the shutting down of the Guantanamo detention centre where a number of international prisoners had been held for several years.

c. Call on Myanmar to release all political prisoners

On 8 January 2007, SG Ban, welcoming Myanmar's release of some political prisoners, urged the Myanmar authorities to release all other political prisoners in the country including Daw Aung San Suu Kyi.[33] On 25 May he deeply regretted the decision of the Government of Myanmar to extend once again the detention under house arrest of the Nobel laureate.[34]

d. Concern over humanitarian impact of US air strikes in Somalia: 10 January, 2007.

On 9 January 2007, SG Ban expressed concern over United States air strikes on Somalia, particularly their humanitarian impact. His spokesman declared:

> "Notwithstanding the motives for this reported military action, the Secretary-General is concerned about the new dimension this kind of action could introduce to the conflict and the possible escalation of hostilities that may result. He is also concerned about the impact this would have on the civilian population movements in and around the border."[35]

e. Zimbabwe

On 12 March 2007, he urged the Government of Zimbabwe to release opposition leaders being held by police "and condemned the reported beatings they suffered while in custody". Through his spokesperson, he called on the authorities to "allow peaceful assembly and to provide a space for the exercise of legitimate political rights".[36]

UN POLICY OF ZERO TOLERANCE ON SEXUAL EXPLOITATION AND ABUSE BY PEACEKEEPING PERSONNEL

At his first press conference on 11 January 2007, SG Ban declared that the UN would uphold a policy of zero-tolerance on sexual exploitation and abuse

---

33 UN News Service, 8 January, 2007.

34 Statement attributable to the Spokesperson for the Secretary-General on Myanmar, 25 May, 2007.

35 UN News Service, "Secretary-General Ban Concerned over Humanitarian Impact of US Air Strikes in Somalia," 9 January 2007.

36 UN News Service, "Zimbabwe : Ban Ki-moon Condemns Reported Police Beating of Opposition Leader," 12 March 2007,

by UN peacekeeping personnel.

As indicated earlier, Secretary-General Ban has taken principled stances on a number of issues and it can be expected that this will continue. All in all the Secretary-General's efforts to be a steadying hand across the board and on human rights issues is understandable and deserving of support.

IX. THE HIGH COMMISSIONER FOR HUMAN RIGHTS

What does the High Commissioner for Human Rights bring to the protection table? Her latest annual report to the General Assembly is a good place to take the pulse on this.[37] The High Commissioner reaffirmed the importance of universality and saw the universal periodic review system as representing an essential step in ensuring a universal application of human rights – whereby all States Members of the UN are reviewed in the same manner. It is to be a constructive process which avoids politicization and exaggeration of discussions.[38]

The High Commissioner indicated that the rule of law and democracy were priority areas of her office.[39] She attached importance to the role of the special procedures: "I will continue to encourage the Council to seize this opportunity to further develop the system in order to maximize necessary protection coverage".[40] She had established a rapid response unit in her office and it had been stepping up its efforts to ensure a timely and systematic response to human rights crises requiring urgent action.[41]

She considered Office of the High Commissioner (OHCHR) country engagement to be one of the main tools for promoting the implementation of human rights. National human rights institutions were a key component of effective national human rights protection systems and indispensable actors for the sustainable promotion and protection of human rights. [42] Her country visits were also an important means of strengthening country engagement, allowing for a more direct dialogue with counterparts.[43] OHCHR regional offices had a key role to play in facilitating the development and implementation of regional engagement strategies.

The High Commissioner attached importance to accountability against impunity: "A common message in all my missions is the need for accountability

37 See, Annual Report of High Commissioner Louise Arbour to the GA, 2007 (A/62/36).

38 Ibid, p. 2.

39 Ibid, p. 16.

40 Ibid, p. 3

41 Ibid, p. 5

42 Ibid, p.5

43 Ibid, p. 7

with a view to ending oft-prevailing impunity for all forms of human rights violations."[44]

OHCHR provided increased support and advice to ensure that the human rights components of 17 peace missions comprehensively carry out the core human rights functions set out in the Secretary-General's Policy Committee decision 2005/24 on human rights in integrated missions.[45] The High Commissioner underscored the importance of regular public reporting, including thematic reporting, by human rights components of peace missions.[46]

The struggle against racism, racial discrimination, xenophobia and related intolerance remained a key priority for her office.[47] Her Office was continuing its efforts to strengthen its expert capacity in the area of economic, social and cultural rights, with a focus on legal protection and advocacy[48].

X. THE RESPONSIBILITY TO PROTECT ECONOMIC, SOCIAL AND CULTURAL RIGHTS

The report of the Independent Commission on Intervention and State Sovereignty, which came up with the concept of the responsibility to protect[49] has received a great deal of attention. On the occasion of the sixtieth anniversary of the United Nations, the General Assembly endorsed the concept of the responsibility to protect and indicated its willingness, in principle, to refer to the Security Council, if need be, situations of genocide, ethnic cleansing, crimes against humanity and war crimes.[50] It is distressing, however, that the Independent Commission's concept of the responsibility to protect no where deals with the responsibility to protect economic, social and cultural rights, even if the Commission acknowledged the relevance of human security in its discussion of the responsibility to protect.

A. THE OBLIGATION TO RESPECT, ENSURE AND PROTECT ECONOMIC, SOCIAL AND CULTURAL RIGHTS.

Economic rights, like political rights, are rights to goods that every human being needs in order to lead a decent human life and to succeed in the pursuit of happiness. The right to life involves more than security of life and limb; it

44 Ibid, p. 7
45 Ibid, p. 8
46 Ibid, p. 8
47 Ibid, p.11.
48 Ibid, p.13.
49 Op. cit. in note 15 above.
50 GA resolution: The Summit Outcome Document, 2005.

is a right not merely to subsist but to live well in human terms.[51] The basic economic right is the right to a decent livelihood by whatever means it can be honestly obtained.[52]

The obligation of a government to protect human rights is regulated by international law: the idea of international obligation[53]. In respect of economic, social and cultural rights, the key international instrument is the International Covenant on this topic (ICESCR).The elements of protection found in the ICESCR are: realization through all appropriate means, including the adoption of legislation, non-discrimination, progressive realization, full realization of the efforts of individual countries to the maximum of its available resources, international assistance and cooperation especially economic and technical.

Each State Party to the Covenant undertakes to take steps, individually and through international cooperation and assistance and cooperation, especially economic and technical, to the maximum of its available resources, with a view to achieving progressively the full realization of the rights recognized in the Covenant by all appropriate means, including particularly the adoption of legislative measures.

The Committee on Economic, Social and Cultural Rights (CESCR) considers that States parties have the following obligations:

a) To respect economic, social and cultural rights – requiring States to refrain from interfering with the enjoyment of economic, social and cultural rights;
b) To protect economic, social and cultural rights – requiring States to prevent violations of such rights by third parties; and
c) To fulfil, promote, facilitate and provide economic, social and cultural rights – requiring States to take appropriate legislative, administrative, budgetary, judicial and other measures towards the full realization of such rights.

There are a number of issues that arise for reflection: Should one activate, nationally, regionally and internationally, the concept of a consistent pattern of gross violations of economic, social and cultural rights? Should one introduce and operationalize a new concept, that of the prevention of gross violations of economic, social and cultural rights, placing the emphasis on the duty of governments, using their available resources, to prevent gross violations of ESCRts? Should one entrust the judiciary more with the protection of economic, social and cultural rights? How can the idea of an international peti-

51 M.J.Adler, Six Great Ideas, MacMillan, 1981, p.168.

52 Ibid., p.169.

53 See the report of the United Nations High Commissioner for Human Rights to the Economic and Social Council in 2006:, E/2006/86, 21 June, 2006. The report focuses on legal protection of economic, social and cultural rights.

tions procedure in respect of ESCRts be advanced further? How should the Human Rights Council, the Economic and Social Council, and the Security Council, react to situations where it is established that a Government is failing in its duty to protect economic, social and cultural rights. What more could the Committee on Economic, Social and Cultural Rights do to protect ESCRts? What protection roles have the Special Rapporteurs on ESCRts played and what more could they do in the future? What roles have regional human rights bodies played in the protection of ESCRts? How can NGOs contribute more to the protection of ESCRts.

The idea of an Optional Protocol to the ICESCR would provide for a petitions procedure under the ICESCR which would be most valuable.

Gross Violations of Economic, Social and Cultural Rights and the Need for Protection

It is beyond question that there are massive violations of economic, social and cultural rights in the world today[54] that go without attention from the principal international and regional human rights bodies. In a report she submitted to the Economic and Social Council in 2006 UN High Commissioner for Human Rights Louise Arbour submitted that modern conceptions of human rights perceive rights in terms of rights of the individual to be free from State interference and abuse of State powers – freedom from the State – as well as rights to State intervention – freedom through the State. Strategies to promote and protect human rights should be multidimensional, covering a range of legal, administrative, financial, budgetary, educational and social measures. However, legal protection of economic, social and cultural rights must be an essential element in this strategy, particularly given the recognition of these rights in legally binding treaties and because of increasing proof that legal protection is effective. The first step in legal protection is the recognition of economic, social and cultural rights in domestic law. This can occur through incorporation of international norms into the domestic legal order and recognition of economic, social and cultural rights in the constitution, in legislation or, in limited cases, by the judiciary. The second step is the provision of remedies:

> "The courts, administration tribunals, quasi-judicial mechanisms such as National Human Rights Institutions or regional and international treaty bodies can provide legal remedies in the case of breaches of economic, social and cultural rights. In this context, the drafting of an optional protocol to the International Covenant on Economic, Social and Cultural Rights

54 See T. Pogge, Recognized and Violated by International Law : The Human Rights of the Global Poor. 19 Leiden Journal of International Law 2005, No. 4, pp 717-745.

should stimulate strengthened legal protection of these rights."[55]

The above-mentioned report by High Commissioner Louise Arbour identified the following criteria from the practice of the Committee on Economic, Social and Cultural Rights in determining whether a State party has acted in conformity with the Covenant in the measures taken to implement a particular right:

a) The severity of the alleged violations – if the claim concerned an alleged violation of a minimum core obligation (or minimum core content), the onus is on the State party to indicate that it had made every effort to use all resources at its disposal in an effort to satisfy, as a matter of priority, those minimum obligations;
b) The development level of the country – the examination is on a case-by-case basis with a wider margin of discretion given to the least developing State parties;
c) Current economic influences – a State with a higher level of development might be going through a period of recession which might have to be considered;
d) Other influences – for example, the presence of a natural disaster might have an impact on available resources and their allocation;
e) The process of allocating resources – whether the allocation was non-discriminatory, directed towards grave threats to the enjoyment of rights and took into account as a matter of priority the needs of vulnerable, disadvantaged and marginalized people; and
f) Proportionality – whether the allocation of resources to social expenditures was reasonably proportional to allocation in other areas.[56]

XI. FUTURE PREVENTIVE STRATEGIES

We are firmly of the view that in the next phase of efforts for the national, regional and international protection of human rights stronger emphasis should be placed on preventive human rights strategies. There are some slender strands of prevention in the work that has been done to promote and to protect human rights since the birth of the human rights movement and more particularly since the establishment of the United Nations. One could say that national human rights charters are aimed essentially at preventing breaches of human rights. The rule of law and the role of the courts in upholding human rights also have a preventive hope. The Convention on the Prevention and

55 Report of the United Nations High Commissioner for Human Rights to the Economic and Social Council in 2006:, E/2006/86, 21 June, 2006 , p.1.

56 E/2006/86, para. 42.

Punishment of the Crime of Genocide was meant to prevent genocide – an objective that has unfortunately not been achieved. The Council of Europe has a Convention on the Prevention of Torture and human rights treaty bodies have developed urgent response procedures and arrangements for reacting to situations of concern.[57] Special procedures of the United Nations Commission on Human Rights also have arrangements for reacting urgently to cases and situations of concern.[58] The United Nations Security Council, these days, meets almost continuously and can respond to emergencies. Regional and sub-regional organizations such as the African Union and ASEAN are developing conflict prevention arrangements.[59] The United Nations High Commissioner for Human Rights can intercede urgently in situations of concern. Some attention is being given these days to the role of human rights considerations in risk analysis.[60]

These are important but still slender strands of protection and it is crucial for the future of the human rights cause that more deliberate attention be given to the development of stronger preventive strategies. We suggest some options for consideration next.

The report of the International Commission on Intervention and State Sovereignty launched the concept of the responsibility to protect. In the view of the Commission, the responsibility to protect embraces three specific responsibilities: (a) The responsibility to prevent: to address both the root causes and direct causes of internal conflict and other man-made crises putting populations at risk. (b) The responsibility to react: to respond to situations of compelling human need with appropriate measures, which may include coercive measures like sanctions and international prosecution, and in extreme cases military intervention. (c) The responsibility to rebuild: to provide, particularly after a military intervention, full assistance with recovery, reconstruction and reconciliation, addressing the causes of the harm the intervention was designed to halt or avert.

The Commission was firm in its view that prevention is the single most important dimension of the responsibility to protect: prevention options should always be exhausted before intervention is contemplated, and more commitment and resources must be devoted to it. The exercise of the responsibility to

57 See Nathalie Prouvez, The Prevention of Racial Discrimination through Early Warning and Urgent Procedures, in B.G. Ramcharan, Conflict Prevention in Practice. Martinus Nijhoff, 2005, pp. 265-280.

58 See L-A Alexander (Ed.), *The Prevention of Gross Violations of Human Rights*. Martinus Nijhoff, 2000..

59 See on this B.G. Ramcharan (Ed.), Conflict Prevention in Practice, Martinus Nijhoff 2005.

60 See, B.G. Ramcharan, The Human Rights Dimension: Human Rights and Risk Analysis, in B.G. Ramcharan (Ed.,), Conflict Prevention in Practice, op. cit. pp. 229-236.

both prevent and and react should always involve less intrusive and coercive measures being considered before more coercive and intrusive ones are applied.

A. A Preventive Orientation for the Future UN Human Rights Council

The emphasis of the international community is rightly placed these days more and more on preventive actions and one should therefore expect the Human Rights council to use it s best endeavours for the prevention of gross violations of human rights. A preventive orientation should therefore characterise the Council. By prevention we mean detecting potential gross violations before they occur and acting to head them off, in cooperation with regional and other partners. The prevention of genocide is a case in point.

A central concept of recent human rights reforms at the UN has been the strengthening of national protection systems. This looks to constitutions and laws that are reflective of international human rights norms, to their application by national and local courts, to human rights education and institutions like human rights commissions, and to early-warning and urgent-response arrangements where needed, particularly in multi-ethnic societies. The Human Rights Council must make it a central part of its work to contribute to the strengthening of national protection systems in every country. It is on this issue of national protection systems that a Peer Review Process can have an important role in the new Council. The national protection system should be expected to take the lead in preventive strategies, supported by regional and international bodies.

B. Risk Analysis

The situation of human rights in a country must be a central dimension of risk analysis pertaining to that country – whether it be for the purposes of the prevention of conflict, assessment of the stability of the country, or assessment of opportunities for business. In the literature on risk assessment, one sees discussion of the meaning of risk, examination of political or investment risks, but one finds very little consideration of the relevance of human rights to risk assessment. In this essay, we shall argue that any risk assessment of a country must start with consideration of its human rights infrastructure, record, and problems.

1. *The Adequacy of the National Protection System*

In the human rights strategies of the United Nations these days, increasing emphasis is placed on the concept of the national protection system[61]. By this concept is meant that one should look at the constitution, laws and courts of a country to see the extent to which they are reflective of the international human rights norms. One must also look to see whether the country has specialized human rights institutions such as a national human rights commission or an ombudsman, whether the country is providing for the teaching of human rights in primary and secondary schools in particular, and whether the country has monitoring arrangements to detect grievances on the part of a group or groups of the population with a view to heading off those grievances.

If significant parts of the national protection system of a country are missing, then one can conclude that the country is likely to be shaky and unstable and, depending on its configuration, could easily erupt into violence.

2. The Degree of Acceptance of the Core International Human Rights Conventions

The role of the Universal Declaration of Human Rights and of the core international human rights conventions is to require States to live up to international minimum standards of human rights protection in key areas, such as respect for civil and political rights; the prohibition of torture; the prohibition of racism and racial discrimination; the prohibition of discrimination against women; protection of the rights of the child; protection against torture; and protection of the rights of migrants. These are all the subjects of major international human rights conventions.

The national protection system of a country should be built on the Universal Declaration of Human Rights and on these core human rights conventions. If a country has not ratified the key conventions, then it is already an indicator that the national consensus within the country might be shaky because the country has not yet begun to internalize what the international community has distilled as the key values that should guide nation-building and that should arbitrate relations between the Government and its subjects or between the subjects themselves.

That a country has not ratified one or more of these conventions may not necessarily indicate potential instability. The United States of America, for example, largely because of the relations between the Federal and State governments, has ratified very few international conventions. Even in such instances, however, it would be fair to say that by staying outside of the conventions, a country is denying itself the opportunity of engaging in a dialogue with the international community on how key values are faring within the country.

61 See on this, B.G. Ramcharan (Ed.), The Protection Role of National Human Rights Institutions. Martinus Nijhoff, 2005.

3. The State of Governance in the Country

If a country is democratically governed under the rule of law, the chances are that the state of respect for human rights might be better – although even this is not assured, depending on the country in question and its political maturity. Nevertheless a good indicator in risk assessment of a country is whether it has genuine periodic elections and whether the courts operate freely and independently of the Government. If either of these conditions is absent, one can be pretty certain that the level of grievances in the country will be high and the risk of instability and even conflict serious. Political corruption and inefficient courts foment dissatisfaction and grievances and invariably lead to a weak social fabric.

4. The National Vision

It is a good indicator of the health of a country to ask whether one can point to a unifying vision embracing all parts of the population – whether they be from different political, economic, social, racial, ethnic or religious backgrounds. In today's multi-cultural world, it is fundamentally important that each country project a national vision that can give all parts of the population a feeling that they have a stake in the future of the country. In countries where there is the danger of ethnic or religious conflict, such a unifying national vision is vital and can only be constructed on the basis of the international human rights norms guaranteeing the principles of the rule of law and non-discrimination and respect for the rights of minorities, indigenous populations, migrants and other such groups.

5. The National Security Doctrine

The national security doctrine of a government can often provide an indicator of how stable or equitable the country is. In the contemporary world, a national security doctrine must be grounded in international human rights norms and must give priority to upholding human rights nationally, regionally and internationally. In a world of terrorist threats and global mobilization against terrorism, it is particularly important that there be safeguards against the risks of trampling upon human rights in protecting national security or of countering terrorism.

6. The State of Freedom of Expression and Freedom of Religion or Belief

If freedom of expression is being stifled and freedom of religion or belief is not respected it would be fairly safe to say that there would be grievances lurking beneath the surface in the country that could erupt at any time. If people cannot practice their religion or give expression to their beliefs they are often ready to fight for it, and, if necessary to die.

7. Findings of International Treaty Bodies

Under the principal human rights conventions, States are required to submit reports on their actions to implement the conventions and these reports are considered by treaty monitoring bodies, such as the Human Rights Committee, the Committee against Torture, the Committee on the Elimination of Discrimination against Women, and the Committee on the Elimination of Racism and Racial Discrimination. The comments, conclusions and recommendations of these treaty monitoring bodies can often be quite telling about the state of protection of human rights in the country and about whether there are seething problems or problems beneath the surface waiting to erupt. Those engaged in risk analysis must therefore have in view for every country what the international human rights treaty bodies are saying about the state of human rights within the country.

8. Findings of United Nations Human Rights Investigations

In the United Nations these days, there are thematic human rights rapporteurs and working groups producing reports once or twice a year on problems such as: extrajudicial executions, torture, enforced disappearances, arbitrary detention, violence against women, religious freedom, the right to food, the right to education, the right to health, and on housing issues. These thematic special procedures of the United Nations Commission on Human Rights, in their annual reports, cover a range of some 60-70 countries per year. In 2003, the Special Rapporteur on Violence against Women did a survey on this problem for every country of the world. The reports of these thematic special procedures can give a pretty good indication of whether or not there are serious problems within a country. Evidence of extrajudicial executions, torture, enforced disappearances or arbitrary detention can tell one straightaway that the storm clouds are over the country and are about to burst if they have not already done so.

9. States of Emergency

If a country has a *de facto* or *de jure* state of emergency, then that would tell that there are particular reasons to look closer at the country. If a country is democratically governed under the rule of law, a state of emergency might not necessarily indicate instability.

Under article 4 of the International Covenant on Civil and Political Rights

> "In time of public emergency which threatens the life of the nation and the existence of which is officially proclaimed, the States Parties to the present Covenant may take measures derogating from their obligations under the present Covenant to the extent strictly required by the exigencies of the situation, provided that such measures are not inconsistent with their other obligations under international law and do not involve discrimination solely on the ground of race, colour, sex, language, religion or social origin."

10. Early Warning and Prevention

Especially in today's world where people are moving across frontiers and cultures are intermingling, it would be advisable for each country to have arrangements to detect and head off grievances that could erupt in a strife or conflict. One way of achieving this might be for a national commission on human rights to provide an annual assessment of the state for respect for human rights within the country. Risk assessment of a country could look at whether such arrangements for early warning and prevention exist within the country.

11. Civilian Control of the Police and the Military

An important question to ask in risk assessment of a country is whether the police and the military are under civilian control. If this is not the case, as night follows day, one can expect that the police and the military will be engaging in excesses on the civilian population leading to potentially explosive situations. Even if there is civilian control of the police and military, it would be important to ask if there is abuse of power by either. Abuse by the police or the military will certainly foment discontent and possibly strife and conflict.

12. Prevention of Genocide, Ethnic Cleansing or Mass Killings

In a recent initiative, the then Secretary-General of the United Nations, Kofi Annan, informed the Commission on Human Rights on 7 April 2004 that he intended to designate a Special Adviser on the prevention of genocide, ethnic cleansing and mass killings. This is a major innovation which leads to the thought that in risk assessment of a country, it would be necessary to ask about the danger of genocide, ethnic cleansing or mass killing. A related indicator is whether there is torture or arbitrary detention or enforced disappearances in the country. If any evidence exists that such pernicious practices are taking place then it can be safely concluded that the country presents major risks of instability and possibly strife or conflict.

To conclude, we would recapitulate the following checklist of issues that might be kept in mind when undertaking risk assessment through human rights lens:

1. What is the ethnic composition of the country? Is there a minority population? Is there an indigenous population? Is there a migrant population?
2. Is there a unifying vision of the country?
3. What is the state of governance? Is there a functioning democracy?
4. What is the state of the rule of law and the courts?
5. Is there an effective national protecting system?
6. Are there major grievances within the population?
7. Is there an internal system of early warming and alert to head off grievances?
8. Is there a *de jure* or *de facto* state of emergency?
9. Are there gross violations of human rights?
10. What is the state of human rights of women?
11. Is there a problem of human trafficking in the country?
12. What is the state of respect for the rights of the child?
13. What is the state of freedoms of expression, religion or belief?
14. What is the national security doctrine of the state?
15. What are the UN human rights treaty bodies and the UN human rights investigations reporting about the country?
16. What are the leading international human rights organizations reporting about the country?
17. Are there reputable human rights NGOs in the country and what are they reporting?
18. Are perpetrators of gross violations of human rights being brought to justice?

C. Strengthening the Preventive Capacity of National Protection Systems

We have already argued earlier in this chapter that the strengthening of national protection systems must be a key element of strategies for the protection of human rights in the future. Within the framework of such national protection systems it is essential to build up a preventive capacity to detect grievances and to respond to them before they deteriorate into disputes, conflicts, or atrocities. This is particularly important in multi-ethnic countries. It is important for all parts of the population to feel that they have a stake in the future of the country and that they have an opportunity for equitable life-chances.

National Human Rights Commissions in the developing countries are relatively new institutions that are feeling their way carefully. The following thoughts may help us move forward to a higher level of protection: preventive strategies, judicial or quasi-judicial approaches to the issue of non-discrimination, in-depth studies into problematic issues, petitions procedures, partnership with the judiciary, and the designation of national, regional and international Commissioners on the Right to Development.

A. Preventive Strategies

In his last report on conflict prevention, submitted to the Security Council and the General Assembly in 2006, former Secretary-General Kofi Annan urged that all countries put into place a national prevention system to detect, ahead of time, potential troublesome issues or situations or to head them off. We would submit that each National Human Rights Commission, in partnership with NGOs, would wish to do a kind of mapping of its country to identify where there are problem areas in the field of human rights, where such problems could arise if left unattended, and offer suggestions how the nation as a whole might act to head off such threats.

B. Non-Discrimination

There is much work to be done on the issue of non-discrimination, particularly in relation to the enjoyment of economic, social and cultural rights. We may assume, for purposes of discussion that the principle of equality is enshrined in the Constitution and is justiciable before the courts when it comes to civil and political rights. But this is rarely the case in respect of economic, social and cultural rights. Yet, this is often precisely the area where the problem exists in many countries.

National Human Rights Commissions would do well to keep horizontal inequalities under review and to open themselves up to a quasi-judicial role, in partnership with the judiciary where possible, in tackling issues of horizontal inequality. NGOs can help them in bringing situations to their attention and in preparing reasoned submissions for their consideration. In this way National Human Rights Commissions can contribute to dealing with structural problems of inequality.

C. Topical Studies

Going beyond issues of equality and non-discrimination, there are often serious human rights problems that require attention inside countries including: prison conditions, respect for human rights by police and prison personnel, arbitrary arrest and detention, the treatment of hardened criminals, the treatment of children and juveniles and gender justice, to mention only a few. National Human Rights Commissions, with the support of NGOs, can make an important contribution to their respective societies in offering up in-depth studies on topics such as these, offered in constructive spirit of dialogue and cooperation. National human rights institutions can be a mirror of the problems of the societies they serve. Over time their contribution can be structural and lasting.

D. Petitions Procedures in respect of situations of consistent patterns of gross violations of human rights.

Whether a National Human Right Commission is able to receive, consider, and pronounce upon, individual petitions will depend on the legislation establishing them. But we would submit that all National Human Rights Commissions should hold themselves competent to receive and consider petitions alleging a situation where there is a consistent pattern of gross violations of human rights. It is here that there is particularly good space for beneficial cooperation between National Human Rights Commissions and NGOs. The concept of a consistent pattern of reliably attested gross violations of human rights is one that is well known to international human rights law and jurisprudence. It is one that can be adopted by National Human Rights Commissions within their existing terms of reference as a matter of natural justice.

In considering submissions alleging a consistent pattern of reliably attested gross violations of human rights, National Human Rights Commissions will offer their views and recommendations. If done with respect for principles of due process and equity, the findings and recommendations of National Human Rights Commissions can go a long way to providing justice in countries and in contributing to stopping gross violations and preventing their recurrence in the future.

E. Partnership with the Judiciary

There are many areas where there could be beneficial partnership with the judiciary. National Human Rights Commissions could play the lead role in organizing information and orientation seminars for members of the judiciary on the norms and jurisprudence of international human rights law. There is a dearth of information on these topics in the judiciary of many countries. Human Rights NGOs and regional organizations could be partners in such an endeavour. The aim is to infuse the judiciaries with the spirit and the culture of international human rights law and jurisprudence with the aim of protection by the judiciary.

F. National Commissioners on the Right to Development.

We have thus far discussed the role of National Human Rights Commissions, in partnership with NGOs. We would like now to suggest the establishment of positions of Commissioners on the Right to Development. We have framed the proposal thus for many reasons. First, we have to see the promotion and protection of human rights in the context of development. Second, the UN Millennium Development Goals represent shared ground for cooperation among all countries. Third, the right to development includes economic, social and cultural rights as well as civil and political rights. Fourth. a Commissioner on the Right to Development would have a wider remit to look at the advancement of human rights in the context of development, to be a voice of conscience in respect of gross violations of economic, social and cultural rights as well as civil and political rights, and to pioneer new paths of cooperation in the partnership between human rights and development.

Furthermore, the Commissioner on the Right to Development would be an invaluable partner of National Human Rights Commissions and NGOs in their quest for the protection of human rights against violations and abuse.

We would recapitulate, in conclusion, the following policy propositions that might be kept in mind when discussing the future role of national human rights commissions:

- Each National Commission could map and analyze the human rights history of the country and the contemporary and future challenges of protection.
- Each National Commissions could do a study on the state of economic, social and cultural rights and identify issues and situations of concern.
- National Commissions could do a study of situations where there is evidence of a consistent pattern of gross violations of human rights.
- National Commissions could do a study of population groups at risk.
- National Commissions could offer policy recommendations for the advancement of women's rights.
- National Commissions could offer policy recommendations for the advancement of children's rights.
- National Commissions could maintain, as a principal focus, policies and strategies for the prevention of gross violations of human rights.
- National Commissions could encourage and support the role of judges in the protection of human rights.
- National Commissions could disseminate the core international human rights norms and jurisprudence to judges and magistrates.
- National Commissions could develop a policy for the spread of human rights education in schools and higher institutions of learning.
- National Commissions could enhance their cooperation with protection partners.

CONCLUSION

In this chapter we have discussed contemporary challenges of international protection as a background against which to discuss, later in this book, the protection roles of special procedures of the UN Human Rights Council. In the chapter following we discuss the origins, essence and foundations of the special procedures.

Chapter II

ORIGINS, ESSENCE AND FOUNDATIONS OF SPECIAL PROCEDURES

INTRODUCTION

In this chapter we provide some historical background on the establishment of the early mandates in order to give an idea of how they came about and what were their objectives. Thereafter, we look at some key features that provide the foundations for the system of special procedures, weaving in, as appropriate, the recently adopted code of conduct for special procedures mandate holders. This code was adopted by the Human Rights Council on 18 June, 2007. Third we look at some of the core principles of human rights fact-finding.

I. THE ESTABLISHMENT AND DEVELOPMENT OF THE EARLY MANDATES

A. The First Country Rapporteur: Chile

The United Nations, in 1977, had three fact-finding working groups in operation: one on southern Africa , one of the territories occupied by Israel in the 1967 war, and a third on Chile. The first and the third, established by the Commission on Human Rights, consisted of five members serving in their personal capacity, while the second, established by the General Assembly, consisted of three governmental members. What this meant was that any time the working group or committee moved, it had to provide interpretation or documentation facilities for five or three members. This was labour-extensive and expensive. The practice of multiple membership had come about in order to spread the acceptability and responsibility for such investigations among the different regional groups of the United Nations. Probably the three investigations would not have been established without multiple membership.

It was evident, however, that because of logistics and cost the United Nations could not investigate gross violations of human rights in many countries with groups of three or five. A formula had to be found to make more fact-finding exercises possible, in more countries, as needed.

The United Nations, in 1967, had experimented with the use of a single Special Rapporteur, who had examined the situations in South Africa and the

Occupied Territories and the International Labour Organization had an established practice of using single investigators to look into complaints in particular countries.

In 1978 the Director of the Division of Human Rights, Theodoor van Boven, launched the idea that one might replace the working group on Chile with a single rapporteur. He proposed this in his opening address to the Commission on Human Rights in 1978. The Commission on Human Rights accepted the idea and the first country rapporteur was appointed that year to continue the investigations into human rights violations in Chile. Mr. Justice Abdoulaye Dieye of Senegal, who had been a member of the working group on Chile, was appointed rapporteur.

Justice Dieye had a fine intellect and a strong personality and he took charge of the investigations into gross violations of human rights in Chile with a firm hand. Soon, however, he would be challenged in legal submissions by the Chilean government. It argued that written complaints received by the Secretariat should be handled in accordance with the confidential procedures for dealing with petitions (ECOSOC resolution 1503). It wished to superimpose on the Special Rapporteur the modalities of a confidential procedure. The Argentine Government would also make similar submissions subsequently when they had to deal with investigators probing into allegations of enforced and involuntary disappearances in that country.

In his report to the General Assembly. Justice Dieye argued that the United Nations had the competence to determine the means and methods of responding to allegations of gross violations of human rights in any given situation. If the competent body, in that instance the Commission on Human Rights, felt that a confidential investigation was called for, it was at liberty to decide accordingly. If it felt that a public investigation was called for it could go that route also. In any event, it was for a fact-finder to choose the means and methods of inquiry he or she deemed appropriate in each instance. This was the first time, as far as we are aware, that the doctrine of free choice of approach and methods had been articulated by a United Nations fact-finder. New ground had been covered by this position of Justice Dieye in his report.

Nowadays the existence and operations of the special procedures of the Human Rights Council, the rapporteurs, working groups and other experts, is well-established. But in the early days it required some struggle to put them on sound footing. Governments such as that of Chile resorted to all sorts of legal subterfuges to obstruct them. Shortly after the adoption of the Universal Declaration of Human Rights in December, 1948, when the General Assembly sought to deal with *apartheid* in South Africa, the South African Government had also pressed in its defence legal arguments that sought to deny the competence of the United Nations to look into its internal affairs. In a historic decision, the General Assembly had brushed aside its objections and established the competence of the United Nations to deal with violations of human rights taking place inside a country[62].

Now it was Chile's turn. In a letter of 15 March, 1979 to the Secretary-General of the United Nations it railed against *ad hoc* procedures which, it contended, had no legal basis in the United Nations system. In a letter of 17 May, 1979 to the Special Rapporteur it informed him that in accordance with the principle of the legal equality of states embodied in the Charter of the United Nations, it would not accept any action or proceeding by the United Nations which was of an *ad hoc* or *ad casum* nature. It would cooperate only in proceedings which were universal in character or applied on a general basis.

Justice Dieye, in his legal response to these submissions, argued that the competence of the General Assembly under the Charter was determined by its membership as a whole and therefore the Chilean Government could not decide on its own that the procedure agreed upon by the General Assembly and the Commission on Human Rights was without legal basis in the United Nations. The Government of Chile could not substitute its judgment of legality for the judgment duly and overwhelmingly pronounced by the membership of the United Nations.

Justice Dieye went on to argue that in the long-standing practice of the United Nations it had been repeatedly confirmed that the United Nations had wide competence to deal with large-scale situations of violations of human rights. That had been established since the inception of the United Nations and had been maintained throughout its existence in the various situations involving violations of human rights it had dealt with in all parts of the world.

It had also been well-established that the United Nations might employ for dealing with situations of violations of human rights all appropriate methods under the Charter, depending upon the circumstances of each situation. Some situations were handled in the Security Council or its subsidiary organs, in the General Assembly or its subsidiary organs, in the Trusteeship Council, in the Economic and Social Council, in the Commission on Human Rights, or in other United Nations organs. Situations were sometimes raised in open debate, or handled under procedures for dealing with communications, or an investigating committee or rapporteur might be appointed to look into a situation. "Whatever the method used, it was a clear principle that the United Nations might utilize for each situation such methods or procedures as it considered best suited to deal with that situation."

Justice Dieye concluded that a Government could not legitimately claim that the situation in its country should be examined under any particular pro-

62 See L.B. Sohn and T. Buergenthal, The International Protection of Human Rights. Bobbs Merril, 1972.

cedure or procedures, or under one procedure to the exclusion of others. The decision in each case was a matter for the United Nations, having regard to all the factors and circumstances involved, including, as appropriate, the views of the Government concerned. These principles were important for subsequent investigations. Similar legal submissions would be made later when the Working Group on Enforced and Involuntary Disappearances began its operations.

On the death of Dag Hammarskjold in September, 1961, Walter Lippman wrote that it had been one of Hammarskjold's historic contributions to take the United Nations from a talking shop to an organization of action. A similar claim can be made that Theodoor van Boven took the human rights programme of the United Nations into the era of responding to gross violations of human rights. But there were obstructions and challenges all along the way. It took some effort to back up these early creations of investigative mechanisms. We published some of the supporting legal papers in a book of 1997 on *The Principle of Legality in International Human Rights Institutions.*[63]

Backing up the investigative role of the United Nations in dealing with situations of gross violations of human rights required resolve, research, discipline, and guts. That the enterprise succeeded we know nowadays. It was not so evident in those days. Van Boven would be fired for his efforts. But he never flinched.

B. The First Thematic Investigation: Disappearances.

It was in the General Assembly in 1978 that the United Nations first addressed the problem of enforced and involuntary disappearances. The initiative came from the British and Canadian delegates to the Third Committee who worked with this author as Special Assistant to the Director of the Division for Human Rights. Together, we prepared what became resolution 33/173 of the General Assembly, adopted on 20 November 1978.

At the Commission on Human Rights some two months later, in February/March, 1979, delegations and NGO observers wished the Commission to express itself on this pressing problem. The resistance of the then Argentinian Ambassador to the United Nations Office in Geneva made that difficult. It will be recalled that it was only in 1978, thanks to ideas put forward by the then Director of the Human Rights Division, Theo Van Boven, that the Commission on Human Rights had appointed the first rapporteurship on a country-situations. The General Assembly, in 1979, again adopted a resolution recalling the concerns it had expressed the previous year on the problem of enforced and involuntary disappearances. At the Commission on Human Rights in 1980,

63 The Hague, Martinus Nijhoff, 1997.

delegations, NGOs and the Secretariat pooled their efforts in a remarkable common endeavour to overcome the stubborn resistance of the Argentinian representative on the Commission: Ambassador Martinez.

Ambassador Van den Heuvel of the US Mission in Geneva met with Van Boven, the Director of the Division of Human Rights, and this author for a working session on how best to tackle the problem. We provided some ideas in the form of a draft resolution and kept in touch with him as the process evolved.

At the Commission on Human Rights itself, the French delegate Mr. Justiti, a good friend, took the lead and circulated a draft resolution that went in the direction of reminding Governments of their responsibilities for law enforcement and approached the issue in terms of the responsibility of the police for investigating reports of disappearances. It was a well-meant initiative but was considered to be approaching the problem from a narrow perspective.

At the technical level three persons would then join in turning around the 'Justiti draft' and coming up with an approach that would address the problem as one of violations of human rights that needed to be investigated, and which required the urgent action and human rights diplomacy of the United Nations. These three persons were: the Canadian delegate, Dan Livermore, the Dutch delegate, Toine Van Dongen and this author as Special Assistant to the Director of the Division of Human Rights. Together we succeeded in getting Justiti to accept a different approach and then made him part of a four-member team that drafted what was eventually adopted as Commission resolution 20 (XXXVI) of 29 February, 1980, which established the Working Group on Enforced and Involuntary Disappearances.

It was quite a task to get the resolution adopted by the Commission. The Eastern Europeans were askance. The Yugoslav delegate, Ivan Tosevski, helped. He subsequently became a leading member of the working Group when it was established. The Africans were sitting on the fence on this issue. This author prepared a speech which he offered to the Ghanian delegate, who delivered it. Africa came on board.

Canadian Ambassador Yvonne Beaulne played a leading role in getting the Argentinian delegate, Ambassador Martinez, to go along with the resolution. He deserves the most credit for the political work to get the resolution adopted. Others helped a great deal. US Representative Jerome Shestack lobbied strongly in favour of the resolution.

Thus was born the first of the thematic procedures: a global investigation into a problem which was then occasioning concern mainly in Argentina. Shaping the implementation of the resolution required a resolute effort. From the inception, the need to take urgent action was registered in the Secretariat.

As the Chileans had done earlier, the Argentine Government also brought into its armoury of defence all sorts of subterfuges and legal submissions. In a note of 10 September, 1980 the Argentinean Government submitted that individual petitions on alleged violations of human rights must fulfil various formal requirements and that when they were transmitted to Governments their form should correspond with rules established by the Economic and Social Council for the handling of petitions. What the Argentinean Government was basically saying was that complaints about disappearances in Argentina should not be handled by the Working Group but under the milder confidential procedure established by ECOSOC resolution 1503 for dealing with petitions (communications as they were termed in UN parlance).

The Government pressed this point when it argued that the establishment of the Working Group on Enforced and Involuntary Disappearances did not mean the adoption of an *ad hoc* system for the consideration of a particular type of complaint, something, it contended, that would go against the structure already specifically accepted by States. It was important to uphold the competence of the Working Group to deal with such complaints and van Boven approved a legal opinion prepared by this author supporting this.

The legal opinion argued that, in support of the goal of improving the capacity of the United Nations to put a stop to gross violations of human rights wherever they occurred, various co-existing procedures had been established in order to deal with different problems or situations. Since these various procedures had been established by, upon the request of, or with the consent or approval of higher United Nations organs such as the General Assembly and the Economic and Social Council, they were all of equal weight and independent status. To argue that one procedure should be governed by another would be to frustrate the intention of the General Assembly, the Economic and Social Council, and the Commission on Human Rights in devising methods and approaches for dealing with specific problem or phenomena.

The legal opinion pointed out that, in the case of the Working Group on Enforced or Involuntary Disappearances, the General Assembly, in requesting the Commission on Human Rights to consider the question of disappeared persons with a view to making appropriate recommendations, had been particularly concerned at reports of difficulties in obtaining reliable information from competent authorities as to the circumstances of missing and disappeared persons. It was clear that the General Assembly and the Commission intended to establish a special procedure for dealing with the problems of missing and disappeared persons, which would be complementary to other existing procedures and which would not be subordinated to any pre-existing procedure.

Thus it was that one sought to back-up the Working Group and to help lay the legal underpinnings for developing the protection role of the United Nations in the field of human rights. Let it be remembered that the drafters of the United Nations Charter had consciously eschewed a protection role for the United Nations. It would have to be developed through practice. During the days of the cold war that was not an easy task. But one went about it with all the heart one could muster.

During the Working Group's early sessions, the issues which it faced included the following: How to respond to a pressing human rights problem, how to deal with the fact that the Eastern Europeans were cautious in their approval of the Group and how to deal with Argentinian submissions on the methods of work of the Group. Because of the attitude of Eastern European countries, and bearing in mind that Yugoslavia was the only country of this group ready to designate a member to serve on the Working Group, the Yugoslav member, Ivan Tosevsky, a man known for his carefulness in diplomacy, was the one who, more than the others set the tone of the Group. His influence increased after he became Chairman of the Working Group. A careful humanitarian approach thus emerged. The reasons for that approach must be understood in the context in which it emerged: Eastern Europe would not go along with more.

The same careful approach influenced the Group's attitude to the handling of telegrams about potential cases of disappearances: the Group adopted the procedure of consultation among the members before action was undertaken on telegrams. In later stages the Chairman would occasionally authorize the Secretariat to take action.

The third issue which the Group had to deal with in its early stages concerned Argentinian submissions about the methods of work of the Group. In written submissions and in oral presentations the Argentinian Government argued that the Group should apply to the complaints that it received the procedural and evidentiary criteria contained in ECOSOC resolution 1503 (XLVIII). This author prepared a legal opinion rebutting the submissions of Argentina. The opinion argued that the Working Group was competent to determine its own methods of work. That became the position of the Group.

In transmitting cases of disappearances, the Working Group dealt exclusively with Governments, basing itself on the principle that Governments must assume responsibility for any violation of human rights on their territory. If, however, disappearances were attributed to terrorist or insurgent movements fighting the Government on its own territory, the Working Group refrained from processing them. The Group considered that, as a matter of principle, such groups may not be approached with a view to investigating or clarifying disappearances for which they were held responsible.

Reports on disappearances were considered admissible by the Working Group when they originated from the family or friends of the missing person. Such reports might however, be channelled to the Working Group through representatives of the family, Governments, inter-Governmental organizations, humanitarian organizations and other reliable sources. They had to be submitted in writing with a clear indication of the identity of the sender.

In order to enable Governments to carry out meaningful investigations, the Working Group provided them with information containing at least a minimum of basic data. In addition, the working Group constantly urged the sources of a report to furnish as many details as possible on the identity of the missing person (if available, identity card numbers) and the circumstances of the disappearance. The Group required the following minimum elements:

a) Full name of the missing person;
b) Date of disappearance, i.e. day, month and year of arrest or abduction or day, month and year when the missing person was last seen in a detention centre; an approximate indication was sufficient (i.e. March or spring 1980);
c) Place of arrest or abduction or where the missing person was last seen (at least indication of town or village);
d) Parties presumed to have carried out the arrest or abduction or to hold the missing person in unacknowledged detention;
e) Steps taken to determine the fate or whereabouts of the missing person or at least an indication that efforts to resort to domestic remedies were frustrated or had otherwise been inconclusive.

Reported cases of disappearances were placed before the Working Group for detailed examination during its sessions. Those which fulfiled the requirements as outlined above were transmitted, upon the Group's specific authorization, to the Governments concerned requesting them to carry out investigations and to inform the Group about their results. The reported cases were communicated by letter from the Group's Chairman to the Government concerned through the Permanent Representative to the United Nations.

Cases that occurred within the three months preceding receipt of the report by the Group were transmitted directly to the Ministers for Foreign Affairs by means of a cable. Their transmission could be authorized by the Chairman on the basis of a specific delegation of power given to him by the Group. Cases which occurred prior to the three-month limit but not more than one year before the date of their receipt by the Secretariat, provided that they had some connection with a case which occurred within the three-month period, could be transmitted between sessions by letter, upon authorization by the Chairman.

At least once a year the Working Group reminded every Government concerned of the cases that had not yet been clarified. Furthermore, at any time during the year, any Government could request the summaries of the outstanding and/or clarified cases which the Working Group had transmitted to it.

All replies received from Governments on reports of disappearances were examined by the Working Group and summarized in the Group's annual report to the Commission on Human Rights. The number of cases on which a Government had provided one or several specific replies was listed in the statistical summary concerning each country in the annual report. Any information given on specific cases was forwarded to the sources of those reports who were invited to make observations thereon or to provide additional details on the cases.

If the reply clearly indicated where the missing person was (whether alive or dead) and if that information were sufficiently definite for the family to be reasonably expected to accept it, the Working Group considered the case clarified at the session following the receipt of that information. The case was accordingly listed under the heading "Cases clarified by the Government's responses" in the statistical summary of the annual report.

If the reply provided definite information on the missing person's fate after the reported date of disappearance, but did not unambiguously specify the person's whereabouts (for instance that the person was released from prison some time ago or that he was free without stating where), a reply from the source was awaited. If the source did not respond within six months of the date on which the Government's reply was communicated to it, the case was considered clarified. If the source contested the Government's information on reasonable grounds, the Government was so informed and invited to comment.

If the source submitted well-documented information that a case had erroneously been considered clarified, because the Government's reply referred to a different person, did not correspond to the reported situation or had not reached the source within the six-month period described above, the Working Group transmitted the case to the Government anew requesting it to comment. In such instances the case was presented in the Group's report to the Commission on Human Rights, describing the above-mentioned errors or discrepancies.

Any substantive additional information which the source submitted on an outstanding case was placed before the Working Group and, following its approval, transmitted to the Government concerned. If the additional information received amounted to a clarification of the case, the Government was informed immediately without awaiting the Group's next session. Clarifications by the sources were summarized in the Group's annual report and listed in the statistical summary under the heading "Cases clarified by non-governmental sources."

The working Group retained cases on its files as long as the exact whereabouts of the missing persons had not been determined, in accordance with the criteria outlined above. This principle was not affected by changes of Government in a given country. However, the Working Group accepted the closure of a case on its files when the competent authority specified in the relevant national law pronounced, with the concurrence of the relatives and other interested parties, on the presumption of death of a person reported missing. .

The methods of the working group, as just seen, were quite careful. It was the first thematic group of its kind and it was important for it to set down a good model. That it did. It also had a good complement of staff who did pioneering work in setting up data-banks of persons reported disappeared.

C. The First Thematic Rapporteur: Arbitrary and Summary Executions

The previous section told how the first thematic working group was established to deal with the problem of enforced and involuntary disappearances. This approach would be used next in dealing with the problem of arbitrary and summary executions, which was then widespread, and remains so, in the world.

At the time, Amnesty International was leading a campaign against arbitrary and summary executions and violations of this type were taking place in many parts of the world, particularly Asia, Africa, and Latin America. Theodoor Van Boven, the Director of the Division of Human Rights, was greatly distressed about this problem of arbitrary and summary executions and wished to take an initiative to address it.

Van Boven decided to advance the idea of a Special Rapporteur on arbitrary and summary executions in his opening address to the Commission on Human Rights in 1979. He made a special plea for the Commission to take action on this problem Before mounting the initiative we had been in close contact with the key NGOs, particularly Amnesty International, and we had also been in touch with key members of the Commission to sponsor a draft resolution calling for the appointment of a Special Rapporteur. The Danish representative, Nils Dyrlund, was the lead delegate on this.

Van Boven and this author worked on a draft resolution, then discussed it with Dyrlund, keeping Amnesty International in the picture throughout. Dyrlund was an effective negotiator and he piloted the resolution to successful passage. Significant new ground had been broken. The rapporteur would look at the problem globally, would be able to undertake urgent actions, would submit findings and recommendations to the Commission.

Amos Wako of Kenya would be appointed the first rapporteur. This was the first time that a thematic rapporteur had to shape a mandate. How would it be done? Wako was determined to present to the Commission country situations where arbitrary and summary executions were taking place. This he did, and a firestorm erupted in the Commission when his first report was published the following year. Governments wanted the report withdrawn and when, with our support, Amos would not accept this, they wanted to adopt a resolution censuring him. Nils Dyrlund of Denmark had by then moved on and the resolution on this topic was being run by Denmark's successor on the Commission, Finland. Marjatta Raasi was the Finnish delegate. This author pleaded with her to reject the idea of a censure. Marjatta, who later became Finnish Permanent Representative to the United Nations and President of the Economic and Social Council, courageously fought off any censure. This author mobilized friendly delegations to ward off any censure. Had the first thematic mandate-holder been censured, it could have marked the end of the thematic rapporteurs.

Fortunately the censure effort did not succeed and Amos Wako went on to be a successful Special Rapporteur succeeded by others who have kept this crucial mandate alive ever since then! Amos Wako, submitted nine reports to the Commission between 1983 and 1991. He found summary or arbitrary executions to persist in all regions of the world, and the largest loss of life due to this phenomenon to be in situations of armed conflict. The Special Rapporteur concluded that in spite of existing international norms designed to control the conduct of armed conflicts, and despite repeated calls by international and regional bodies for parties to conflicts to respect the right to life of innocent civilians, the loss of human life continued to be considerable. This was due to a fundamental absence of understanding and respect for the right to life among those responsible for the direction of military operations in such conflicts.

A second principal cause of loss of life, according to the Special Rapporteur, was attributable to indiscriminate violence, the victims of which were very often innocent civilians. In addition, the absence of safeguards to protect the accused during judicial proceedings had led to a climate that contributed to summary executions. Still another principal cause was the inability of the authorities to control the groups concerned and to enforce order and respect for the right to life.

The Special Rapporteur's reports contained recommendations on such questions as the need to develop international standards designed to ensure effective legislation and other domestic measures so that the proper investigations were conducted by appropriate authorities in all cases of suspicious death, including provision for adequate autopsy.

On 24 May, 1989, on the recommendation of the Committee on Crime Prevention and Control, the Economic and Social Council, in its resolution 1989/65, adopted the Principles on the Effective Prevention and Investigation of Extra-legal, Arbitrary and Summary Executions. The United Nations Secretariat also prepared a Manual on the Effective Prevention and Investigation of Extra-legal, Arbitrary and Summary Executions.[64]

64 This summary is taken from UN Action in the Field of Human Rights. UN publication, Sales No.E.94.XIV.11, pp.72-73.

D. The Second Thematic Rapporteur: Torture

In 1982 van Boven left the United Nations. Secretary-General Perez de Cuellar, under US and Latin American pressure because of van Boven's exposure of gross violations of human rights in Latin America, did not renew his contract. It was a traumatic time for the human rights programme.

It was a difficult task for his successor, Kurt Herndl of Austria, to follow him. There was universal outrage among the human rights NGOs at van Boven's sacking. Kurt Herndl was a thoughtful, careful diplomat, devoted to the ideals of the United Nations. At a very young age he had served as the Director of the Security Council Division of the United Nations Secretariat and had also served in the Executive Office of the Secretary-General, after which he had returned to the foreign service of Austria.

There had been much creativity in the van Boven period and Kurt Herndl, following in the wake of the former's dismissal, had to calm down the human rights programme. He did this with diplomatic skill. This was a period to consolidate the gains that had been made in the previous five years and to put down some building blocks of promotion and protection to the extent that one could. In the United States, the Carter Presidency, which had been so favourable to human rights, had been replaced by the Reagan Presidency. Jeanne Kirkpatrick was US Ambassador to the United Nations. She had played a leading role in the sacking of van Boven.

As Kurt Herndl's special assistant and drafter of his speeches, as we had been for van Boven and Marc Schreiber before him, this author began to emphasize human rights education and human rights technical assistance. The traffic could bear these items, while we sought to let the special procedures on disappearance and summary executions take root. Kurt Herndl, a former Legal Adviser to the Austrian Foreign Ministry, himself took a strong interest in the implementation of the human rights treaties. He was also a firm believer in professional services to the human rights bodies. He had great experience in this as Director of the Security Council Division.

In 1984 we thought that the moment was ripe for a major protection initiative, the establishment of a Special Rapporteur against torture. Herndl was a believer in human rights and shared the view that torture was an abhorrent phenomenon. He thus agreed to propose the establishment of a Special Rapporteur against torture.

At the time, the Commission on Human Rights was engaged in the drafting of a convention against torture. After the Commission had completed its work on the draft convention Herndl launched the idea in his closing address to the Commission in 1984. Delegations took action on the idea in 1985, when it succeeded. The second thematic rapporteur, against torture, was thus established long the lines of the Special Rapporteur against arbitrary and summary executions.

With a view of promoting "the full implementation of the prohibition under international and national law of the practice of torture and other cruel, inhuman or degrading treatment or punishment" the Special Rapporteur was mandated to "examine questions relevant to torture." The resolution authorised the Special Rapporteur to "seek and receive credible and reliable information from governments, as well as specialized agencies, intergovernmental organizations and non-governmental organizations." He had to bear in mind "the need to respond effectively to credible and reliable information that comes before him and to carry out his work with discretion." Finally, the Special Rapporteur was also requested "to submit a comprehensive report" to the Human Rights Commission on his activities "regarding the question of torture, including the occurrence and extent of its practice, together with his conclusions and recommendations." [65]

Dutch Professor Peter Kooijmans, a former Chairman of the Commission, and later a judge on the International Court of Justice, was appointed the first rapporteur and served with distinction for many years. The rapporteurship has continued to this day. Nigel Rodley and Theodoor van Boven, served with dedication. The position is now held by Professor Manfred Novak.

The Special Rapporteur's mandate authorizes him to seek and receive information from "Governments, specialized agencies, intergovernmental organizations and non-governmental organizations." Kooijman interpreted his mandate flexibly and received information from all kinds of sources, including victims of torture and ill-treatment, victims' families, lawyers and eyewitnesses.[66] As early as 1986, the Special Rapporteur mentioned holding consultations not only with Governments and NGOs but also with individuals, including an individual who claimed to be a victim of torture while in the custody of the army.[67]

The Special Rapporteur sought information from Governments through consultations with their representatives in Geneva to obtain data on national legislation and measures implementing the prohibition of torture and ill-treatment. But most information was received by the Special Rapporteur in the form of *communications* from organizations and individuals. The Special Rapporteur examined the credibility and reliability of the information according to a set of criteria developed by him before transmitting communications to Governments alleging individual cases of torture or some forms of ill-treat-

65 I have drawn here on factual information from the research papers of my students at the Geneva Graduate Institute of International and Development Studies.

66 Supra note 20, pp. 101-102.

67 Supra note 3, para. 61.

ment as well as a generalized pattern of torture.

In his second report to the Commission,[68] Kooijmans stressed the necessity of *never* disclosing the identity of his sources in order to protect the person or organisation concerned against retaliatory measures. He also stated that because most cases of torture and ill-treatment occurred in a political context, it was essential for the Special Rapporteur to assume sole responsibility for the assessment of the reliability and credibility of the information that came before him. For the Special Rapporteur, the fact that most allegations of torture and ill-treatment came from opposition and other politically-motivated groups was insufficient grounds for dismissing them. He considered that it was essential to look at these allegations against the background of information received from other sources and the general human rights situation of the country concerned.

Upon receiving credible information suggesting that an individual or a group of individuals was at risk of torture at the hands, consent, or acquiescence of public officials, the Special Rapporteur sent an *urgent appeal* in the form of a letter to the Minister of Foreign Affairs of the country concerned, urging the Government to ensure the physical and mental integrity of the person(s). It was the practice of the Special Rapporteur to issue appeals when an individual was feared to be at risk of any of the following: [69]

- corporal punishment;
- means of restraint contrary to international standards;
- prolonged incommunicado detention;
- solitary confinement;
- "torturous" conditions of detention;
- the denial of medical treatment and adequate nutrition;
- imminent deportation to a country where there was a risk of torture;
- the threatened use or excessive use of force by law enforcement officials, and
- the enactment of legislation that could undermine the prohibition of torture (e.g. providing impunity for acts of torture)

The urgent appeals procedure, has become one of the most important features of the thematic special procedures. According to Kooijman, this procedure was " not per se accusatory, but essentially preventive and humanitarian in nature and purpose." Due to the "extremely time sensitive" information contained in an urgent appeal, the direct transmission of the information to the Government in question was entirely justified.[70]

68 E/CN.4/1987/13, paras. 5-7.

69 See http://ohchr.org/english/issues/torture/rapporteur/appeals.htm (last visited on 28.11.2007).

70 Supra note 19, paras. 4-5.

The Special Rapporteur also made numerous press statements with regard to pressing matters relating to his mandate. This practice aimed to raise public awareness and attract Governments' attention to crucial issues. The Special Rapporteur's approach to his mandate and the working methods developed over the years has received the approval of the General Assembly. In A/RES/51/86 of February 7, 1997, the GA stated that it:

> "Approves the methods of work employed by the Special Rapporteur, in particular as regards urgent appeals, reiterates his need to be able to respond effectively to credible and reliable information that comes before him, invites him to continue to seek the views and comments of all concerned, including Member States, in the elaboration of his report, and expresses its appreciation of the continuing discrete and independent way in which he carries out his work."[71]

The Special Rapporteur has also been actively involved in the promotion of the right of victims of torture to remedy and reparation. The Special Rapporteur actively participated in the drafting of the Basic Principles and Guidelines on the Right to a Remedy and Reparation for Victims of Gross Violations of International Human Rights Law and Serious Violations of International Humanitarian Law.[72] In addition, the Special Rapporteur also continues to support the work of the Board of Trustees of the Voluntary Fund for Victims of Torture by encouraging States to make contributions to its resources and disseminate, as appropriate, information on the Board's work to those that could benefit from the assistance it offers.[73]

Since the events of September 11, 2001, the Special Rapporteur has also paid attention to the implications anti-terrorism measures implemented by States might have.[74] As the Special Rapporteur noted, the provisions of some new anti-terrorist legislation at the national level may not provide sufficient legal safeguards as recognized by international human rights law in order to prevent human rights violations, in particular those safeguards preventing

---

71 A/RES/51/86 of February 7, 1997, para. 7.

72 Adopted by GA Resolution 60/174 of December 16, 2005.

73 The General Assembly created the United Nations Voluntary Fund for Victims of Torture in 1982. The purpose of the Fund is to receive voluntary contributions and distribute them to non-governmental organizations and treatment centres for assisting victims of torture and their relatives whose human rights have been severely violated as a result of torture, as well as for the funding of projects for training healthcare professional specialized in the treatment of victims of torture. It is administered by the United Nations Secretary-General with a Board of Trustees acting in an advisory capacity and comprising five members with wide experience in the field of human rights.

74 See the following reports: E/CN.4/2003/68; A/57/173; A/58/120, A/59/324; A/60/316; E/CN.4/2006/6.

and prohibiting torture and other forms of ill-treatment.[75] In this regard, the Special Rapporteur stated that the following basic legal safeguards should remain in any legislation relating to arrest and detention of suspected terrorists: the right to habeas corpus; the right to have access to a lawyer within 24 hours from the time of arrest; and the right to inform a relative or friend about the detention. The Special Rapporteur also addressed the issues of the places and length of pre-trial detention and of admissibility of confessions in court, as well as the necessity to ensure that impunity would not prevail in cases of torture in all circumstances. In addition, he recalled the obligation of States to respect the principle of non-refoulement in relation to extradition cases. The Special Rapporteur called attention to the use of diplomatic assurances in such cases and stressed that they were insufficient guarantees against torture and ill-treatment.

II. KEY FEATURES OF THE SPECIAL PROCEDURES SYSTEM

A. Functions

According to the Manual which they themselves produced, special procedure mandate holders consider that their principal functions are to:

- analyse the relevant thematic issue or country situation on behalf of the international community;
- advise on the measures which should be taken by the Government(s) concerned and other relevant actors;
- alert United Nations organs and agencies and the international community in general to the need to address specific situations and issues. In this regard they have a role in providing 'early warning' and encouraging preventive measures
- advocate on behalf of the victims of violations through measures such as requesting urgent action by relevant States and calling upon Governments to respond to specific allegations of human rights violations and provide redress;
- activate and mobilize the international and national communities to address particular human rights issues and to encourage cooperation among Governments, civil society and inter-governmental organizations.[76]

75 E/CN.4/2003/68, para. 5 and ff.

76 Manual of the Special Procedures, p. 5.

B. Status

Mandate holders are legally classified as 'experts on mission' for the purposes of the Convention on Privileges and Immunities of the United Nations. While they are working on their mandates, experts enjoy functional privileges and immunities that are specified *inter alia* in article VI, section 22 of the Convention. These include:

a. Immunity from personal arrest and detention and from seizure of their personal baggage.
b. In respect of words spoken or written and acts done by them in the course of the performance of their missions, immunity from legal process of every kind. This immunity is to be accorded notwithstanding that the persons concerned are no longer employed on missions for the United Nations.
c. Inviolability for all papers and documents
d. For the purpose of their communications with the United Nations, the right to use codes and to receive papers or correspondence by courier or in sealed bags;
e. The same facilities in respect of currency or exchange restrictions as are accorded to representatives of foreign governments on temporary official missions;
f. The same immunities and facilities in respect of their personal baggage as are accorded to diplomatic envoys."[77]

They enjoy privileges and immunities 'with a view to the independent exercise of their functions. ...They may be invoked as against the State of nationality or of residence...'[78] The International Court of Justice held in the Cumaraswamy case that a Special Rapporteur was 'entitled to immunity from legal process of every kind' for the words spoken by him during an interview.[79]

C. Genre

According to their own Manual, "Unlike the requirements of communication procedures established under human rights treaties, the exhaustion of local remedies is not a prerequisite for the consideration of an allegation by the Special Procedures. The Special Procedures are not quasi-judicial mechanisms. Rather they are premised upon the need for rapid action, designed to protect

77 Ibid.

78 Manual prepared by the Special Procedures mandate-holders, para. 14. See also the Mazilu case , ICJ Reports, Advisory Opinion (1989).

79 Manual, op cit., para. 15. See also the Cumaraswamy case, ICJ Reports, Advisory Opinion, 1999.

victims and potential victims, and do not preclude in any way the taking of appropriate judicial measures at the national level."[80]

D. The Essence of the System

The *Lund Statement to the UN Human Rights Council on the Human Rights Special Procedures* (2007), which was drafted under the chairmanship of the author of this book, brought out well the essence of the system of special procedures:

The Essence of the System

"15. The system of human rights special procedures of the United Nations has been developed to carry out mandates assigned by the former Commission on Human Rights, now the Human Rights Council, and other policy-making organs dealing with the promotion and protection of human rights in accordance with internationally recognized human rights law. They pay particular regard to the universality, indivisibility, interdependence and interrelatedness of human rights and the principles of equality and non-discrimination and gender equality, and are mindful of the importance of the implementation of the right to development. The system consists of independent experts implementing thematic and country mandates.

"16. Special procedure mandate holders discharge their functions with independence, impartiality, integrity and in accordance with standards of fairness and due process and in the quest for justice.

"17. The special procedures place the protection of those in need high among their priorities and pursue a victims-oriented perspective. They have the tasks of analysing human rights situations, making relevant recommendations and striving for justice for the victims, actual and threatened.

"18. Special procedure mandate-holders operate on the basis of international cooperation with governments, specialized agencies, regional organizations, national human rights institutions, non-governmental organizations, civil society and other partners and also pursue cooperative approaches among themselves…

"19. The functions of special procedures include the gathering and analysis of information and trends on emerging and actual human rights issues, acting upon the recommendations of human rights treaty bodies, contributing to the development of international standards, respond-

80 P. 11.

ing to urgent situations referred to them by the Human Rights Council, gathering and reacting to reliable information concerning allegations of human rights violations, reporting on State implementation of human rights obligations, identifying best practices, undertaking country visits, making recommendations for improved enforcement of human rights at the national level and communicating on behalf of victims.

"20. The special procedures are also attentive to the importance to their work of contributing to human rights education and training and to the dissemination of information on human rights. They communicate with, respond to and interact with, civil society, national human rights institutions, non-governmental organizations, media and other actors in the implementation of their mandate.

"21. The efficacy of the work of special procedures depends upon effective and timely cooperation from governments, particularly in providing relevant information expeditiously, responding effectively to their communications, enabling them to have unhindered access to the country to assess the field situation, and in giving effect to their recommendations in a sustained and faithful manner.

"22. The standing invitations by countries pledging to accept visits of thematic special procedures is an important way of strengthening the system and all countries should consider issuing such standing invitations."[81]

III. HUMAN RIGHTS FACT-FINDING

Fact-finding in the field of human rights possesses distinct characteristics generally not found in traditional fact-finding or in fact-finding in other areas of international law. First, the approach of fact-finding in the field of human rights is not primarily to judge or to condemn but to assist in the restoration of human rights. Second, fact-finding is nevertheless partisan in favour of human rights. Third, it proceeds from the basis that governments have a responsibility to guarantee human rights in their respective countries and, therefore, once *prima facie* evidence is established that violations of human rights have occurred, the government has the burden to disprove the allegations or to show that it has taken, is taking, or intends to take measures to guarantee respect for human rights and fundamental freedoms. Fourth, fact-finding in the field of human rights is frequently inquisitorial rather than adversarial, in the sense that often there are no parties as such to fact-finding.

Bar Yaacov also points out that certain rules applicable to traditional fact-

81 See UN document HRC/5/18 Of 13 June, 2007, paras. 15-22.

finding may not be suitable to fact-finding in the field of human rights:

> "The practice of the United Nations with regard to inquiries into alleged violations of human rights reveals the following basic differences from the Hague system: joint initiative of the parties in dispute is not necessary for the appointment of a commission of inquiry; the state requesting an inquiry need not claim direct injury; the consent of the accused states is not a prior condition for the conduct of the inquiry; the accused state is not necessarily consulted on the membership of the commission, or its mode of operation; the commission of inquiry is responsible not to the states in conflict, but to the United Nations organ that has appointed it; the scope of investigation includes legal as well as factual issues; the report contains not only findings, but also recommendations; action on the report is expected, not only by the state or states directly concerned, but also the competent United Nations organs.[82]

Dr. N. Valticos presented some of the salient features of human rights fact-finding in an excellent way:

> "Fact-finding in the field of human rights has a special importance, and also encounters special difficulties, both because of the subject-matter and because of the importance attached to it by public opinion, which regards it as the acid test of the effectiveness of international organizations. Fact-finding in respect of human rights is however all the more difficult, because it frequently concerns the action and essential interests, if not indeed the very structure, of the States involved, which are therefore less inclined to accept international intervention in such matters. The issues often have political aspects and are the subject of discussion in political bodies, a factor which necessarily complicates their examination. Lastly, although the United Nations have primary responsibility for the protection of human rights as such (and especially civil and political rights), human rights problems are also frequently dealt with by other organizations, whether universal (such as the International Labour Organization, which has played and continues to play a pioneering role in this field) or regional (such as the Council of Europe and Organization of American States). Consequently, fact-finding on questions concerning human rights has been undertaken by various organizations and bodies in differing contexts, and the methods used have not always been similar."[83]

82 N. Bar Yaacov cited in Ramcharan, op.cit., pp.6-7.

83 Foreword to B.G. Ramcharan (Ed.), *International Law and Fact-Finding in the Field of Human Rights* (1982), p.viii.

A. The role of human rights fact-finding

With respect to the role of fact-finding in human rights we may ask: What is its objective? One answer could be that the objective is to promote and to protect human rights effectively, i.e. to prevent violations, to stop them if they are taking place, and to restore respect for human rights. At what stage, it may be asked, does one generally resort to fact-finding? In practice, resort is made to fact-finding at the stage of trying to halt violations, or of restoring respect for human rights, or in dealing with complaints of violations of human rights in the context of established procedures such as those in the ILO. What are the specific goals of fact-finding? Fact-finding, it may be suggested:

- may help to clarify disputed facts arising in the context of complaints of violations human rights;
- may assist the deliberations of international organizations in their consideration of human rights situations;
- may be a means of bringing an international presence to bear upon a situation;
- may assist the government involved to become aware of excesses committed by its agents or its security forces;
- may record violations which have taken place in the past so as to assist future governments in taking appropriate remedial or compensatory measures or in filling in gaps in laws or in strengthening protecting institutions;
- may assist in discovering and examining phenomena of, or trends in violations; for example, torture enforced or involuntary disappearances and arbitrary or summary executions.

Another question that may be asked is: In what types of situations is fact finding most appropriate? A possible answer is: in relation to situations of gross violations of human rights or to phenomena such as torture or enforced or involuntary disappearances, or arbitrary and summary executions. There are other questions which come to mind. For example, when is a group preferable to a lone fact-finder? Is it wise to entrust fact finding to the Secretary General of the United Nations or to the Secretariat of an international organization? Can fact-finding mechanisms be made more structured or do *ad hoc* arrangements facilitate different approaches to different situations?

B. Principles and rules of fact-finding

In the contemporary international law of human rights there are certain clearly established principles by which fact-finding should be guided on all occasions. Among these may be mentioned:

- the independence, objectivity, and impartiality of fact-finders;

- propriety in form and in substance;
- legality and due process;
- equity and fairness;
- responsiveness to, and effectiveness in dealing with, humanitarian problems.

As Dr. Valticos emphasized, fact-finding:

"...must be based on certain rules and respect certain principles...

The principles must be such that, having regard to the procedure followed and the persons entrusted with it, the fact-finding process enjoys the confidence of the international community as well as of the State concerned. It thus becomes possible more readily to obtain the cooperation of the latter, while not leaving the international community in any doubt about the integrity and reliability of the findings.

These principles must naturally be based on the principal concepts of due process of law in domestic procedures (such as the age-old rule "*auditor et altera pars*"), but they must also make allowance for the special features of this kind of international action. Thus, in the event of on-the-spot-visits, it will not normally be possible for a representative of the party complained against to take part in interviews with private individuals. The latter party should, however, be given an opportunity to comment on allegations received in the course of such visits. Similarly, precautions have sometimes to be taken to ensure the safety of witness and to protect them against intimidation or reprisals (or the mere fear of reprisals). More generally, one must bear in mind that the proceedings are aimed at ensuring observance of standards adopted by the world community (or by a regional organization): they should therefore be investigatory in nature, particularly as regards the gathering of evidence, and should seek to obtain the fullest possible information on the matters at issue.

A process as difficult as human rights fact-finding calls not only for procedural safeguards. In a divided and distrustful world, and on questions where there exist profound differences of views, fact-finding itself and the conclusions and recommendations emanating from it are more likely to find acceptance if it is entrusted to independent and impartial persons. Not only logic, but also several decades of experience led to that conclusion."[84]

Aside from the basic principles of fact-finding in the international law of human rights, the following questions deserve to be posed:

- Are detailed rules of fact-finding necessary or should it be left to com-

84 Valticos in Ramcharan, International Law and Fact Finding, op.cit., p.ix.

mon sense, pragmatism, and a sense of fairness so as to ensure maximum feasibility?
- May rigid rules of fact-finding even obstruct the protection of human rights?
- If rules are relevant, should they be binding rules, or guides to conduct, which may be applied in a flexible manner from case to case?

Let us seek aid again from Dr. Valticos, who argued that:

> "...as we are on the frequently unstable terrain of international law, it is necessary, as has previously been recognized, not to confine oneself within unduly rigid categories or rules. In international law, functions intertwine – at times, indeed, too much – and judicial aspects cannot always be distinguished clearly from non-judicial ones. It is therefore not always possible, in international fact-finding, to transpose internal judicial procedures in full. Nor is it always possible – or even desirable – to establish unduly detailed rules which may turn out not to be applicable in practice. If procedures are too formal and judicial rules too detailed, they may prove not to be adapted to the great variety of situations, to the susceptibilities and objections of the States concerned, or to practical needs."[85]

C. Questions of Policy

If fact-finding is taking place within the context of an established or quasi-judicial complaints procedure, such as those existing in the ILO the task of the fact-finder may be a more straightforward one, namely to examine whether or not certain asserted facts are true. However, if fact-finding is taking place within the context of the efforts of an international organization such as the United Nations to deal with a situation of violations of human rights within a country, then the fact-finder faces certain crucial policy choices. For example:
- Should the strategy be one of ascertaining the truth and exposing violations – truth exposure? Here the emphasis will be on attracting the force of public opinion.
- Should the objective be to establish the truth, but at the same time to engage in a dialogue with the government – truth and dialogue? Here more emphasis will be placed on dialogue than on public opinion.
- Should the objective be principally one of pursuing a diplomatic dialogue with the government – dialogue and diplomacy? In this case, while the facts may be found, they will be even more guarded by the fact-finders and even greater reliance will be placed on diplomacy.

As opposed to "country situations", if the problem being investigated is a global one such as arbitrary and summary executions, should the fact-finder

85 Valticos in Ramcharan, International Law and Fact Finding, op.cit., p.viii.

merely describe the problems in global terms or should he or she also deal with specific situations in individual countries? This issue arose in relation to the first report of the United Nations Commission on Human Rights' Special Rapporteur on arbitrary and summary executions in particular countries. During the debate on this question at the thirty-ninth session of the Commission on Human Rights, governments opposed the Special Rapporteur's discussion of a number of country situations. Difficult choices are involved here. Is it possible to discuss a problem without being mindful of its manifestation in particular instances? May too much emphasis on diplomatic niceties serve to mask the truth?

Other important policy questions which may arise in practice are: How should a fact-finder deal with a deceitful government? How should a fact-finder approach his task if the government concerned refuses to allow a visit on the spot? In all of this, the ultimate objective already referred to must be kept uppermost in mind: to protect human rights effectively. This is the acid test.

D. Elements of Fact-Finding in International Law and Practice

Having raised some issues touching on the role of fact-finding, principles for the conduct of fact-finding, and fundamental policy questions which may be involved for the fact-finder, let us now proceed to offer an examination of certain elements of fact-finding which may be distilled from international law and practice.

a) Sources of international fact-finding standards and models

In a path-finding work on human rights fact-finding the following conclusions were offered on the question of standards:

1. Fact-finding being, in principle, a quasi-judicial process, fact-finding bodies in the field of human rights should be guided, as appropriate, by the relevant rules of international law.
2. However, a flexible approach should be adopted by fact-finding bodies and legal criteria should usually yield to humanitarian considerations. Nevertheless, the rules of procedure in international fact-finding should remain consistent with principles of due process in order to retain the credibility of the procedure.
3. The sources of law applicable by fact-finding bodies are:
   a. Sources indicated by any particular constitutional or treaty regime within which the fact-finding body may have been established;
   b. Sources expressly mentioned in the constitutive instrument;
   c. Relevant legal pronouncements of parent organs;

d. The laws of the State concerned, in so far as they are consistent with international standards;
e. The sources of law enumerated in article 38 of the Statute of International Court of Justice, namely, international conventions, international custom, the general principles of law, judicial decisions, and the teachings of highly qualified publicists;
f. The binding parts of international human rights standards.

4. The international standards of human rights are fully invocable by fact-finding bodies. In so far as they represent binding rules of international law they may be applied by the fact-finding bodies. In so far as they represent standards of conduct they may be, and frequently have been used by fact-finding bodies to guide them in their assessment of a situation or the conduct of a Government."[86]

b. Sources of Information

In the same work to which we have just referred, the following conclusion were offered on matters of evidence:

1. The rules of evidence applicable to any fact-finding exercise depend in the first place upon any relevant provisions in the constitutive instrument initiating the exercise. If the constitutive instrument gives the fact-finding body the power to draw up its own rules of procedure, then the fact-finding exercise will be governed by such rules of evidence as are included in the rules of procedure.
2. In the absence of any, or sufficiently express, provisions in the constitutive instrument, fact-finding bodies should be guided by the following general principles, both in drawing up their rules of procedure and in their practical operations:
   a. The standard of proof is usually a "balance of probability". Probability in this sense may be defined as an evaluation of the likelihood of a past event having happened, given the facts and assumptions expected or adopted for the purposes of the evaluation. However, in adversarial contexts, the standard "beyond all reasonable doubt" may be applied.
   b. Fact-finding exercises in the field of human rights often being more inquisitorial than adversarial, there is usually no onus or burden of proof upon any particular complaint. However, upon the establishment of a prima facie case in which breaches of human rights have occurred, a burden of proof may rest upon the government concerned to show that this was not the

86 Ramcharan, International Law and Fact Finding, op.cit., pp.38-39

case or that government agents were responsible for such violations.

c. Flexible admissibility criteria should be applied. A fact-finding body is free to employ, for enlightening itself, all the kinds of evidence that it deems necessary. It has the unlimited right of admitting all methods of proof that may be considered in conscience as sufficient and necessary.
d. As regards the communication of evidence to the government concerned, a fact-finding body should, as a general rule, communicate to the government concerned for its comments such evidence as it may receive. However, it is within its discretion to communicate a particular piece of evidence to the government or not. It may decide not to do so, in order to protect the source of information or to protect other persons from reprisals.
e. As regards the evaluation of evidence, this is a matter that rests exclusively within the competence of the fact-finding body, or, after it has submitted its report, upon its parent organ (if any).

c. On-site observations and hearings

Certain basic principles regarding on-the-spot visits may be detected in United Nations practice:

i. Freedom of investigation and freedom to determine programme, itinerary and methods: Although the itinerary and programme is usually the subject of consultations with the government concerned, especially in view of the government's responsibility to guarantee the safety and security of members of the visiting mission, the final decision on the nature of the programme rests with the fact-finding organ, which is also free to determine its methods of operation.
ii. Freedom of movement throughout the country concerned is insisted upon.
iii. Guarantees of safety and security as well as of privacy and security of premises, possessions, records: Fact-finding organs usually insist on written guarantees of safety and security for their members and the accompanying secretariat staff.
iv. Independence of premises and accommodation is also insisted upon.
v. Privacy of interviews or hearings: Persons interviewed are usually heard in the absence of government representatives.
vi. Protection of witnesses: Fact-finding missions usually insist upon writ-

ten guarantees by the host government that no person who has been in contact with the mission will for that reason be subjected to coercion, sanctions, punishment, or judicial proceedings.

vii. Privileges and immunities of the members of the Group and Secretariat staff are insisted upon.

viii Maintenance of records: Fact-finding missions may keep such records of their visits, interviews, hearing, meetings, etc. as they consider necessary.

ix. Press communiqués: It is generally accepted that the visiting mission may issue information communiqués on its visit to the media. Sometimes, if appropriate, the government concerned may be consulted.

In so far as hearings are concerned, the late Mr. Justice Dieye, on the basis of an examination of the practice of fact-finding bodies in the field of human rights, offered the following basic elements for the conduct of hearings:

i. Hearings, be they in an inquisitorial or adversarial context, should be conducted in a quasi-judicial manner.

ii. After establishing their identity, witnesses should be required to make an oath or affirmation to tell the truth.

iii. Witnesses should preferably give an oral account of their story instead of reading out prepared statements.

iv. Witnesses should be examined by the fact-finder with a view to checking for reliability, veracity, or corroboration.

v. The fact-finding body may decide whether its hearing shall be public or private.

vi. Due attention should be paid to the need to protect witnesses against reprisals. If necessary, hearings may be conducted in locations or in circumstances designed to protect witnesses.

vii. A fact-finding body may decide on witnesses whom it wishes to hear and may call witnesses on its own volition.

viii A fact-finding body may indicate interim measures of protection, if necessary, or may suggest that urgent measures be taken in order to ensure respect for human rights.

ix. In hearings in an adversarial context, the principle of equality of arms should be respected.

x. Appropriate arrangements should be made for maintaining records of hearings.[87]

On the issue of legal representation Professor R. Clark suggested that

"...as a general principle, a fact-finding body should, if possible, and if it considers this desirable, allow the party or parties involved to utilize the

87 Ramcharan, *International Law and Fact Finding*, op.cit., pp.102-103

services of legal experts, eg. In order to make submissions to the fact-finding body or perhaps, in appropriate cases, to examine witnesses."

Bearing in mind the mixture of adversarial and inquisitorial elements usually found in fact-finding in the field of human rights, it may be valuable for fact-finding bodies to consider ways and means of drawing upon legal expertise in the examination of witnesses or in the marshalling of evidence. It may be desirable for fact-finding organs, for example, to designate one of their members or a member of the secretariat to act as counsel to elicit the story of persons appearing before them, and also to attempt to probe such persons for reliability, veracity, character, possible motives, etc.[88]

d. Reporting and dissemination

Theo van Boven offered the following general thoughts on the reports of fact-finding bodies in the field of human rights:

i. As a minimum, the reports of fact-finding bodies should contain a summary of: the facts alleged, the human rights affected, the submission of the parties, if any, the evidence obtained, the facts established, and the conclusions reached.
ii. If the fact-finding body is so empowered, it may offer appropriate recommendations. In any case, it may offer advice or views on measures which need to be taken with a view to the speedy restoration of respect for human rights.
iii. It seems fairly well-established that separate or dissenting opinions may be entered by members who have participated in the inquiry in question.[89]

As regard the dissemination of fact-finding reports, a question which may be considered is the desirable length of the report. If the report is unnecessarily long, the chances of its being read by many people may be diminished. This applies to members of organs such as the United Nations Commission on Human Rights Council or the United Nations General Assembly. The position may be even worse for members of the public. The more concise the report, the greater may be its chances of being read and of having an impact. There has, unfortunately, been a tendency in some instances for fact-finding reports to go into hundreds of pages. If such great length is considered unavoidable, it may be desirable for a concise summary of each report to be inserted at the beginning. This summary can then be widely disseminated.

88 R. Clark "Legal Representation" in B.G.Ramcharan, International Law and Fact Finding, op.cit., p.130

89 T. van Boven , "The Reports of Fact-Finding Bodies", in Ramcharan, International Law and Fact Finding, op.cit., p.185

IV. THE POLICY FRAMEWORK ESTABLISHED BY THE HUMAN RIGHTS COUNCIL (2007)

On 18 June 3 2007, the Human Rights Council (HRC) as part of its package of institutional modernization, adopted a code of conduct for special procedures mandate holders. The Council considered that the efficiency of the system of special procedures should be reinforced through the consolidation of the status of mandate-holders and the adoption of principles and regulations taking the specificities of their mandate into consideration. It underlined the centrality of the notions of impartiality and objectivity, as well as the expertise of mandate-holders, within the context of special procedures, along with the need to give the required degree of attention to all human rights violations, wherever they may be taking place.

The Council considered "that one should distinguish between on the one hand, the independence of mandate-holders, which is absolute in nature, and on the other hand, their prerogatives, as circumscribed by their mandate, the mandate of the Human Rights Council, and the provisions of the United Nations Charter."[90]

The Council urged all states to cooperate with, and assist, the Special Procedures in the performance of their tasks and furnish all information as well as respond to communications transmitted to them by the Special Procedures without undue delay.

GENERAL PRINCIPLES OF CONDUCT

According to Article 3 of the Code of Conduct, mandate holders are independent United Nations experts. While discharging their mandate, they shall:

a) act in an independent capacity; and exercise their functions in accordance with their mandate, through a professional, impartial assessment of facts based on internationally recognized human rights standards, free from any kind of extraneous influence, incitement, pressure, threat or interference, either direct or indirect, on the part of any party, whether stakeholder or not, for any reason whatsoever, the notion of independence being linked to the status of mandate-holders, and to their freedom to assess the human rights questions that they are called upon to examine under their mandate;

b) keep in mind the mandate of the Council which is responsible for promoting universal respect for the protection of all human rights and fundamental freedom for all, through dialogue and cooperation as specified

90 Code of Conduct, Human Rights Council resolution, 18 June, 2007, Preambular Paragraph 13.

in General Assembly Resolution 60/251;

c) exercise their functions in accordance with their mandate and in compliance with the UN Regulations governing the Status of Experts on mission as well as with the present Code;

d) focus exclusively on the implementation of their mandate, constantly keeping in mind their fundamental obligations of truthfulness, loyalty and independence pertaining to their mandate;

e) uphold the highest standards of efficiency, competence and integrity, meaning, in particular, though not exclusively, probity, impartiality, equity, honesty and good faith;

f) neither seek nor accept instructions from any Government, individual, governmental or non-governmental organisation or pressure group whatsoever;

g) adopt a conduct that is consistent with their status, at all times;

h) be aware of the importance of their duties and responsibilities, taking the particular nature of their mandate into consideration and behaving in such a way as to maintain and reinforce the trust they enjoy from all stakeholders;

i) not use their office or knowledge gained from their functions for private gain, financial or otherwise, or for the gain and/ or detriment of any family member, close associate, or third party;

j) not accept any honour, decoration, favour, gift or remuneration from any governmental or non-governmental source for activities carried out in pursuit of his/her mandate.

Status of Mandate-Holders

Article 4 of the Code of Conduct stipulated the following on the status of mandate-holders.

a) Mandate-holders exercise their functions on a personal basis, their responsibilities not being national but exclusively international;

b) When exercising their functions, the mandate-holders are entitled to the privileges and immunities provided for under relevant international instruments including under section 22 of Article VI of the United Nations Convention on Privileges and Immunities;

c) Without prejudice to these privileges and immunities, the mandate-holders shall carry out their mandate while fully respecting the national legislation and regulations of the country wherein they are exercising their mission. Where an issue arises in this regard, mandate-holders shall adhere strictly to the provisions of Regulation 1(e) of the Regulations Governing Status, Basic Rights and Duties of Officials and Experts on

Mission, adopted by General Assembly resolution 56/280.

Solemn Declaration

Prior to assuming their functions, mandate-holders shall, in accordance with Article 5 make the following solemn declaration in writing:

> "I solemnly declare that I shall perform my duties and exercise my functions from a completely impartial, loyal and conscientious standpoint, and truthfully, and that I shall discharge these functions and regulate my conduct in a manner totally in keeping with the terms of my mandate, the United Nations Charter, the interests of the Organization of the United Nations and with the objective of promoting and protecting human rights, without seeking or accepting any instruction from any other party whatsoever".

Prerogatives

Article 6 of the Code of Conduct laid down that without prejudice to prerogatives for which provision is made as part of their mandate, the mandate-holders shall:

a) always seek to establish the facts, based on objective, reliable information emanating from relevant credible sources, that they have duly cross-checked to the best extent possible;
b) take into account in a comprehensive and timely manner, in particular information provided by the State concerned on situations relevant to their mandate;
c) consider all information in light of internationally recognized human rights standards relevant to their mandate, and of international conventions to which the State concerned is a party;
d) be entitled to bring to the attention of the Council any suggestion likely to enhance the capacity of Special Procedures to fulfil their mandate.

Observance of the Terms of the Mandate

According to Article 7, it is incumbent on the mandate-holders to exercise their functions in strict observance of their mandate and in particular to ensure that their recommendations do not exceed their mandate or the mandate of the Council itself.

Sources of Information

According to Article 8, in their information-gathering activities the mandate-holders shall:

a) be guided by the principles of discretion, transparency, impartiality, and even handedness;

b) preserve the confidentiality of sources of testimonies if their divulgation could harm witnesses;

c) rely on objective and dependable facts based on evidentiary standards that are appropriate to the non-judicial character of the reports and conclusions they are called upon to draw up;

d) give representatives of the concerned State the opportunity of commenting on mandate-holders' assessment and of responding to the allegations made against this State, and annex the State's written summary responses to their reports.

Letters of Allegations

According to Article 9, with a view to achieving effectiveness and harmonization in the handling of letters of allegations by special procedures, mandate-holders shall assess their conformity with reference to the following criteria:

a) The communications should not be manifestly unfounded or politically motivated;

b) The communication should contain a factual description of the alleged violations of human rights;

c) The language in the communication should not be abusive;

d) The communication should be submitted by a person or a group of persons claiming to be victim of violations or by any person or group of persons, including NGOs, acting in good faith in accordance with principles of human rights, and free from politically motivated stands irrelevant or contrary to, the provisions of the UN Charter, and claiming to have direct or reliable knowledge of those violations supported by clear evidence; and

e) The communication should not be exclusively based on reports disseminated by mass media.

Urgent Appeals

Mandate-holders may, under Article 10, resort to urgent appeals in cases where the alleged violations are time-sensitive in terms of involving loss of life, life-threatening situations or either imminent or ongoing damage of an irreparable nature to victims that cannot be addressed in a timely manner by the procedure under article 9.

Field Visits

According to Article 11, Mandate-holders shall:

a) Ensure that their visit is conducted in compliance with the terms of reference of their mandate;

b) Ensure that their visit is conducted with the consent, or at the invitation, of the concerned State;

c) Prepare their visit in close collaboration with the Permanent Mission of the concerned State accredited to the United Nations Office in Geneva except if another authority is designated for this purpose by the concerned State;

d) Finalize the official programme of their visits directly with the host country officials with administrative and logistical back-up from the local United Nations Agency/Representative of the High Commissioner for Human Rights who may also assist in arranging meetings with private witnesses;

e) Seek to establish a dialogue with the relevant Government authorities and with all other stakeholders, the promotion of dialogue and cooperation being a shared obligation of the mandate-holders, the concerned State and the said stakeholders;

f) Have access upon their own request, in consultation with OHCHR and after approval by the host Government or upon the decision of the latter, in light of its assessment of the security situation, to official security protection during their visit without prejudice to the privacy and confidentiality that mandate-holders require to fulfil their mandate and to their freedom of movement within the itinerary agreed to with the host Government;

PRIVATE OPINIONS AND THE PUBLIC NATURE OF THE MANDATE

According to Article 12, mandate-holders shall:

a) Bear in mind the need to ensure that their personal political opinions are without prejudice to the execution of their mission, and base their conclusions and recommendations on objective assessments of human rights situations;

b) in implementing their mandate, therefore, show restraint, moderation and discretion so as not to undermine the recognition of the independent nature of their mandate or the environment necessary to properly discharge the said mandate.

RECOMMENDATIONS AND CONCLUSIONS

According to Article 13, mandate-holders shall:

a) while expressing their considered views, particularly in their public statements concerning allegations of human rights violations, report fairly on the responses of the concerned State;

b) while reporting on a concerned State, ensure that their declarations on the human right situation in the country are at all times compatible with their mandate and the integrity, independence and impartiality which their status requires, and which is likely to promote a constructive dialogue among stakeholders as well as cooperation for the promotion and protection of human rights;
c) ensure that the concerned Government authorities are the first recipients of their conclusions and recommendations concerning the State and are given adequate time to respond, and that likewise the Council is the first recipient of conclusions and recommendations addressed to it.

Communication with Governments

According to Article 14, mandate-holders shall address all their communications to concerned Government through diplomatic channels unless agreed otherwise by individual Government with the OHCHR;

Accountability to the Council

According to Article 15, in the fulfilment of their mission, mandate-holders are accountable to the Council.

CONCLUSION

This chapter has traced the origins, essence and foundations of the special procedures system. As was seen, there is a substantial body of law and practice for the conduct of human rights fact-finding. In the next chapter we shall begin an exploration of the protection roles of special procedures, beginning with the country mandates.

Chapter III

THE PROTECTION ROLES OF COUNTRY MANDATES

INTRODUCTION

From 1967 until the end of the *apartheid* regime, for some twenty five years, the Commission on Human Rights' Working Group on Southern Africa consistently documented the shocking violations of human rights under the *apartheid* regime in South Africa, violations of human rights in *apartheid*-ruled Namibia, and violations of human rights in the former Portuguese colonies in southern Africa until their independence. The Group was not allowed to visit South Africa and therefore went to neighbouring countries to listen to witnesses, heard witnesses in Geneva and New York, published reports and communiqués, and generally supported the peoples of southern Africa in their quest for justice. The reports of the Group are a historical record of the suffering of the southern African peoples. At times the Group named specific individuals whom it accused of committing the crime of *apartheid* and other gross violations of human rights.

The peoples of southern Africa certainly achieved their independence because of their own struggles, but international support was without a doubt of great assistance to them. It gave them encouragement, it provided fora for them to tell their stories, drew attention to their plight, and documented the criminal violations of human rights from which they suffered. One cannot say how much, but the Working Group on southern Africa decidedly contributed to the protection of human rights.

Country mandates of the former Commission on Human Rights, now the Human Rights Council, similarly accompanied and supported the peoples of other countries in their travails, as they underwent gross violations of human rights. The Working Group on Chile accompanied the people of that country following the military overthrow of the democratically elected government of President Salvador Allende. The Working Group, succeeded by the Special Rapporteur on Chile, documented the violations of human rights in Chile, drew the attention of the United Nations General Assembly and the Commission on Human Rights to terrible violations, such as making people disappear, summarily executing them, torturing them and ill-treating women and children. The Working Group decried the failure of the Chilean judiciary to come to the protection of Chileans in distress. At the time, the representatives of the Chilean government of President Pinochet denounced the UN human rights investigators. Later, when democracy returned, the people of Chile thanked the investigators and the evidence they had gathered was used in the trials of some of the perpetrators. People who were imprisoned in Chile at the time said that they drew moral support in their plight from knowing that they were being morally supported by the UN human rights investigators.

On Tuesday 20 November, 2007, the trial began in Cambodia of persons accused of having committed crimes against the Cambodian people. Thirty years earlier, as the genocidal regime of Pol Pot had ravaged the Cambodian people, a United Nations investigator produced a report informing the Commission on Human Rights that a genocide was taking place in Cambodia. The evidence that United Nations investigators gathered would help those pressing for justice for the victims to build up the cases to prosecute the perpetrators. UN human rights investigators might not have made a difference in Cambodia at the time, but their work contributed to the search for justice.

As regards the Arab territories occupied by Israel in 1967, United Nations human rights investigators have, for four decades, recorded numerous violations of human rights and drawn attention to the plight of the victims. The latest Special Rapporteur, John Dugard, has been forthright in his denunciation of certain practices of the occupying regime. Here also, the work of the United Nations in documenting the violations of human rights in the Occupied Territories stands as part of the historical record of the suffering of the Palestinian people.

For years, a United Nations Special Rapporteur investigated the situation of human rights in Afghanistan under Soviet occupation. Another rapporteur investigated the situation of human rights in the Iraq of Saddam Hussein. United Nations human rights investigators have documented violations of human rights in country situations in many parts of the world. The designation of such country mandates is nowadays criticized by representatives of some countries, who argue for dialogue and cooperation in dealing with situations of gross violations of human rights. But for the people who underwent gross violations of human rights in the different situations of the past, and for those undergoing them now, international support and fact-finding at least lets them know that they are not abandoned and that there are people outside who are championing their causes. The work of UN human rights investigators with country mandates brings the facts of particular situations to the attention of the international community, enables interested Governments and non-governmental organizations to rally in support of the victims, and provides a historical record of the suffering of the victims for the purposes of justice in the future. This is work of inestimable importance.

Since the Commission on Human Rights first began the system of special procedures in 1967, the following country situations have been the subject of human rights investigations, presented in alphabetical order: Afghanistan, Belarus, Bolivia, Burundi, Cambodia, Chad, Chile, Cuba, Democratic Republic of Congo (formerly Zaire), Equatorial Guinea, El Salvador, Guatemala, Haiti, Iran, Iraq, Liberia, Myanmar, Nigeria, Occupied Palestinian Territories, Occupied Kuwait, Rwanda, Somalia, Sudan, and Yugoslavia.

Human Rights special procedures examining country situations, like thematic special procedures, contribute to protection through: dialogue with Governments concerned, making country visits, discreet and public appeals, offering recommendations, contributing to rallying the international community in favour of the victims, documenting, recording and denouncing the violations, and contributing to the quest for justice for the victims. However, the development of the role of the country rapporteurs has shared the difficulties experienced by the United Nations generally in dealing with allegations of gross violations of human rights and it is important to begin this examination of their protection role by setting the evolution of their role in historical perspective.

I. PROBLEMS FACED BY THE UNITED NATIONS IN DEALING WITH ALLEGATIONS OF VIOLATIONS OF HUMAN RIGHTS

From its inception, to the present day, the United Nations has experienced severe problems in dealing with allegations of gross violations of human rights and this has had a direct bearing on the development of the role of country and thematic procedures as well. We summarize the problems encountered over the years in the following paragraphs.

In 1947, the Commission on Human Rights adopted an infamous decision that it lacked competence to deal with the petitions reaching it complaining of gross violations of human rights.[91] The UN Secretary-General, Trygve Lie and the UN Assistant Secrertary-General for Human Rights, Henri Laugier, denounced the Commission for this decision, which was adopted with the support of leading representatives such as Mrs Eleanor Roosevelt. This was the period of segregation in the USA, gulags in the USSR, and colonies held by Britain and France. They all vigorously protected their interests.

In 1948, shortly after the adoption of the Universal Declaration of Human Rights, the General Assembly helped restore the reputation of the United Nations when it held that it was competent to discuss the situation of apartheid in South Africa. The occasion was a motion by India and others to discuss the situation of *apartheid* in South Africa. The South African Government made dogged submissions that the General Assembly could not discuss the mat-

91 See on this J.Th. Moller "Petitioning the United Nations" Universal Human Rights (Now Human Rights Quarterly), Vol. I, No. 4, 19.., pp. 57-72.

ter on the ground that it would interfere in the internal affairs of a member State. The General Assembly, in a historic decision, overruled this and adopted a resolution expressing concern over the situation. Subsequently the General Assembly established investigations and mandated the Special Committee Against *Apartheid* to monitor the situation of human rights in that part of the world.

In 1965, with the arrival of the newly independent countries in the United Nations, the Special Committee on Decolonization requested that the Commission on Human Rights take action on violations of human rights in colonial and dependent territories and in apartheid-ruled South Africa. This was endorsed by the General Assembly and the Economic and Social Council, with the result that in 1967 the Commission on Human Rights decided that henceforth it would inscribe an item on its agenda under which it would discuss the question of violations of human rights and fundamental freedoms in any part of the world, including in colonial and dependent territories and in apartheid-ruled South Africa. The parent body of the Commission, the Economic and Social Council endorsed this and by its resolution 1235(XLII) authorized the Commission to conduct through studies of any situation of concern from the point of view of allegations of gross violations of human rights. Shortly thereafter, the Council would establish a confidential procedure by its resolution 1503 (XLVIII), authorizing the Commission to act on petitions showing a consistent pattern of gross violations of human rights. The Commission could conduct a thorough study or initiate a process of direct contacts with the government involved.

Thus began two parallel procedures, a public one whereunder the Commission could discuss any situation, and a confidential one whereunder it could discuss petitions appearing to show a consistent pattern of gross violations of human rights. Under both procedures the Commission authorized its subsidiary body, the Sub-Commission on Prevention of Discrimination and Protection of Minorities, to undertake the groundwork to assist it in the performance of its responsibilities.

Under the pubic procedure, the Commission requested the Sub-Commission to bring to its attention situations of alleged gross violations of human rights occasioning concern. When the Sub-Commission first submitted some situations to the Commission in 1968 it was subjected to a fire-storm of criticism inside the Commission and never repeated this exercise again, although it did adopt resolutions of its own expressing concern and even initiating some gathering of information, as it did in the cases of Chile and Cambodia. In the end result the Commission would instruct the Sub-Commission to desist from considering such 'country situations' in the future. This restrictive approach would culminate with the establishment of the Human Rights Council, which superseded the Commission, in 2006. The Human Rights Council has placed the accent on 'dialogue and co-operation' in dealing with allegations of gross violations of human rights.

The first country and thematic special procedures were thus born within the 'violations item' in the Commission on Human Rights and they were meant in principle to conduct thorough studies of situations of international concern from the point of view of the commission of gross violations of human rights. Shifting from a 'violations perspective', many of them would subsequently, because of political pressures inside the Commission, perform from the perspective of advisory services and technical assistance, namely to assist countries experiencing problems with advice and technical assistance in dealing with those problems. Sometimes this was no more than political chicanery inside the Commission. Some mandate-holders appointed under an advice and technical assistance mandate still used their mandates to undertake investigations into gross violations of human rights.

The first country mandates, some of which we discussed earlier, namely those on South Africa, the Occupied Territories in the Middle East, and Chile, enjoyed broad political support and were given much latitude to denounce violations. Others, where Governments lobbied their friends for support. were subject to greater political control. Nevertheless, depending on the mandate-holder, there has been a fair measure of dynamism, as we shall see later in this chapter. To begin with, we look at how some of the early mandate-holders approached their tasks, especially the preparation of studies of alleged violations.

II. STUDIES AND INVESTIGATIONS UNDER ECOSOC RESOLUTION 1235(XLII)

In its resolution 7(XXIII) of 16 March, 1967, entitled "Action effectively to combat racial discrimination and the policies of apartheid and segregation" the Commission on Human Rights appointed a Special Rapporteur, Mr Manouchehr Ganji of Iran "to survey past action in its efforts to eliminate the policies and practices of apartheid in all its forms and manifestations, to study the legislation and practices in South Africa, South-West Africa[92] and Southern Rhodesia, including such matters as forced labour, inequality of opportunity in the economic, social and educational fields, arrest, detention and treatment of prisoners, right to counsel and fair trial, and to report with recommendations to the Commission.

In presenting his report to the Commission the following year, the Special

92 Report of the Commission on Human Rights on its twenty fourth session, E/4475, 1968, p. 20.

Rapporteur concluded that the situations in all the countries falling within his mandate was "an affront to humanity" and called for practical steps to be taken by the Commission as a matter of the greatest urgency.

Also at its twenty-third session, the Commission, by resolution 2(XXIII) of 6 March, 1967, had decided to establish an *ad hoc* Working Group of Experts composed of eminent jurists and prison officials to:

> "(a) Investigate the charges of torture and ill-treatment of prisoners, detainees or persons in police custody in South Africa;
>
> (b) Receive communications and hear witnesses and use such modalities of procedure as it may deem appropriate;
>
> (c) Recommend action to be taken in concrete cases;
>
> (d) Report to the Commission on Human Rights at the earliest possible time."

The *Ad Hoc* Working Group of Experts reported to the Commission that, in addition to examining documentary evidence, it had heard twenty-five witnesses, nearly all of whom had been South African citizens at the time of their imprisonment or detention.[93] "They had been people who had committed no crime and wanted only to live like human beings in dignity and justice, but had been subjected to torture and ill-treatment and were now forced to live separated from their families." The Group had met in New York, London, Dar es Salaam and Geneva but had been denied entry to South Africa.[94]

These were dramatic efforts to protect the peoples of southern Africa and the group was given wide latitude regarding its methods of work. It was also specifically authorized to act on individual cases. As we shall see below, the special procedures of the Commission on Human Rights would take on dynamic roles in coming to the protection of the peoples of southern Africa. Altogether, in addition to the annual and special reports of the *ad hoc* Working Group of Experts, the following studies were done at the request of the Commission:

- Study of apartheid and racial discrimination in southern Africa, prepared by Mr Manouchehr, Special Rapporteur appointed by the Commission on Human Rights in its resolution 7(XXIII) of 16 March, 1967.[95]
- Study concerning the question of apartheid from the point of view of international penal law, prepared by the *Ad Hoc* Working Group of Experts on southern Africa under Commission on Human Rights reso-

93 E/CN.4/950.

94 Report of the Commission on Human Rights on its twenty fourth session, E/4475, 1968, pp. 50-51.

95 E/CN.4/979 and Adds. 1 – 8

lution 8 (XXVI) of 18 March, 1970.[96]

- Study on ways and means of ensuring the implementation of international instruments such as the International Convention on the Suppression and Punishment of the Crime of Apartheid, including the establishment of the international jurisdiction envisaged by the Convention, prepared by the *Ad Hoc* Working Group of Experts on southern Africa.[97]
- Reports on the effects of the policy of apartheid on black women and children in South Africa, prepared by the *Ad Hoc* Working Group of Experts on southern Africa in accordance with Commission on Human Rights resolution 5(XXXVII) of 23 February, 1981.[98]
- Study of the criminal effects of apartheid, prepared by the *Ad Hoc* Working Group of Experts on southern Africa pursuant to Commission on Human Rights resolution 1983/9.[99]

One could also note a related study done for the Commission's subsidiary body, the Sub-Commission, on Adverse Consequences for the Enjoyment of Human Rights of Political, Military, Economic, and Other Forms of Assistance Given to the Colonial and Racist Regimes in Southern Africa, by Mr Ahmed Khalifa, Special Rapporteur of the Sub-Commission.[100]

As we shall see below, these studies staked out important normative, policy and jurisprudential ground regarding the international protection of human rights. Denunciation of crimes under the apartheid regime in South Africa were a highlight of these studies, as we shall see next.

III. DETERMINATION OF CRIMINAL AND GENOCIDAL VIOLATIONS IN SOUTHERN AFRICA

In its study of violations of human rights in southern Africa prepared by the *Ad Hoc* Working Group of Experts in southern Africa in accordance with resolution 1983/9 of 18 February, 1983, the Working Group examined the extent to which acts of apartheid might be likened to acts of genocide under the Convention on the Prevention and Punishment of the Crime of Genocide of 1948. The Working Group concluded that the practical implementation of apartheid, forty years after its institutionalization, had resulted in certain criminal consequences that coincided with the acts prohibited under article II (a), (b), and (d) of the Convention against genocide, and that the policy of apartheid, viewed as a whole and in the long term, would ultimately produce con-

96 E/CN.4/1075

97 E/CN.4/1426

98 E/CN.4/1497 and E/CN.4/1983/8.

99 E/CN.4/1985/14.

100 United Nations Publication, Sales Nos. E.85.XIV.4 and E.86.XIV.4

sequences identical with those of the acts of genocide prohibited under Article II (c) of the Convention. The Working Group recommended that "the way in which the South African regime implements the policy of apartheid should henceforth be considered as a kind of genocide" and suggested that consideration should be given to possible revision of the Convention against genocide to embrace practices "bordering on genocide". Genocide, it concuded, had acquired new aspects, not only in South Africa, but in other countries.[101]

IV. IDENTIFYING AND PURSUING THOSE ACCUSED OF CRIMINAL VIOLATIONS

The Commission on Human Rights, in its resolution 7(XXXIV) of 22 February, 1978, had called upon the competent United Nations organs to provide it with information relevant to the preparation of a list of individuals, organizations, institutions and representatives of States alleged to be responsible for the crimes of apartheid enumerated in article II of the International Convention on the Suppression and Punishment of the Crimes of Apartheid, as well as those against whom legal proceedings had been instituted by States Parties to the Convention.

The *Ad Hoc* Working Group of Experts on southern Africa, which had earlier included in its reports a list of persons deemed guilty of the crime of apartheid or of serious violations of human rights in Namibia pursuant to mandates received from the Commission, prepared a special report on the application of the anti-apartheid convention. The report, submitted to the Commission at its thirty sixth session, examined thirty seven cases of murder, torture and deprivation of freedom and of fundamental rights and concluded as follows:

> "...torture by the Security Police is common practice and, moreover, that the Government seems to acquiesce in it and to cover it up by all possible means.... The Group has been particularly struck by the continuance of the acts of torture and murder committed by the South African police, especially since July 1976. It considers that these acts can constitute only a huge campaign of intimidation of African nationalists and that the attitude of the South African Government, which endeavours in almost every case to cover up the acts with which it is charged, can but lead to the conclusion that this is the true policy of South Africa."[102]

Annex III of the report contained a list of persons implicated. The Working Group recommended that the list of persons accused of the crime of apart-

101 E/CN.4/1985/14. The Commission on Human Rights reflected this approach in its resolution 1985/10 of 26 February, 1985.

102 E/CN.4/1366.

heid should be published in the greatest possible number of newspapers and brought to the knowledge of the public by all other information means. The General Assembly of the United Nations expressed its appreciation to the *Ad Hoc* Working Group for the compilation of the list and called for its periodic updating.[103]

It could be seen from the above that when it came to dealing with *apartheid* and racial discrimination in southern Africa the Commission was willing to give its special procedures wide latitude. As we shall see in a later chapter, the Commission also gave wide latitude to its *Ad Hoc* Working Group on the situation of human rights in Chile, established in 1975. The Commission, however, was far more cautious in dealing with other situations, as we shall see when the Commission first considered country situations referred to it under the confidential procedure established by ECOSOC resolution 1503(XLVIII).

V. THE FIRST COUNTRY SITUATIONS TO REACH THE COMMISSION ON HUMAN RIGHTS UNDER ECOSOC RESOLUTION 1503 (XLVIII) (1974-75)

On Monday, 27 January, 1975, a Working Group of the Commission on Human Rights met for the first time under the '1503 procedure'. The Director of the Human Rights Division, Marc Schreiber, opened the meeting. In an injunction that is forgotten these days, he told the five members that whereas, in the Commission on Human Rights, they sat as representatives of Governments, in the Group they sat in their personal capacities. Four of the five regional groups at the Commission had designated a member. The Eastern European (Communist) group had not done so and the Chairman of the Commission, in consultation with the group, had designated a member, a Yugoslav national.

Those attending the meeting were Ghulam Ali Allana (Pakistan), Alexsandar Bozovic (Yugoslavia), Annan Arkyin Cato (Ghana), and Theodoor C. van Boven (The Netherlands). The fifth member, Didimo Rios (Panama), was unable to attend.

In opening the session, Dr Schreiber emphasized the importance of the body and advised it: "It is up to you to determine to what extent you will be able to help the Commission. That could go up to the point of advising the Commission on the course of action it should take with respect to each of the cases before you." The Chilean Government, he continued. had sent two representatives who had asked to be heard by the Working Group. It would have to decide how to proceed on this matter.

The Ghanaian representative, Annan Arkyin Cato was elected Chairperson.

---

103 G.A. resolution 35/39 of 25 November, 1980.

He noted that the subject-matter was very delicate, and the documentation very heavy. "But motivated by the best interests of human rights we shall try our best." On the mandate of the group, he shared the view of the human rights director that it should make proposals to the Commission.

The Dutch representative, Theodoor van Boven, was 'happy to see that we are sitting behind plates in our names. In my view I am sitting in my personal capacity. I agree with the Director of the Division of Human Rights that this is the character of our group as intended by the last session of the Commission".

The Working Group had to consider the following situations that had been referred to it by the Sub-Commission under the procedure established by the Economic and Social Council: situations in Brazil, Burundi, Chile, Guyana, Indonesia, Iran, Israel, Portugal, Tanzania, the United Kingdom, and Uganda.

When the issue came up whether an absent member could be replaced by a diplomat from his country's embassy in Geneva the members took the view that the designation of an alternate had to be done by the Chairperson of the Commission. Service on the groups was in a personal capacity. How times have changed since then!

The name of the group came up and the members insisted on changing the name that had been used by the Secretariat. They thus took charge from the outset. Could the group revisit the issue of admissibility? The members decided that the admissibility stage was dealt with in the Sub-Commission and could not be revisited in the group. Would the members of the group listen to governmental observers. One member, van Boven, felt that if Government observers were heard, the petitioners were also entitled to be heard. A sense of fair-play could be detected here.

Could the Secretariat be asked to follow-up with petitioners to seek clarifications or additional information? This, it was held, was not envisaged in the procedure. It would have to be authorized by the Economic and Social Council! The group registered that the fact that a government had not replied would not deter it from dealing with a situation.

The attitudes of the members of the group were instructive from this very first session. The Chairman, Mr Cato, opined, "*We do not sit in judgment or as an appellate court. We try to dialogue with Governments*." A diplomatic approach was thus taken from the outset. On the situation in Burundi, van Boven asked whether the Commission on Human Rights might ask the then Organization of African Unity to have a watching brief over the situation. The Chairman, Cato, asked whether the Commission had any relationship with the OAU that would permit this. The matter was not pursued. The mood of the prevailing wind of the times was expressed by the Yugoslav members: "Are we interested in apportioning blame? No. Are we to look to the past or the future. The future."

The problems that the group had to deal with probably tell us that the world has not moved on much when it comes to the prevention of gross violations of human rights or to dealing with the balance between security and human rights. Members of the group acknowledged that torture was widespread in Brazil at the time even if some of them bent over backwards not to have to condemn the Government of Brazil outright. In that period, Governments of the right were endeavouring to torture and wipe out dissent on the left, literally! Sadly, we see this in our time as well.

Indonesia then had thousands of prisoners in detention, some of them for many years. Van Boven noted, "Tens of thousands of prisoners are now for eight or more years in detention. The machinery of justice is working so slowly. This is not satisfactory." The Yugoslav member, Mr Bozovic, noted: "A Government is entitled to take security measures. Some of the facts complained of are admitted by Indonesia. What is worrisome is the slow pace of bringing people to the Courts. Secondly, are we sure that the wish to protect the security of the State is well-founded?" Today's questions indeed, in the war against terrorism.

The Chairman, Cato, noted, "None of us would want to deny that Indonesia, like any other country, has a right to protect its interests. We are nevertheless faced with a situation which reveals that large numbers of people have been detained for long periods of time" Today's agonies indeed!

Widespread, genocidal violence in Burundi in 1972 was passed over lightly because they were deemed matters of the past. The same occurred in relation to past violations by Portugal, where the Government had just been overthrown. This led van Boven to ask: "Should wrongs which took place in the past be completely overlooked?" His question was never answered.

Problems in Chile and the Israeli-occupied Palestinian territories came up. The group was conscious that these two situations would be dealt with also in public procedures in the Commission. Van Boven, as on so many other issues, provided the policy framework: "The fact that there is a war-time situation or political tension would not discharge us from our duties." Thirty three years later this remains a valid statement of policy.

In the report it eventually submitted to the Commission, in the drafting of which this author was involved, the Working Group told the Commission that in performing its task it was conscious of the fact that it was not sitting as a court to pass judgments on Governments, nor to apportion blame. The members were motivated by the need to ascertain the facts in the communication before them, to make recommendations to the Commission and to create a climate in which a dialogue could be established between the Commission and Governments.

The Working Group recommended that the Commission make an appeal to governments stressing the need for them to cooperate in the consideration of petitions (communications) concerning their countries and to submit their observations on those petitions promptly. It made specific recommendations to the Commission on procedural aspects of the implementation of the petitions system, including that the Commission should set up an annual working group to examine petitions referred to the Commission by the Sub-Commission.

The recommendations of the Working Group to the Commission on the country situations were a mixed bag. On Brazil, it recommended that the Commission further study the situation – even though it knew that torture was widespread. On Burundi, it recommended that the United Nations provide assistance in the fields of education and social services with a view to reducing the causes of future tribal conflict.

On Chile, the group considered that the petitions disclosed a catalogue of well-documented violations of human rights in the country. It decided to inform the Commission of the willingness of the Government's request to be represented by accredited observers during the Commission's consideration of the situation. It further decided that the petitions and the situation revealed by them were of such a nature as to be relevant to any action the Commission might wish to take regarding that situation.

On Guyana, the Group considered that the petition did not disclose the existence of a consistent pattern of gross and reliably attested violations of human rights. On Iran, the group found that the allegations made against the Government were sketchy and unsubstantiated.

On Indonesia, the group expressed concern about the slowness with which the machinery of justice was working in Indonesia, particularly in relation to detainees. While recognizing the right of Indonesia to take measures required for national security, it recommended that the Commission call on the Indonesian Government to take steps to bring to trial those detainees who could be brought before the courts and to speed up the process of releasing those detainees against whom no evidence appeared to exist.

On Israel, the petitions concerned the situation in the occupied Palestinian territories. The group decided that the situation revealed by the petitions was of such a nature as to be relevant to any action the Commission might wish to take in its consideration of the situation in its public debates on the situation in the Occupied Territories.

On Portugal, the group considered that the change of government in that country had radically altered the situation complained about and that no further action was called for. On Tanzania, the petition under consideration dealt with reports of forced marriages in Zanzibar. The group decided that though the forced marriages that were the subject of the petitions constituted violations of individual human rights and were therefore 'regrettable', nevertheless the situation did not constitute a consistent pattern of gross violations of human rights.

On Uganda, the group decided that the petitions revealed a consistent pattern of violations of human rights and called upon the Commission to act upon them. On the United Kingdom, the petitions related to the situation in Northern Ireland. The group was of the view that the Government of the United Kingdom had taken steps to investigate the situation and to institute corrective measures. It recommended that the government of the United Kingdom, and also the Council of Europe, provide relevant information for the consideration of the Commission.

It bears mentioning that when the recommendations of the working group went before the Commission on Human Rights it, regrettably, took an almost entirely political approach to the consideration of the various situations referred to it, thereby establishing a precedent that would, alas, be repeated in subsequent years.

Going back over these results thirty three years later one can detect some encouraging positions on the part of members of the group and also the politico-diplomatic approach that would, unfortunately, come to dominate this and other United Nations procedures for dealing with allegations of gross violations of human rights. Nevertheless, it is a fact that under this procedure the Commission on Human Rights, with varying degrees of effectiveness, would, over the next thirty years, invite some 80 Governments to come before it and explain the human rights situation in their countries. The dialogue that took place in the plenary Commission iwss sometimes probing, sometimes superficial. Nevertheless, the 80 Governments in question were put on notice that the international community was concerned about the human rights situation in the country concerned.

Sometimes the Commission went further and authorized a thorough study on the ground. The first such mission was initiated with the Government of Uganda. For this, the services of a respected former judge of the International Court of Justice was used, Mr Justice Onyeama (Nigeria).

VI. THE FIRST THOROUGH STUDY UNDER ECOSOC RESOLUTION 1503(XLVIII): UGANDA (1978)

In a confidential decision concerning Uganda, adopted on 3 March, 1977, the Commission on Human Rights requested the Secretary-General, in consultation with the Chairman of the Commission on Human Rights, to designate an eminent African personality to enter into contact with the Government of Uganda and, under the procedure provided for under ECOSOC resolution 1503 (XLVIII), to undertake a thorough study of the situation with regard to human rights in Uganda and report to the Commission on Human Rights as soon as possible, through the Secretary-General. The Secretary-General, after consultation, appointed Mr Justice Onyeama of Nigeria to undertake the contacts and to do the thorough study.

This was the first time that such a mission was being undertaken under the '1503 procedure' and it was important to establish its policy parameters – even if great precedents had been established by the *Ad Hoc* Working Group of Experts on southern Africa. The majority of the members of the Commission were far more restrictive in dealing with 'country situations' than they were willing to do in respect of southern Africa, the Occupied Arab Territories and Chile. One had to proceed with great caution.

As Special Assistant to the Director of the Division of Human Rights this author drafted in cooperation with the head of the petitions team in the Division, Mr Jakob Moller of Iceland, an 'Analysis of the mandate and possible approaches to its execution' which we eventually made available to Mr Justice Onyeama for his consideration.

The first issue that needed to be addressed was what was the situation to the examined. We examined the pertinent documentation of the Commission that helped define the situation in question. We then considered what was meant by 'entry into contact, the undertaking of a thorough study, and the preparation of a report as soon as possible'. On the meaning of entry into contact we took the view that the task of the eminent personality would be to discuss with the Ugandan authorities and other Ugandan citizens questions concerning the situation of human rights in Uganda raised in materials that had been before the Commission and its Sub-Commission under resolution 1503; issues raised in public debate in the Commission, the Sub-Commission or the General Assembly; and, having regard to the fact that the eminent personality was required to undertake a thorough study, he would also be entitled to raise with the Ugandan authorities questions raised in other reliable reports that came to his attention in publications, newspapers, or from reputable non-governmental organizations.

We enumerated the following minimum requirements necessary for carrying out meaningful contacts:

- Guarantees of safety and freedom of movement to the eminent personality and his staff.
- Freedom of visit: freedom of the eminent personality and his staff to visit Government institutions and to interview Government personnel.
- Access to official records, including medical and police records.
- Authority to request Government personnel to attend interviews.
- Freedom to interview private citizens confidentially.
- Guarantees of personal safety to persons interviewed.

On the concept of a 'thorough study', we pointed out that paragraph 6(a) of resolution 1503 authorized the Commission on Human Rights, after its examination of any situation referred to it by the Sub-Commission, to determine "whether it requires a thorough study by the Commission and a report and recommendations thereon to the Council in accordance with paragraph 3 of Council resolution 1235 (XLII)." We drew to the attention of the eminent personality a report that had just been published by the ILO dealing with Committees of Inquiry. That study submitted that such Commissions of highly qualified independent persons had determined their own procedure:

> "The proceedings before a commission of inquiry are essentially of a judicial nature and are designed to enable the commission to prepare a report embodying its findings on questions of fact and containing its recommendations on any steps to be taken to meet the complaint. Commissions of inquiry, in addition to considering documentary material emanating from the parties and other qualified sources, have heard witnesses and, in some cases, have supplemented the information and evidence so obtained by on-the-spot investigations."[104]

The ILO report continued that the procedure followed by such commissions had been designed to ensure that they had at their disposal thorough and objective information concerning the questions at issue. They had not, therefore, confined themselves to examining only such information as might be submitted by the parties. They had invited other governments that might possess factual information relevant to the complaint as well as the international organizations of employers and workers having consultative status with the ILO – and in certain cases national organisations of employers and workers and other non-governmental organizations – to submit any relevant factual information in their possession to the Commission of Inquiry. In particular, they had themselves drawn up lists of the witnesses they wished to hear in addition to those put forward by the parties, and, in the cases in which they had visited the country against which the complaint was made, they had drawn up their own itineraries and, as well as meeting persons whom the government wished them to see, had themselves selected the persons they wished to interview and the establishments they wished to visit. The witnesses heard in Geneva or interviewed in the country normally included representatives of the trade unions and employers' organizations of the country concerned, who were given every opportunity to put forward their views.[105]

The report added that the procedure followed by commissions of inquiry contained a number of safeguards designed to ensure respect of the princi-

104 ILO document GB.205/21/7 : Past practice concerning special inquiries with particular reference to human rights questions, para. 14.

105 Ibid, para. 15.

ples of due process of law. Thus all written statements, whether received from the other party, or from other governments or organisations invited to submit information were communicated to the parties, and the government against which the complaint was made was given an opportunity to submit its observations on them. Witnesses were heard in private sittings in the presence of the agents of the parties and, in the case of witnesses appearing on behalf of an organisation, of a representative of that organisation. Each witness had to make a solemn declaration identical to that made by witnesses before the International Court of Justice, and was given an opportunity to make a statement, following which questions were put to him or her by the representatives of the parties (and, where he or she was being heard on behalf of the organisation, also by its representative). All questions were subject to control by the commission. The members of the commission might put questions to the witness at any stage.[106]

Continuing with the analysis prepared for Mr Justice Onyeama, we noted that the sources of information was an important issue to be thought through. We submitted that the eminent personality could look "at all materials which are relevant to a thorough study". The eminent personality could even solicit information submitted from potential sources and could certainly use any information voluntarily submitted to him. Furthermore the eminent personality could undertake confidential contacts with entities such as the Organization of African Unity and the Commonwealth Secretariat, which had also had the situation in Uganda under consideration.

As regards the submission of a report 'as soon as possible' we submitted that this did not necessarily mean the final report and that the Commission intended to leave this to the judgment of the eminent personality.

Mr Justice Onyeama certainly took these elements of guidance into account in the conduct of his visit to Uganda and in the preparation of his confidential report to the Commission on Human Rights. Alas, the government of Uganda, under President Idi Amin Dada, continued to wreak havoc on the people of Uganda until Tanzanian forces entered the country and rid the 'pearl of Africa' of the rule of the 'last king of Scotland'!

VII. A SUBSTANTIVE DIRECT CONTACT MISSION UNDER ECOSOC RESOLUTION 1503: HAITI (1986).

In the preceding section we looked at how one had to navigate the first thorough study under the 1503 procedure, keeping in mind the sensitivity of the majority of members of the Commission. Another window for peering into the processes involved in undertaking direct contacts with governments could

106 Ibid, para. 16.

be seen in the visit of a representative of the Commission on Human Rights to Haiti after the fall of the younger Duvalier in 1986.

The human rights situation in Haiti had been a subject of international concern for many years and had been under consideration for several years under the confidential procedure established by the Economic and Social Council. A representative of the Commission on Human Rights, the late Jonas Foli of Ghana, visited the country for a few years and one had the impression that he had become somewhat relaxed with the leaders there. The Commission therefore decided in 1986 to take a new tack and appointed Michel Gauvin, a retired Canadian Ambassador, to undertake a mission of direct contact with the new authorities in Haiti. This author accompanied him on his mission.

A human rights mission to Haiti is a journey into one's soul. A proud and independent people had been the first in South America and the Caribbean to fight for their independence and had won it from France. They had then lent support and assistance to Bolivar in his fight for the independence of Latin American countries. Haiti was once the bread-basked of the Caribbean. Now its soil was denuded of trees and it could hardly afford to feed its people. Emigration to the USA seemed the only route of salvation for its people.

Haiti had been ruled by a succession of dictatorships, especially the father and son Duvalier duo. Baby Doc Duvalier had been forced from the country in 1986. It had phenomenal illiteracy and unemployment rates and one did not know how the country could pull itself out of its predicament. It would need international support and assistance. Good governance and the rule of law would be starting points.

Undertaking such a mission involves deep research and contacts with those in a position to assist. Before going out on the mission one sought to gather as much information as one could on the human rights situation in Haiti and met with a number of human rights representatives specializing in Haiti. One should go on such a mission with a fairly good grasp of the contours of the situation, while keeping an open mind on the situation on the ground. That is to be determined only when one is there and has seen and heard first hand.

Michel Gauvin had fought as a young man in the battle of the Ardennes and had been decorated by both the British and the French for his valour. He had been stationed in Congo at the time of the crisis there in the 1960s and had also seen duty on a Mixed Commission on Vietnam. He was a seasoned soldier/diplomat who had been to many trouble spots. He and this author spent two weeks in Haiti. At the outset of our mission he declared, "Remember, we are not here to make our names!" He was more for diplomacy and a quiet approach.

While in Haiti, Gauvin saw all the political leaders in the country save one, Jean Aristide. Aristide was then a very popular priest calling for in-depth political, economic and social reforms that could aid the poor in Haiti. Gauvin thought that he was too much of a leftist firebrand and choose not to ask to see him!

The political leaders we met in Haiti were stunning for their personal qualities. One by one, Gauvin met them and had in-depth discussions with them. Mark Bazin, an economist who had worked with the World Bank seemed the favourite of the US Government. Professor Leslie Mannegat was by far the most scintillating intellect. He gave the most lucid presentation of the situation in Haiti, historical, political, economic, social. He was formidable. Unfortunately, he would later make some unfortunate choices in throwing his lot in with the military and would lose ground for that. But he was without a doubt a superb thinker and leader.

The Church leaders with whom Gauvin met were reluctant to open up at first. It took them a while to get going. But when they did open up, one got an in-depth account of the need for political reforms and what could help the poor people of the country.

Business leaders were more interested in commercial opportunities and in having political leaders who would be favourably disposed to business. The gulf between the rich and the poor in Haiti was wide. It is one of the agonies of the soul to see the chasm between the rich and the poor in Haiti.

The military had pushed Baby Doc Duvalier out of the country. At the time one could not sense whether they intended to hold on to power or to pass it in on in democratic elections. They professed to want to hand over. But, as events turned out, they would hold on to power, directly or through surrogates for some years into the future.

The judiciary was in a sorry state, the legacy of dictatorship, and the Bar, though having superb lawyers, was largely without influence in the affairs of the nation.

How could one take forward the human rights cause in such a situation? Gauvin was the leader and this author was his substantive adviser. Based on what this author saw and heard, he set his sights on three objectives: Haitian ratification of the International Covenants; the separation of the military from the police. Haiti up to that point had only the military, which also carried out policing functions; and human rights training for prison officials.

Gauvin took a very careful approach and he was reluctant to push for the ratification of the covenants. He stated: "This country has such fine leaders; who am I, a person from outside, to tell them what to do?" When one pressed him that the ratification of the covenants would be the start of a human rights process for Haiti, he still stuck to his guns!

In the report he eventually presented to the Commission on Human Rights, on which this author worked, Gauvin advised the Commission that malnutrition in Haiti was widespread, especially in the rural areas. Haiti also appeared to be the most disadvantaged country in the American hemisphere in terms of health conditions. Infant mortality was high, largely the result of malnutrition. Life expectancy was only 53 years. With the lowest regional *per capita* protein and calorie consumption, nutritionally related diseases in Haiti were especially severe. 77 per cent of children 0-5 years were malnourished, 30 percent in moderate to severe categories. In addition, 30 per cent of pre-school children and 38 per cent of women were found to be anaemic. 45 per cent of recorded deaths were due to infectious diseases, a large proportion of which could have been prevented with immunizations. Diarrhoeal disease alone was estimated to account for 25,000 infant and childhood deaths annually.

Gauvin further reported that Haiti had passed through nearly 30 years of a brutal and self-serving dictatorship. Its largely illiterate population had suffered from large-scale poverty, neglect and misery. He had received complaints of arrests without warrants, intimidation of citizens by individual members of the army, particularly in the rural areas, acts of maltreatment during detention, cases of disappearances of persons and reported incidents of torture. Gauvin called upon the Government to increase training of the armed forces in order to improve respect for human rights. The need for a trained and more efficient police force was a priority need, he assessed.

Among the recommendations he made to the Commission were that the flagrant past abuses of human rights should be investigated. For the future peace of mind of the Haitian people it might be helpful that a panel of eminent Haitian personalities be created and entrusted with a mandate to report on major past abuses of human rights in Haiti in order to draw lessons for the future. He further recommended that an independent and vigorous National human rights commission could do much to promote respect for human rights and fundamental freedoms.

Gauvin basically took a diplomatic approach to the situation, keeping in mind western interests in the country and the Commission found this convenient. It went on for years to maintain direct contacts with the Government. Subsequently it would appoint independent experts to provide advice and technical assistance to the Government of Haiti. The 'violations approach' had elided into an 'advice and assistance approach.'

Nevertheless, there were mandate holders who would be quite dynamic and innovative in dealing with their country situations, including insisting on the responsibility of governments to act for the protection of their people. In today's parlance this is termed the responsibility to protect.

VIII. THE RESPONSIBILITY OF GOVERNMENTS TO PROTECT

Special procedures mandate holders have on numerous occasions drawn attention to, and condemned, gross violations of human rights. In his report to the Commission on Human Rights in 1985, for example, the Special Representative on El Salvador, Mr Pastor Ridruejo, reported:

> "As concerns the violations of civil and political rights attributable to the State apparatus and armed paramilitary organizations, presumably tolerated by, or connected with, that apparatus, the Special Representative is morally convinced that, during 1984, serious violations have continued; there is still concern about the numbers of violations of the right to life through political murders of civilians that are not combat-related. ... The Special Representative ... feels obliged to point out the inescapable obligation of the authorities in El Salvador, – legislative, executive and judicial – to adopt the necessary measures for the total eradication of violations of the fundamental right of human beings, namely, the right to life."[107]

He continued:

> "The Special Representative is also morally convinced that different branches of the opposition guerilla forces have committed grave violations of such basic human rights as the right to life and liberty – through murders and abductions ...[108]

Furthermore,

> "The Special Representative believes that the capacity of the Salvadorian judicial system to investigate violations of human rights committed in the country continues to be patently inadequate."[109]

Based on the reports[110] of the Special Representative, the Commission on Human Rights, echoing the General Assembly, condemned the persistence of murders, abductions, terrorist acts, and other grave violations of human rights and fundamental freedoms in El Salvador perpetrated by governmental paramilitary organizations and other armed groups, and noted that the Special Representative had underlined the general attitude of passivity and inactivity on the part of the Salvadorian authorities with regard to constant violations of human rights. In the language of today, the Special Rapporteur, the Commission and the General Assembly were asserting the duty of a government to protect the rights of its people.

107 E/CN.4/1985/18, para. 175.

108 Ibid, para. 176.

109 Ibid, para. 177.

110 A/36/608, annex; E/CN.4/ 1502

IX. DENOUNCING GOVERNMENTS COMMITTING GROSS VIOLATIONS

The publication, United Nations Action in the Field of Human Rights, last updated and published in 1994,[111] has summaries of the work of special procedures mandate holders on country situations up to that time. It cites several occasions in which mandate holders condemned gross violations of human rights in different countries and also the follow-up resolutions of the Commission on Human Rights in condemning those responsible. For example, based on the work of its Special Rapporteur on Afghanistan, Professor Felix Ermacora[112], the Commission on Human Rights repeatedly expressed its profound concern at grave and massive violations of human rights in Afghanistan after the entry of Soviet forces into that country.

At the outset of his mandate Mr Ermacora assessed the situation in Afghanistan as follows:

> "With the advent of the current regime, in December 1979, three significant factors appeared which have had and continue to have serious consequences for the human rights situation in the country. In the first place, the regime which was installed in December 1979, like its immediate predecessors, was a regime which was not elected by the people and which had never submitted to a free expression of will by the population and was therefore unrepresentative. In the second place, the regime instituted a series of reforms of which the least that can be said is that they proceeded at a pace that was apparently unacceptable to the population at large and were stoutly resisted by large segments of the Afghan people. Thirdly, the regime not only applied its reforms with severity, but requested and accepted that foreign armed forces join in their imposition, thus creating a situation of conflict.
>
> "At the present stage, it is difficult to ascertain whether, under the rules of international law, the armed conflict is an international or a non-international one. However, the Special Rapporteur would draw attention to the fact that both Afghanistan and the Union of Soviet Socialist Republics are parties to the Geneva Conventions ...and are therefore at least bound by common article 3 of those Conventions. Notwithstanding this, the following practices have taken place:
>
> a. The use of anti-personnel mines and of so-called toy bombs;
> b. The victimization of the civilian population, particularly women and children;

111 United Nations publication, Sales No. E.94.XIV.11

112 E/CN.4/1985/21

c. The non-acceptance of members of the Afghan opposition forces as prisoners of war.

...

"As a result of this situation which is to be considered as a situation of gross violations of human rights, some 4 million Afghans have fled the country and sought refuge abroad in several countries, particularly Pakistan, the Islamic Republic of Iran and India.

"The result of this situation is that many lives have been lost, many people have been incarcerated in conditions far removed from respect for human rights and fundamental freedoms, many have been tortured and have disappeared, humanitarian norms have been flouted in the conflict taking place, and the resulting situation is fraught with danger for the population as a whole.

...

"In the light of the situation described above, the Special Rapporteur is of the view that as a first step the Government ought to make every effort to re-establish a national consensus..."[113]

X. CALLING THE ATTENTION OF THE INTERNATIONAL COMMUNITY TO ISSUES OF CONCERN IN A NON-COOPERATING COUNTRY

In its resolution 1984/54 of 14 March, 1984, the Commission on Human Rights mandated the appointment of a Special Representative to establish contact with the Government of the Islamic Republic of Iran and to make a thorough study of the human rights situation in Iran. The Special Representative, Mr Andres Aguilar, submitted a preliminary report to the Commission in 1985 in which he indicated that he had not been able to establish dialogue and cooperation with the Government. However, he submitted to the Commission a list of issues on which he invited the Commission to invite the reaction of the Government. This author helped prepare the list and the idea was that if the Government would not cooperate with a mandate-holder, he could, in all objectivity, indicate issues on which the Commission could carry out a dialogue with the Government.

Mr Aguilar stated:

"The Special Representative has received from various sources, including non-governmental organizations in consultative status with the Economic

113 E/CN.4/1985/21, paras. 174 – 183.

and Social Council, communications and documents containing information on alleged violations of human rights in the Islamic Republic of Iran... (T)he Special Representative noted with great concern the number and gravity of the alleged violations of human rights and, in particular, those related to the right to life – as laid down in article 6 of the International Covenant on Civil and Political Rights; the right to freedom from torture or cruel, inhuman or degrading treatment or punishment (article 7); the right to liberty and security of person and to freedom from arbitrary arrest or detention (article 9); the right to a fair trial (article 14); the right to freedom of thought, conscience and religion and to freedom of expression (article 18 and 19, respectively) and the right of religious minorities to profess and practice their own religion (article 27)."[114]

A subsequent special representative, Maurice Copithorne, would continue this approach. In an annex to his report to the Commission on Human Rights in 2002, Mr Copithorne drew the attention to the following "Representations concerning the Status of the Azeris":

"The following is a list of specific complaints received by the Special Representative

Denial of cultural autonomy;
Harassment and imprisonment of cultural activists;
The banning of the use of the Azeri language in schools;
The use of Farsi-Azeri hybrid, rather than pure Azeri, on television and radio.
Teaching in schools that the birth of the Iranian people came with the arrival of the Persian tribes and that the Azeri people are Iranian Aryans, forced to change their language upon the arrival of the Mongolians;
Changing or distorting Azeri geographical names;
Refusal to register a child with an Azeri name."[115]

Another annex to the report contained the following "Representations Concerning the Status of the Kurds":

"The following is a list of specific complaints received by the Special Representative:

Violent deaths of individual Kurds, apparently the result of reckless or intentional acts of the law-enforcement forces;
The recent kidnapping and death of a popular local cultural figure;

114 E/CN.4/1985/20, para. 10.
115 E/CN.4/2002/42, Annex III.

Death sentences imposed and in most cases carried out against Kurdish activists;
The continuing refusal of the authorities to allow Kurdish programming, which is 'drastically shorter' than it was before 1979;
Various forms of economic discrimination, including access to jobs in general; in the case of the Piranshehr Sugar Company, the discharge in May 2001 of 80 *per cent* of the Kurdish employees by a non-Kurdish president and their replacement by workers of other ethnicities, "and those who collaborate with the Pasdaran";
The use of Kurdish territory, particularly Kermanshah province, as a 'resting place' for drug addicts, criminals and other difficult groups from around the country;
A Kurd activist in Sardasht who ran for the municipal council on a platform of improving the conditions of the Kurdish community found himself in jail four months after his election, denounced as an enemy of the Islamic Republic;
The disallowance of the election to the Majlis of two Kurds representing Orumieh and Naghade districts;
The gross under-representation of Kurdish districts in the Majlis, as also perhaps other districts dominated by other ethnic groups, as seen for example in the failure to add any new seats for Kurdish districts in the latest 5th Majlis redistribution."[116]

XI. INTERCESSIONS IN PARTICULAR CASES

The reports of country mandate holders, as indeed, thematic mandate holders, are replete with examples of urgent intercessions in particular cases in an effort to call for protection of those at risk. We discuss these urgent intercessions in a separate chapter below. A dynamic practice intended to generate protection for those at risk could be seen, for example, in the reports submitted to the Commission on Human Rights by the mandate holders on Myanmar and Iran.

In an annex to his report on Myanmar, Mr Sergio Paulo Pinheiro, Special Rapporteur, included an annex of "Humanitarian cases" on whose behalf he was seeking the intercession of the Government. The list contained nine specific cases with details of their arrest and incarceration. One of the cases read as follows:

"3. U Aye Tha Aung – Secretary of the CRPP representing four ethnic nationality parties; arrested and reportedly given three sentences of seven years on three separate charges (21 years in prison) and detained in Insein

116 Ibid, Annex IV.

prison; reportedly seriously ill and held in the section of the Yangon General Hospital reserved for prisoners."[117]

Another annex to his report listed the names of thirteen persons who reportedly received prison terms for communicating, trying or intending to communicate, or being suspected of communicating human rights information to the United Nations.[118]

The report of Maurice Copithorne, Special Representative on Iran, discussed earlier, also contained an annex with 'Information on the Situation of the Bahais' with the following entry, among others:

> "Other Baha'is remaining in Iranian prisons include Bihnam Mithaqui and Kayvan Khalajabadi (arrested on 29 April 1989 and sentenced to death); Dhabihu'llah Mahrami (arrested on 6 September 1995, charged with apostasy and sentenced to life imprisonment, following commutation of a death sentence by the President; Sirus Dhabihi-Muquaddam, Hidayat Kashifi Najafabadih and Ata'u'llah Hamid Nasirizadih (arrested inNovember 1997, sentenced to seven, five and four years' imprisonment, respectively, following commutation of death sentences in the case of the first two).[119]

XII. PUBLIC STATEMENTS AND APPEALS

Public statements and appeals are part of the armoury of country and thematic mandate holders in attempting to generate protection for those in need. A good example of this is the following statement issued on 18 January, 2008 by John Dugard, the Special Rapporteur on the situation of human rights in the Palestinian territories occupied since 1967:

> "The killing of some forty Palestinians in Gaza in the past week, the targeting of a Government office near a wedding party venue with what must have been foreseen loss of life and injury to many civilians, and the closure of all crossings into Gaza raise very serious questions about Israel's respect for international law and its commitment to the peace process. Recent action violates the strict prohibition on collective punishment contained in the Fourth Geneva Convention. It also violates one of the basic principles of international humanitarian law that military action must distinguish between military targets and civilian targets. Israel must have known about the wedding party in Gaza near to the interior ministry when it launched missiles at the ministry building. Those responsible for such cowardly action are guilty of serious war crimes and should be prosecuted and pun-

---

117 E/CN.4/2002/45, Annex II.

118 Ibid, Annex III.

119 E/CN.4/2002/42, p. 24.

ished for their crimes. The United States and other states which attended the Annapolis conference are under both a legal and a moral obligation to compel Israel to cease its actions against Gaza and to restore confidence in the peace process, ensure respect for international law and protect civilian life."[120]

CONCLUSION

The reports of country-mandate holders represent thousands of pages submitted over the years to the Commission on Human Rights and the Human Rights Council. Listing and discussing all their protection practices would take up considerable space. The selection provided above does bear out that in a sometimes inhospitable political environment in the United Nations, mandate holders have sought to do their utmost to come to the protection of those in need. Efforts do not always translate into actual protection. But in a cruel world, effort is salutary. In any event, the reports of the mandate holders constitute a record for history. Dictators in Argentina, Chile, Cambodia, Rwanda, South Africa and elsewhere have already discovered this. The reports of the mandate holders constitute invaluable information for the prosecutor of the International Criminal Court.

120 Press statement by the UN Special Rapporteur on the situation of human rights in the Palestinian territories occupied since 1967, United Nations, 18 January, 2008.

Chapter IV

THE PROTECTION ROLES OF THEMATIC MANDATES

INTRODUCTION

Like the country mandate-holders, thematic mandate holders also contribute to protection by documenting violations, engaging in dialogue with Governments concerned, visits to countries discreet and public appeals, offering recommendations, contributing to rallying the international community in favour of the victims, recording and denouncing violations, and contributing to the quest for justice for the victims. They also contribute to the development of international standards needed for the better protection of potential victims.

Since the first thematic mandate was established in 1980, the following thematic mandates have been established by the Commission on Human Rights/ Human Rights Council, listed in alphabetical order: Arbitrary detention, arbitrary and summary executions, development, education, enforced and involuntary disappearances, environmental issues such as toxic waste, food, freedom of expression, housing, health, independence of judges and lawyers, indigenous peoples, internally displaced persons, mercenarism, migrant workers, minorities, poverty, racial discrimination, religious intolerance, rights of women, sale of children, slavery, torture, trafficking in human beings.

In discussing country mandates in the preceding chapter we noted that they began from the 'violations perspective', evolved to include the 'advice and technical assistance perspective' and nowadays are being invited by the Human Rights Council, on essentially political grounds, to operate through a 'dialogue and cooperation perspective'. In the case of the thematic mandates it would be accurate to say that they began in the 'violations context' but with a humanitarian and facilitation approach, (disappearances) developed an awareness-raising approach in a violations context and also an advisory perspective (arbitrary executions, torture, religious intolerance), pioneered an advocacy approach (violence against women), took on in one instance a remedy approach (arbitrary detention), and, as they embraced economic and social rights, combined a study and analysis function with violations and advocacy approaches (food, health, education, shelter). More recently, they are performing on 'new frontier issues', a topic we discuss at the end of this chapter.

In seeking to distil the protection roles of thematic mandate holders, one might start with their role as channels for representations about violations, actual or potential.

I. CHANNELS FOR REPRESENTATIONS

Historically, United Nations petitions procedures such as those established under ECOSOC resolution 1503 and now updated by the Human Rights Council have received mixed assessments. This is understandable. They do not work wonders. Yet, depending on the country concerned, they can be helpful. During the days of the cold war, petitions claiming the right to leave one's country which reached the United Nations from countries such as Romania led to marked increases in the numbers of persons allowed to emigrate.[121] Nowadays, petitions reaching United Nations special procedures and transmitted to Governments for their attention can similarly lead to protective measures. The reports of the principal thematic mandate holders submitted to the Commission on Human Rights, and now the Human Rights Council, contain voluminous annexes detailing complaints transmitted to governments for their attention. In an interview with Professor Manfred Novak, the Special Rapporteur against Torture, in Geneva on 3 April, 2008, he related that, in his view, his intercessions had saved the lives of fifteen persons who might otherwise have been tortured to death[122].

Thematic mandate holders also contribute to protection through their efforts to clarify the applicable norms, as we shall see below.

II. SOURCES OF NORMATIVE CLARIFICATION AND DEVELOPMENT

A. The Working Group on Enforced and Involuntary Disappearances

In December 1992, the UN General Assembly adopted the Declaration on the Protection of All Persons from Enforced Disappearance (resolution 47/133). The Working Group on disappearances 'welcomed [the declaration] as a milestone' and considered it 'an important basis for [the group's] own future work'.[123] The working group had played an active role in the elaboration of the declaration, and the definition of enforced disappearances contained

121 Interview with Jakob Moller, Chief of the Petitions Unit 1970 – 1996, Geneva, 15 January, 2008.

122 Interview at the Graduate Institute of International and Development Studies, Geneva.

123 http://www.ohchr.org/english/about/publications/docs/fs6.htm

therein.[124] Some of the Working Group's recommendations in its annual annual reports had also been also included in the declaration.[125]

The Working group subsequently decided to formulate general comments on provisions of the declaration that, based on its experience in communicating with governments, necessitated further explanation.[126] To date, the Working Group has offered general comments on six articles. These are Article 3 on taking effective measures to prevent and terminate acts of enforced disappearance, Article 4 on criminalizing all acts of enforced disappearances, Article 10 on holding detainees in officially recognized detention centres and bringing them before a judge, Article 17 on considering an enforced disappearance as a continuing offence so long as the perpetrator has not clarified the fate and whereabouts of the missing person(s), Article 18 on refraining from enacting amnesty laws that exempt perpetrators from criminal proceedings, and Article 19 on giving adequate compensation to victims and their families.[127] Most recently, the Working Group offered a general comment on the definition of enforced disappearance, noting that it aims to 'construe the definition provided by the Declaration, in a way that is most conducive to the protection of all persons from enforced disappearances'.[128]

The Working Group played a leading role in the drafting of the International Convention for the Protection of All Persons from Enforced Disappearances, which was opened for signature in 2007 and will enter into force on the thirtieth day after the twentieth ratification or accession.[129] In its resolution 2001/46, the former Commission on Human Rights had '[stressed] the importance of the working group' and explicitly asked it to 'continue to formulate comments on the draft international convention on the protection of all persons from enforced disappearance'. Moreover, it had requested the appointment of an independent expert to examine the existing international criminal and human rights framework for the protection of persons against enforced disappearances.[130] The chairman of the Commission on Human Rights had selected

124 *Interview with Tonie van Dongen, Member of the United Nations Working Group on Enforced or Involuntary Disappearances*, SIM newsletter No. 14/15, August 1986.

125 http://www.ohchr.org/english/about/publications/docs/fs6.htm

126 UN Doc. E/CN.4/1996/38, at 47; UN Doc. E/CN.4/1997/34, at 395. I have drawn in parts of this chapter for factual information on research papers prepared by my students at the Geneva Graduate Institute of Internacional and Development Studies.

127 http://www.ohchr.org/english/issues/disappear/docs/GeneralCommentsCompilation May06.pdf

128 http://www.ohchr.org/english/issues/disappear/disappearance_gc.doc

129 International Convention for the Protection of All Persons from Enforced Disappearances, Art. 39(1).

130 CHR resolution 2001/46, at 2, 2(j) and 11.

Manfred Nowak, one of the members of the Working Group, to perform this task. The group welcomed this decision, noting that 'in this way, the Working Group is in a position to make its expertise available to this important drafting process'.[131]

B. The General Principles on Internal Displacement

Francis M. Deng, Special Representative on Internally Displaced Persons (IDPs), made a leading contribution to the development of international standards for the protection of the rights of IDPs. He noted, that the protection deriving from refugee law in regard to IDPs was limited by the fact, that they remained within the borders of their countries and that the causes of their displacement were not always identical to those of refugees. As a consequence, an extension of refugee law to IDPs could only be partial and therefore only partially protective.

Based on his work, in 1998 the Guiding Principles on Internal Displacement were presented to the Commission on Human Rights. They contained 30 principles structured in five sections: general principles, protection from displacement, protection during displacement, humanitarian assistance and return and settlement.

The principles prohibited arbitrary displacement. However, once persons had been displaced, the principles attributed to them various civil, political, economic social and cultural rights, including the right to basic humanitarian assistance (e.g. food, medicine, shelter), the right to be protected from physical violence, the right to education, freedom of movement and residence. They also had the right to accept assistance from competent authorities, to return safely to their original places or dignified and safe resettlement by local integration, including help to recover lost property and possessions. If that was not possible, the Guiding Principles advocated compensation or reparation. The Guiding Principles on Internal Displacement made a useful contribution to the protection of IDPs.

C. Torture and other cruel, inhuman or degrading treatment or punishment

The Special Rapporteurs against torture have helped clarify the scope of the the prohibition of torture and other cruel, inhuman or degrading treatment or punishment (CIDTP) which represents a significant contribution to the development of international human rights law.[132] The Special Rapporteurs have made many valuable observations on a variety of issues ranging from patterns

131 UN Doc. E/CN.4/2002/79, at 26 (2002).

132 Nifosi, p. 101.

of State behaviour, factors conducive to torture and other ill-treatment such as *incommunicado* detention, and national legal and administrative measures for the prevention of violations as well as national measures for redress where a violation has occurred. On the basis of these, the Special Rapporteurs have formulated recommendations aimed at states generally with the goal of prevention.

D. Arbitrary Detention

In its first report to the Commission on Human Rights (E/CN.4/1992/20 chapter IV) the Working Group on Arbitrary detention identified a number of situations involving questions of principle which required the Working Group's special consideration. At its third session, in March 1992, the Working Group decided to consider such issues and adopt decisions thereon (referred to as "deliberations") By adopting these deliberations the Working Group clarifies the meaning and application of the law and develops a jurisprudence facilitating the consideration of future cases.

By resolution 1997/50, the Working Group was requested by the then Commission on Human Rights to devote all necessary attention to reports concerning the situation of immigrants and asylum seekers allegedly being held in prolonged administrative custody without the possibility of administrative or judicial remedy. The Working Group elaborated deliberation no. 5 contained in its report in 2004.[133] Since then, administrative detention of foreigners has been included as a part of the Working Group's mandate. In 2005 the Working Group adopted deliberation no. 7 on issues related to psychiatric detention.[134]

III. PROTECTION OF THOSE IN NEED

The efforts of the Special Representative on human rights defenders is a good example of efforts for the protection of those in need. The Special Representative is mandated to:

- seek, receive, examine and respond to information on the situation and the rights of anyone, acting individually or in association with others, to promote and protect human rights and fundamental freedoms;
- establish cooperation and conduct dialogue with governments and other interested actors on the promotion and effective implementation of the Declaration on human rights defenders;
- recommend effective strategies better to protect human rights defenders

133 E/CN.4/2000/4, Annex II, Deliberation No. 5

134 E/CN.4/2005/6, pp16-20) and deliberation no.8 on deprivation of liberty linked to/resulting from the use of the internet (see E/CN.4/2006/7, pp.14-18.

and follow up on these recommendations.[135]

IV. ALERT AND PREVENTION

Early warning and prevention are the subjects of a separate chapter below. Several thematic mandates engage in preventive efforts. The Working Group on Disappearances, for example, has identified both broad and specific preventive measures. In terms of the former, the group has affirmed the importance of 'tackling root factors' that lead to internal instability. It thus considers 'well-thought out policies and action aimed at breaking the vicious cycle of increasing poverty' as 'essential preventative measures'.[136] In its set of specific recommendations, the group offers more immediate measures that can provide protection against enforced disappearances, including:

1) implementing the declaration at the national level;
2) keeping up-to-date registries of detainees;
3) giving information on the whereabouts of a detainee to that person's relatives and granting them access to the detention center;
4) ensuring that detainees are brought before a judicial authority promptly after their arrest;
5) strengthening civil society organizations; and
6) prosecuting perpetrators of acts of enforced or involuntary disappearances, trying them in ordinary courts (as opposed to military tribunals).

V. URGENT INTERCESSION

Almost all of the special procedures mandate holders make urgent intercessions in order to help protect those in need. In its first year of existence, the Working Group on Disappearances began making urgent appeals. Recalling the mandate to carry out its work effectively and expeditiously, the group reported that one of its first actions had been to '[authorize] its Chairman to transmit urgent reports of enforced or involuntary disappearances, received between sessions of the Group and requiring immediate action...'[137] Cases requiring immediate action were considered to be those in which reliable information indicated that a person had recently been subjected to enforced disappearance and consequently faced serious danger to his/her health or life.[138]

A report of the Working Group on disappearances assessed that 'there [was]

---

135 Commission on Human Rights resolution E/CN.4/2000/61 of 26 April, 2000.

136 UN Doc. E/CN.4/2005/65, at 378.

137 UN Doc. E/CN.4/1435, at 30.

138 UN Doc. E/CN.4/1992/17, at 14, quoted in Nifosi, *supra* note 13, 63.

some indication that this procedure [had] saved lives'.[139] It also voiced the hope that the urgent appeals 'may also have had a deterrent effect in preventing a disappearance from happening at all'.[140] Second, the urgent appeals procedure has been integrated into the mandates of other UN special procedures, thereby allowing the possibility of saving lives or deterring violations in relation to a wide range of human rights issues. Third, some have offered the assessment that 'prompt international expression of concern can be effective in helping to clarify reports of recent disappearances'.[141] The Working Group on disappearances confirmed this, stating that it had been possible to clarify 'a considerably higher percentage' of the urgent appeals cases than those transmitted under the standard procedure.[142]

Nowadays, the Working Group on disappearances sends via urgent appeal disappearance cases that have reportedly occurred within the three months preceding its receipt of the report and that meet its criteria for admissibility They are submitted to the Ministry of Foreign Affairs of the concerned country via the most rapid and direct means. The working group sends reminders twice a year on all urgent action cases submitted during the past six months to which no reply has been offered.[143]

The Special Rapporteur on Torture has followed similar practices. If the Special Rapporteur finds that the allegations of torture he receives do not require immediate action, these are sent to Governments in the form of "allegation letters" whereby the Special Rapporteur requests the Government to clarify the substance of the allegations and to forward information on the status of any investigation (i.e. the findings of any medical examination, the identity of the persons responsible for the torture, the disciplinary and criminal sanctions imposed on them, and the nature and amount of compensation paid to the victims or their families). Allegation letters are also sent in relation to systematic patterns of torture and where a specific legislation may impact on the occurrence of torture.

According to the first Special Rapporteur against torture, the urgent action procedure "is not *per se* accusatory, but essentially preventive and humanitarian in nature and purpose." Due to the "extremely time sensitive" information contained in an urgent appeal, the direct transmission of the information to the Government in question is entirely justified.[144]

The Working Group on Arbitrary Detention has developed an "urgent ac-

139 UN Doc. E/CN.4/1492, at 7 (1981).

140 Ibid., at 7.

141 UN Doc. E/CN.4/1983/14, at 13.

142 UN Doc. E/CN.4/1984/21, at 84, quoted in Rodley, *supra* note 22, 711.

143 UN Doc. E/CN.4/1435, at 7 (1981).

144 Supra note 19, paras. 4-5.

tion procedure for cases in which there are sufficiently reliable allegations that a person is being detained arbitrarily and that the continuation of the detention may constitute a serious danger to that person's health or life. The urgent action procedure may also be resorted to in other circumstances when the Working Group deems that that situation warrants such an appeal ("In cases in which, even when no such threat is alleged to exist, there are particular circumstances that warrant an urgent action"). In such cases, an urgent appeal is sent, by the most rapid channel of communication, to the Minister for Foreign Affairs of the State concerned, requesting that his or her Government should take appropriate measures to ensure that the detained person's right to life and to physical and mental integrity are respected. In addressing such communications, the Working Group emphasizes that such urgent appeals are of purely humanitarian character and in no way prejudge the Working Group's final assessment of whether the deprivation of liberty is arbitrary or not.

VI. HUMANITARIAN INTERCESSION

The Working Group on Enforced and Involuntary Disappearances, from its inception, has continuously reiterated that its mandate is humanitarian, emphasizing that the group serves first and foremost 'as a channel of communication between family members and Governments'.[145] The enormity of the task of clarifying old cases led the group to deepen its engagement with concerned governments, urging them to define legal requirements for the presumption of death and to exhume bodies for identification so that victims' relatives could receive compensation for the disappearances. Attaching great importance to this issue, the working group developed a questionnaire that it sent out in June 1997 to countries with more than twenty unresolved cases.[146] It posed a set of five questions with the aim of determining each country's system of compensation. In its subsequent annual report, the group presented the replies received to the questionnaire comparing legislation and practices across countries[147] and expressed its intention to continue to devote attention to the compensation issues.[148] In addition to financial compensation, the Working Group stressed that other forms of redress may also be appropriate; these included 'medical, psychological, legal and social rehabilitation; restoration of personal liberty, employment and property; and other forms of restitu-

145 See, for example, UN Doc. A/HRC/4/41, at 3 (2006).

146 Ibid., at 23.

147 UN Doc. E/CN.4/1998/43, at 25-64. These were Argentina, Chile, Ethiopia, Guatemala, Honduras, India, Morocco, Peru, the Philippines, Sri Lanka, Turkey, and Uruguay.

148 Ibid., at 65 (1998).

tion, satisfaction and reparation, which may remove the consequences of the enforced disappearance'.[149]

The Working Group's efforts have achieved some success. In 2000, for example, the Sri Lankan government acted on more than 6,000 outstanding cases, reporting that it had issued certificates of presumption of death and provided compensation to the families of victims 'in accordance with the Working Group's mandate and its methods of work'.[150] In many other cases, however, the group continues to express concern over amnesty legislation that denies compensation to victims' families and thereby violates Articles 17 and 18 of the Declaration on the Protection of All Persons from Enforced Disappearance.

VII. MITIGATION

The special procedures' advocacy, urgent intercessions, humanitarian intercessions, and visits on the spot or to neighbouring countries have had mitigatory effects. The first thematic mandate, the Working Group on Enforced and Involuntary Disappearances, in a message to governments of countries where disappearances were alleged to have taken place, asked the governments if they would 'in principle be disposed to invite the Group to visit the country in order to establish direct contacts'.[151] Mexico responded in the affirmative to the request and two members of the Working Group travelled there in January 1982, marking the group's first on-site (***in situ***) visit. The Working Group has subsequently continued the practice of country visits, travelling to fifteen countries over the course of twenty-five years.

As in the instances of Mexico and Peru in the early 1980s, the Working Group on disappearances has continued to hold meetings with government officials, NGOs, legal advocates and relatives of disappeared persons during these visits. Visits are carried out once the government has extended an invitation, but the group has stated its policy of seeking out such an invitation when 'factors such as the number, credibility and gravity of the reports received, and the potential impact that the mission may have on the overall human rights situation' make a visit imperative.[152] The Working Group also carries out follow-up visits to assess whether its recommendations to the government presented after the first visit have been implemented.

149 UN Doc. E/CN.4/2002/79, at 22.

150 UN Doc. E/CN.4/2001/68, Executive Summary para 3. More recently, however, the Human Rights Commission of Sri Lanka decided to halt inquiries into 2,000 cases of disappearances out of fear that they could lead to findings that required monetary compensation. See UN Doc. A/HRC/4/41, at 389 (2006).

151 UN Doc. E/CN.4/1435, at 31 (1981).

152 http://www.ohchr.org/english/issues/disappear/visits.htm#completed

VIII. REDRESS

The activities of the Working Group on Arbitrary Detention are a good example of efforts for redress. We discuss this separately in a later chapter in this volume. The Special Rapporteur against torture has consistently pointed out that the practice of torture is still widespread. Impunity was one of the major reasons for this state of affairs.[153] The Special Rapporteur observed in 2006 that one of the main reasons why many acts of torture remained unpunished was because States continued to be reluctant to fulfil their obligation to exercise universal jurisdiction under the 2nd paragraph of Article 5 of the Convention against torture.[154] He therefore encouraged States to exercise universal jurisdiction, in compliance with their obligations under the Convention.[155]

The Special Rapporteur has also been actively involved in the promotion of the right of victims of torture to a remedy and reparation. The Special Rapporteur actively participated in the drafting of the Basic Principles and Guidelines on the Right to a Remedy and Reparation for Victims of Gross Violations of International Human Rights Law and Serious Violations of International Humanitarian Law.[156] In addition, the Special Rapporteur also continues to support the work of the Board of Trustees of the Voluntary Fund for Victims of Torture by encouraging States to make contributions to its resources and to disseminate, as appropriate, information on the Board's work to those that could benefit from the assistance it offers.[157]

IX. CONDEMNATION

Where needed, special procedures mandate holders often condemn gross violations of human rights. The Working Group on Enforced and Involuntary Disappearances, for example, even though it pursues a humanitarian approach,

153 A/HRC/4/33, summary.

154 Article 5 para. 2 of the CAT Convention states : *Each State Party shall... take measures as may be necessary to establish its jurisdiction over (torture) offences in cases where the alleged offender is present in any territory under its jurisdiction and it does not extradite him...* This is the so-called "aut dedere aut iudicare" principle.

155 Ibid., para. 47.

156 Adopted by GA Resolution 60/174 of December 16, 2005.

157 The General Assembly created the United Nations Voluntary Fund for Victims of Torture in 1982. The purpose of the Fund is to receive voluntary contributions and distribute them to non-governmental organizations and treatment centres for assisting victims of torture and their relatives whose human rights have been severely violated as a result of torture, as well as for the funding of projects for training health care professional specialized in the treatment of victims of torture. It is administered by the United Nations Secretary-General with a Board of Trustees acting in an advisory capacity and comprising five members with wide experience in the field of human rights.

has been ready to apply a 'name and shame' strategy. In two recent reports, the Working Group has published the names of all persons newly reported missing for countries with ten or more such cases during the reporting period. The names appear in an annex to the report. The listswere reported in Algeria during this period' and provided tangible information that those thirty-one people, listed by name, had reportedly been disappeared and that their families waited in agony for news of their loved ones' fate and whereabouts.[158]

X. DOCUMENTING VIOLATIONS FOR JUSTICE INITIATIVES IN THE FUTURE

Like country mandate-holders, the reports of thematic mandate holders document violations for the historical record and for use in any future initiatives for truth and reconciliation, or for justice. Each year their reports contain thousands of pages of reported violations.

XI. NEW FRONTIER ISSUES

As some special procedures wrestle with protection challenges in the face of actual situations of violations of human rights, others are analyzing and pointing up new issues requiring attention or systemic issues affecting the universal realization of human rights. Two examples of these are the representative of the Secretary-General on Business and Human Rights and the Independent Expert on Solidarity and Human Rights. We look at the efforts of these two mandate-holders below.

A. Human Rights, Corporations and Businesses

In 2005 the then Commission on Human Rights requested the UN Secretary-General to appoint a Special Representative on the issue of human rights and transnational corporation and other business enterprises. The Commission asked the Special Representative to identify and clarify standards of corporate responsibility and accountability with regard to human rights, to elaborate on the role of States in effectively regulating and adjudicating business activities, to research and clarify the implications of concepts such as complicity, and to identify some prevailing if not best practices by States and companies.

In his progress report to the Human Rights Council,[159] the Special Representative noted that the State duty to protect against non-State abuses was part of the very foundation of the international human rights regime. This

158 See Annex I of UN Doc. A/HRC/4/41.

159 A/HRC/4/35.

duty required States to play a key role in regulating and adjudicating abuse by business enterprises or risk breaching their international obligations. (18). Corporations were increasingly recognized as 'participants' at the international level, with the capacity to bear some rights and duties under international law. They had certain rights under bilateral investment treaties, they were also subject to duties under several civil liability conventions dealing with environmental pollution.

Furthermore, corporate responsibility was being shaped through the interplay of two developments: one was the expansion and refinement of individual responsibility by the international *ad hoc* tribunals and the ICC Statute, the other was the extension of responsibility for international crimes to corporations under domestic law. The complex interaction between the two was creating an expanding web of potential corporate liability for international crimes, imposed through national courts.

In principle, public authorities set the rules within which business operate. But at the national level some Governments may simply be unable to take effective action, whether or not the will to do so was present. And in the international arena States themselves competed for access to markets and investments, thus collective action problems may restrict or impede their serving as the international community's 'public authority'. The most vulnerable people and communities paid the heaviest price for these governance gaps. There were large protection gaps for victims as well as predictability gaps for companies who may still get tried in the courts of public opinion. Not all State structures as a whole appeared to have internalized the full meaning of the State duty to protect, nor its implications with regard to preventing and punishing abuses by non-State actors, including business. Nor did States seem to be taking full advantage of the many legal and policy tools at their disposal to meet their treaty obligations. Insofar as the duty to protect lay at the very foundation of the international human rights regime, this uncertainty gave rise to concern.

B. Independent Expert on Human Rights and International Solidarity.

In 2005 the then Commission on Human Rights appointed an independent expert on human rights and international solidarity who submitted his first report in 2006[160]. After considering this report, the Human Rights Council, in September, 2007, resolved to strive to ensure that the present generation is fully aware of their responsibilities toward future generations, and that a better world was possible for the present and future generations. The Human Rights Council reaffirmed the recognition set forth in the declaration adopted by

160 A/HRC/4/8.

the Heads of State and Government at the Millennium Summit of the United Nations of the fundamental value of solidarity to international relations in the twenty-first century, in stating that global challenges must be managed in a way that distributes costs and burdens fairly, in accordance with basic principles of equity and social justice, and that those who suffer, or who benefit least, deserve help from those who benefit most.

The Council expressed its determination to contribute towards the solution of current world problems through increased international cooperation, to create such conditions as will ensure that the needs and interests of future generations are not jeopardized by the burdens of the past, and to hand on a better world to future generations. It urged the international community to consider urgently concrete measures to promote and consolidate international assistance to developing countries in their endeavours for development and for the promotion of conditions that make possible the full realization of all human rights.

The Council recognized that the so-called 'third-generation rights', closely interrelated to the fundamental value of solidarity, needed further progressive development within the United Nations human rights machinery in order to be able to respond to the increasing challenges of international cooperation in this field. It requested all States, UN agencies, other relevant international organizations and non-governmental organizations to mainstream the right of peoples and individuals to international solidarity in their activities. It further decided, taking into account the urgent need to further develop guidelines, standards, norms and principles with a view to promoting and protecting the right of peoples and individuals to international solidarity, to request the independent expert on human rights and international solidarity to continue his work in the preparation of a draft declaration on the right of peoples and individuals to international solidarity.

CONCLUSION

Even more than in the case of country mandate holders, the reports of thematic mandate holders represent a historical record of gross violations of human rights worldwide since the first thematic mandate was established in 1980. It would require considerably more space to highlight all of the protection approaches and practices of these courageous and dynamic special procedures. In this chapter we have sought to provide samples of their efforts for protection that we consider noteworthy. In their cases also, effort does not always result in protection. But striving for justice is a universal yearning. The thematic mandate holders certainly do a great deal of striving – and achieve some results. In the ensuing chapter we highlight some of their principles of responsibility and accountability.

Chapter V

STATE, INDIVIDUAL, CORPORATE AND INTERNATIONAL RESPONSIBILITY

INTRODUCTION

From the outset, special procedure mandate holders have set a high standard of protection in insisting on State, individual, corporate and international responsibility for violations of human rights. One of the earliest special procedures, the Working Group of Experts on Southern Africa, basing itself on the then International Convention on the Suppression and Punishment of the Crime of Apartheid (1973), which had declared apartheid a crime against humanity, listed in its reports the names of persons alleged guilty of the crime of apartheid, called for the dissemination of the lists internationally, and advocated the trial and punishment of the persons named for international crimes. The Working Group and a related Special Rapporteur of the then Sub-Commission on the Prevention of Discrimination and Protection of Minorities cited companies allegedly collaborating with the apartheid regime and called for the waging of campaigns against them internationally. The Working Group on Chile also listed some names of individuals allegedly responsible for gross violations of human rights and a member of the Working Group, carrying out an additional task entrusted to him by the then Commission on Human Rights, made detailed submissions to the Commission on Human Rights about the international legal responsibility of the Government of Chile for gross violations of human rights. In this chapter we outline some of these ground-breaking precedents of special procedures mandate holders.

I. STATE RESPONSIBILITY FOR GROSS VIOLATIONS OF HUMAN RIGHTS

In resolution 3219 (XXIX) of 6 November, 1974, the General Assembly endorsed the recommendation made by the Sub-Commission on Prevention of Discrimination and Protection of Minorities, in resolution 8 (XXVII) of 21 August, 1974, that the Commission on Human Rights should study the reported violations of human rights in Chile at its thirty-first session. In resolution 8 (XXXI) of 27 February 1975 the Commission decided to appoint an *Ad Hoc* Working Group of five of its members to inquire into the situation of human rights in Chile on the basis of oral and written evidence to be gathered from all relevant sources, and of a visit to Chile. In 1979 the Working Group was succeeded by a Special Rapporteur on human rights in Chile. That year the Commission on Human Rights in resolution 11 (XXXV) of 6 March, 1979 also mandated two experts to undertake a study on the fate of missing and disappeared persons in Chile. In the end result the study was done by Prof. Felix Ermacora. These three special procedures of the Commission on Human Rights put down landmark foundations on the concepts of international accountability and responsibility for gross violations of human rights.

The Special Rapporteur, Mr Abdoulaye Dieye, dealing with legal and political submissions of the Government of Chile, took the following firm position of principle on the competence of the United Nations and its special procedures to deal with gross violations of human rights:

> "The competence of the General Assembly under the Charter is determined by its membership as a whole, and therefore the Chilean Government cannot decide on its own that the procedures decided upon by the General Assembly and the Commission on Human Rights 'have no legal basis in the United Nations' and 'will have no legal or moral force'. The Government of Chile cannot substitute its judgment of legality for the judgment duly and overwhelmingly pronounced by the membership of the General Assembly. Insofar as the Commission on Human Rights is concerned, it may be pointed out that the actions decided upon by the Commission, with the approval of the Economic and Social Council, were taken with the approval of the Economic and Social Council, were taken upon the express request of the General Assembly ..."

> "... In the long-standing practice of the United Nations it has been repeatedly confirmed that the United Nations has wide competence to deal with large-scale situations of violations of human rights. This has been established since the inception of the Organization and has been maintained throughout its existence in the various situations involving violations of human rights dealt with by the United Nations in all parts of the world. It has also been established that the United Nations may employ for dealing with situations of violations of human rights all appropriate methods under the Charter, depending upon the circumstances of each situation. Some situations are handled in the Security Council or its subsidiary organs, in the General Assembly or its subsidiary organs, in the Trusteeship Council, in the Economic and Social Council, in the Commission on Human Rights, or in other United Nations organs. Situations are sometimes raised in open debate, or handled under procedures for dealing with communications, or an investigating committee or rapporteur may be appointed to look into a situation. Whatever the method used, it is a clear principle that the United

Nations may utilize for each situation such methods or procedures as it considers best suited to deal with that situation."[161]

The Report of the Expert on the Question of the Fate of Missing and Disappeared Persons in Chile submitted to the General Assembly in 1979[162] dealt squarely with the responsibility of the Government of Chile under international law. The author of the report, Prof. Felix Ermacora began by pointing out that there could be no doubt that the phenomenon of missing persons in Chile amounted to a real situation of gross violations of human rights and was not a question of a few, individual cases. There was also evidence, as regards missing persons in Chile, of 'administrative practices' within the meaning given to that term by the European Commission on Human Rights, inasmuch as there was a repetition of acts throughout the country by government agents and that such acts were officially tolerated or sanctioned.

Where a serious situation of missing persons existed, as in Chile, there were firm international obligations upon the State in question, which was responsible for the fulfilment of those obligations. In so far as the acts leading to the disappearance of persons also violated specific obligations under national or internationally established human rights, the State was likewise responsible for those violations of human rights.

In support of his submissions he analysed relevant works of the International Law Commission, the jurisprudence of the International Court of Justice and the applicable international law. He concluded:

"The Government of Chile has not been willing to cooperate fully with the United Nations and other international organizations in the process of clarifying the fate of missing persons ...

"The fact that at least 600 persons remain missing following acts of the State security system shows that in Chile there has continuously existed a 'situation' of massive and systematic violation of human rights, including the right to life and other rights connected with the fact of missing persons. This 'situation' is of a continuing nature. As long as the Government cannot show that it has taken effective action to clarify the fate of the missing persons, the Government continues to be responsible for the fate of missing persons ...

"The Expert therefore comes to the conclusion that the Chilean Government is responsible under international law for the fate of at least 600 cases of missing persons whose basic rights as human beings have been infringed and violated as indicated in the present report. The Government is also responsible for those missing persons who met their deaths in suspicious

161 UN doc. A/34/583, paras. 6 and 9.

162 UN doc. A/34/583/Add.1, 21 November, 1979.

circumstances imputable to agencies of the Government. The Chilean Government owes it to the international community to explain and clarify the fate of these missing persons, to punish those responsible for the disappearances, to compensate the relatives of the victims and to take measures to prevent such acts from recurring in the future."[163]

In a follow-up report, Prof. Ermacora added:

"The information received on the activities of the DINA reinforces the findings of the report to the General Assembly that the Government of Chile established and permitted to function an organization which in theory and practice systematically violated the right to liberty and security of person. Further, this new information shows that many persons died as a result of torture by government agents and that, in addition, the headquarters of the DINA, responsible directly to the President of Chile, made decisions that certain persons were to be killed which were reflected in the code words 'Puertomont' – elimination on land and 'Moneda' elimination at sea. It may be doubted if the documents in which such decisions were reflected have been allowed to continue in existence, especially in light of the report that registers of detainees of the DINA detention centre Cuatro Alamas have been burned. The Government of Chile, if this reliable information is indeed true, is not only responsible for the arrest and detention of the missing persons, but also for the deaths of persons eliminated by decision of the DINA or killed under torture."[164]

In 1985, the Special Representative on Iran, Mr Andres Aguillar dealt in a magisterial way with submissions of the Iranian Government claiming superiority of national or religious law:

"12. In its resolution 1984/54 which established the mandate of the Special Representative, the Commission on Human Rights was expressly guided by the principles embodied in the Charter of the United Nations, the Universal Declaration of Human Rights and the International Covenants on Human Rights. The Commission further reaffirmed that all Member States had an obligation to promote and protect human rights and fundamental freedoms and to fulfil the obligations they had undertaken under various international instruments in that field.

"13. This position of principle, as expressed in the above-mentioned resolution, is in line with the Charter of the United Nations of which Iran is an original member. The purposes of the United Nations as spelled out in Article 1, paragraph 3, of the Charter expressly include the achievement

163 Ibid, paras. 176 and 177,

164 UN doc. E/CN.4/1363, 2 February, 1980, para. 89. The DINA was the state security agency.

of international cooperation in solving international problems of an economic, social cultural or humanitarian character, and in promoting and encouraging respect for human rights and for fundamental freedoms for all without distinction as to race, sex, language, or religion. Moreover, under Article 56 of the Charter, all Member States pledge themselves to take joint and separate action in cooperation with the Organization for the achievement of the purposes set forth in Article 55 which, in turn, includes the promotion or universal respect for, and observance of, human rights and fundamental freedoms for all without distinction as to race, sex, language, or religion.

"14.The Universal Declaration of Human Rights gave expression to the human rights principles contained in the Charter of the United Nations. The Universal Declaration is thus an emanation of the Charter, providing as it does common standards of achievement for *all* peoples and *all* nations. Through practice over the years, the basic provisions of the Universal Declaration of Human Rights can be regarded as having attained the status of international customary law and in many instances they have the character of *jus cogens*. This is, for example, the case with the right to life, freedom from torture, freedom of thought, conscience and religion and the right to a fair trial.

"15. Such fundamental guarantees of the Universal Declaration of Human Rights cannot be open to challenge by any State as they are indispensable for the functioning of an international community based on the rule of law and respect for human rights and fundamental freedoms.

"16. States of all political, economic, social, cultural and religious persuasions participated in the drafting of the Charter, the Universal Declaration of Human Rights and the International Covenants on Human Rights. The Universal Declaration of Human Rights and the International Covenants thus contain norms which, distilled from the collective experiences and the common heritage of the world's peoples, represent universal standards of conduct for all peoples and all nations.

"17. Within the framework of the International Covenants on Human Rights, States of all religious, cultural or ideological persuasions co-operate in the implementation of universal standards of human rights in their respective countries. The General Assembly has repeatedly emphasized the importance of the strictest compliance by States parties with their obligations under the International Covenants and has further stressed the importance of uniform standards of implementation of the International Covenants.

"18. Therefore it must be concluded that no State can claim to be allowed to disrespect basic, entrenched rights such as the right to life, freedom from torture, freedom of thought, conscience and religion, and the right to a fair trial which are provided for under the Universal Declaration and the International Covenants on Human Rights, on the ground that departure from these standards might be permitted under national or religious law.

"19. It is the firm conviction of the Special Representative that the following fundamental principles are applicable to the situation in the Islamic Republic of Iran as indeed to the situation, present or future, in any other country:

States members of the United Nations are bound to abide by universally accepted standards of conduct in so far as the treatment of their population is concerned, particularly as regards the protection of human life, freedom from torture and other cruel, inhuman or degrading treatment or punishment, freedom of thought, conscience and religion and the right to a fair trial;

In so far as the basic rights and freedoms of the individual are concerned, the Universal Declaration of Human Rights gives expression to the human rights principles of the Charter of the United Nations and essential provisions such as those referred to above represent not only rules of international customary law but rules which also have the character of *jus cogens*;

The International Covenants on Human Rights give added conventional force to those provisions of the Universal Declaration of Human Rights which already reflect international customary law. Since the Islamic Republic of Iran is a party to the International Covenants on Human Rights, the latter's provisions in their entirety are legally binding upon the Government of the Islamic republic of Iran. They must be complied with in good faith."[165]

II. INDIVIDUAL RESPONSIBILITY FOR GROSS VIOLATIONS OF HUMAN RIGHTS

In its resolution 6(XXXIII) of 4 March, 1977, the Commission on Human Rights requested its *Ad Hoc* Working Group of Experts on southern Africa to institute an inquiry in respect of any person who had been suspected, in Namibia, to be guilty of the crime of apartheid or of a serious violation of human rights, in accordance with article II of the International Convention on the Suppression and Punishment of the Crime of Apartheid. Furthermore, the General Assembly of the United Nations, by its resolution 37/47 of 3 December, 1982, invited the Commission on Human Rights to compile pe-

165 E/CN.4/1985/20, pp. 8-9.

riodically a progressive list of individuals, organizations, institutions and representatives of States deemed responsible for crimes enumerated in article II of the International Convention on the Suppression and Punishment of the Crime of Apartheid, as well as of those against whom or which legal proceedings had been undertaken. The General Assembly also called on the United Nations Secretary-General to distribute the list among all States Parties to the Convention and all Member States of the United Nations and to bring such facts to the attention of the public by all means of mass communication.

In accordance with the foregoing mandates, the Ad Hoc Working Group periodically published a list of persons whom it accused of the crime of apartheid.[166] The list published in 1984 contained the names of over three hundred persons deemed guilty of the crime of apartheid.[167]

III. RESPONSIBILITY FOR COLLABORATION WITH GROSS VIOLATORS OF HUMAN RIGHTS.

On 9 March, 1977, the Sub-Commission on Prevention of Discrimination and Protection of Minorities, at the invitation of the General Assembly and the Commission on Human Rights entrusted one of its members, Prof. Antonio Cassese to undertake a study on the impact of foreign economic aid and assistance on respect for human rights in Chile. The Sub-Commission asked Mr Cassese to analyse the volume, origins, development and significance of the assistance given to the regime in Chile and to study whether a quantitative or qualitative change in such aid might contribute to restoring respect for human rights in Chile. The Special Rapporteur concluded that foreign economic assistance to Chile helped to maintain human rights violations and to uphold the oppressive political system. He presented his report to the Sub-Commission, the Commission and the General Assembly.

In relation to the situation in South Africa under the then *apartheid* regime, the Economic and Social Council in its resolution 1864(LVI) of 17 May, 1974, had condemned the activities of States which continued to give political, military, economic and other assistance to the racist and colonial regimes in southern Africa, or which refrained from taking any steps to prevent natural or juridical persons within their jurisdiction from assisting those regimes and thus encouraging them to continue violating fundamental human rights.

With the endorsement of the General Assembly and the Commission on Human Rights, the Sub-Commission on Prevention of Discrimination and Protection of Minorities mandated one of its members, Mr Ahmed Khalifa,

166 See UN Action in the Field of Human Rights. UN Publication, Sales No. E.83.XIV.2, p. 221.

167 E/CN.4/1984/8

to prepare and publish an annual list of banks, firms, and other organizations which gave assistance to the colonial and racist regimes in southern Africa.[168]

At its thirty-fifth session in 1980 the General Assembly considered the list of Mr Khalifa and adopted resolution 35/32 of 14 November, 1980 in which it called upon the Governments of the countries where the banks, transnational corporations and other organizations named and listed in the Special Rapporteur's report were based to take effective action to put a stop to their trading, manufacturing and investing activities in the territory of South Africa as well as the Territory of Namibia – then illegally occupied by South Africa.

Mr Khalifa continued to publish the list annually for several years and the General Assembly, the Commission on Human Rights and the Sub-Commission consistently condemned those responsible for collaborating with the apartheid regime in South Africa.

More recently, in 2007, the Special Representative of the Secretary-General on the issue of human rights and transnational corporations and other business enterprises presented to the Human Rights Council a report on State responsibilities to regulate and adjudicate corporate activities under the United Nations core human rights treaties.[169] Reviewing the practice of human rights treaty bodies, the Special Representative, Professor John Ruggie, noted that the treaties, as interpreted by their respective treaty bodies, required States to play a key role in effectively regulating and adjudicating corporate activities with regard to human rights. This role is generally considered as being part of the State duty to protect against abuse by third parties. Treaty body commentaries showed a trend towards increasing pressure on States to fulfil this duty in relation to corporate activities, regardless of whether the entities in question were privately or publicly-owned or controlled.

The treaty bodies, he continued, also tended to focus on certain types of companies and business sectors requiring regulation, although this did not detract from the broad duties of States to protect against all abuse by all types of entities. For example, in providing recommendations to particular States in the employment context, the treaty bodies not only referred generally to 'employers', but had also expressed particular concern about the mining, manufacturing and agricultural industries. The treaty bodies also frequently recommended that States take steps to regulate and adjudicate the acts of mining, extractive, logging and property development companies, especially in the context of resource exploitation in the lands and territories of indigenous peoples. In relation to health, the treaty bodies not only referred to private health-care providers but also to pharmaceutical companies, marketing companies and extractive and manufacturing companies engaging in activities which

168 The first study was contained in UN doc. E/CN.4/Sub.2/425 and Corr. 1 and Add. 1-7.

169 A/HRC.4/35/Add.1, 13 February, 2007.

could threaten food and water resources. Furthermore, the media and communication networks were discussed with respect to the sexual exploitation of children, and to their role in preventing or spreading prejudice on the basis of race, sex, or in relation to persons with disabilities.

The Special Representative found that the human rights treaty bodies required States to take a variety of measures in order to effectively protect against corporate abuse. They must generally monitor compliance by third parties and in most cases introduce legislative measures to prohibit abuse and proscribe certain behaviour; establish and bring perpetrators to justice; and facilitate the provision of effective remedies, including the provision of reparation to victims, where appropriate. The treaty bodies had also called for measures to increase awareness amongst the private sector of the human rights impact of their activities and to encourage the development by private businesses of codes of conduct in respect of human rights.[170]

IV. INTERNATIONAL RESPONSIBILITY

In a report that it submitted to the former Commission on Human Rights, the *Ad Hoc* Working Group of Experts on southern Africa reported that it had found that *apartheid*, its policies and practices had most of the elements of genocide and largely corresponded to the crime of *apartheid* and proceeded to present the following issue:

> "The issue of international responsibility for violations of human rights deserves further attention, since the principle of individual responsibility was confirmed at Nuremberg. It would be necessary to undertake a thorough study of the question in the light of the development of theory and practice concerning international responsibility for gross violations of human rights resulting from *apartheid.* In the present context, the Ad Hoc Working Group of Experts was not able to undertake such a study due to the complexity of the problem, which comprises elements of individual responsibility, the responsibility of members of organizations, and institutions and representatives of a State, and even the responsibility of the State itself. The question of committing and attempts to commit, participation in and incitement to commit *apartheid* should also be taken into consideration. The problem of responsibility should therefore be studied on another occasion.

The Working Group was ahead of its time, but its line of reasoning would lead eventually to the establishment of the International Criminal Court. The Working Group was a pioneer in this quest for international justice for the victims of criminal violations of human rights.

170 Ibid, pp. 2-3.

CONCLUSION

We have seen in this chapter dramatic evidence of how special procedures mandate-holders, at the outset of the system, upheld the governing laws regarding the obligations of governments to uphold, respect, protect, and ensure human rights and insisted on the competence of the United Nations to investigate situations of international concern. We have also seen examples from the practice of mandate-holders, more recently, to hold States responsible for the conduct of corporations that impact adversely on the enjoyment of human rights. This is new-frontier work in the endeavour to protect human rights in an evolving world.

In the next chapter we look at how special procedures engage in efforts to prevent and respond urgently to violations of human rights.

Chapter VI

PREVENTION, URGENT ACTION AND APPEALS

INTRODUCTION

The International Commission on Intervention and State Sovereignty, in launching the concept of the responsibility to protect, placed high emphasis on prevention. In the view of the Commission the responsibility to protect has three specific dimensions:

(a) The responsibility to prevent: to address both the root causes and direct causes of internal conflict and other man-made crises putting populations at risk.

(b) The responsibility to react: to respond to situations of compelling human need with appropriate measures, which may include coercive measures like sanctions and international prosecution, and in extreme cases military intervention.

(c) The responsibility to rebuild: to provide, particularly after a military intervention, full assistance with recovery, reconstruction and reconciliation, addressing the causes of the harm the intervention was designed to halt or avert.[171]

The Commission was firm in its view that prevention was the single most important dimension of the responsibility to protect: more commitment and resources must be devoted to prevention. The exercise of the responsibility to both prevent and react should always involve less intrusive and coercive measures being considered before more coercive and intrusive ones are applied.

In establishing the Human Rights Council the United Nations General Assembly entrusted to it a responsibility to prevent gross violations of human rights.[172] As subsidiary entities of the Human Rights Council, special procedures mandate holders are expected to act for the prevention of gross violations of human rights.[173]

---

171 See the report of the International Commission on Intervention and State Sovereignty, Ottawa, The International Development Research Center, 2001.

172 General Assembly Resolution 60/251?

173 E. Stamatopolou, "Integrating Human Rights into the Preventive Action of the United Nations," in L-A Sicilianos (Ed.), *The Prevention of Human Rights Violations, Contribution on the Occasion of the Twentieth Anniversary of the Maragopolous Foundation for Human Rights*, International Studies in Human Rights, Vol. 67 (Athens: Ant. N. Sakkoulas Publishers, and The Hague/New York/London: Martinus Nijhoff Publishers, 2001), pp.181-194.

I. DIMENSIONS OF PREVENTION

Sicilianos has identified three levels of prevention: "Prevention in the narrow sense of the term is the activity which manifests itself before or more accurately, independently of any human rights violations ... At a second level prevention manifests itself on the occasion of sporadic violations and/or converging indications of the existence of structural problems which are in danger of taking on significant dimensions ... The third level of prevention concerns those cases in which gross and systematic violations are being committed."[174]

Special procedures mandate holders contribute to prevention by:

- Studying and alerting the world to threats to humanity such as environmental degradation and the spread of toxic waste.
- Studying issues or situations that require urgent corrective action and making recommendations for the prevention of such situations in the future.
- Contributing to the development of standards for the protection of people in need and for the prevention of human rights violations in the future
- Sounding the alert about practices and trends that are violative of human rights, for example, the growth of arbitrary detention in the "war against terror"
- Studying and alerting the world to violations of human rights stemming from mass poverty
- Sounding the alarm on specific situations
- Undertaking urgent action intercessions
- Contributing to the development of early warning systems

II. STUDYING AND ALERTING THE WORLD TO THREATS TO HUMANITY: ENVIRONMENTAL DEGRADATION AND THE SPREAD OF TOXIC WASTE.

A Special Rapporteur of the former Commission on Human Rights studied for a number of years the adverse effects of the illicit movement and dumping of toxic and dangerous products and wastes on the enjoyment of human rights. In her reports she presented a series of analyses, conclusions and recommendations some of which serve the purposes of early warning and preventive ac-

174 L.-A. Sicilianos, "The Prevention of Human Rights Violations: Utopia or Challenge," in Sicilianos (Ed.), *The Prevention of Human Rights Violations, Contribution on the Occasion of the Twentieth Anniversary of the Maragopolous Foundation for Human Rights*, International Studies in Human Rights, Vol. 67, Athens: Ant. N. Sakkoulas Publishers, and The Hague/New York/London: Martinus Nijhoff Publishers, 2001. pp. 285-286.

tion. In the report she submitted to the Commission on Human Rights on 16 January 2003 she highlighted a new trend concerning the export of hazardous electronic waste from developed countries to countries in Asia:

> As documented by many reports received from different sources, these wastes are being processed in operations that are extremely harmful to human health and the environment, with severe implications for human rights. Improper disposal of electronic waste that contains heavy metals and pollutants poses a significant threat to human health. The Special Rapporteur shares the view that the gravity of the problem points to the need for the strict application of existing international instruments and for the elaboration of international standards to ensure that electronic wastes are recycled in a manner that is neither harmful to workers, nor destroys the environment.[175]

III. STUDYING ISSUES OR SITUATIONS THAT REQUIRE URGENT CORRECTIVE ACTION AND MAKING RECOMMENDATIONS FOR THE PREVENTION OF SUCH SITUATIONS IN THE FUTURE

In a report which she submitted to the Human Rights Council on 2 March, 2007, Ms Gay McDougall, Independent Expert on Minority Issues, alerted the Human Rights Council that there was an urgent need to take the situation of persons belonging to minorities fully into account in the efforts of the international community to achieve the Millennium Development Goals (MDGs) and to implement the Millennium Declaration. Her review of MDG country reports revealed a serious lack of attention to the situation of persons belonging to minorities, who disproportionately experienced poverty and lower levels of human development. Only a third of reports she had reviewed mentioned minorities one or more times and barely 20 per cent of the reports discussed the situation of minorities under four or more of the Goals. In none of the reports was the situation of minorities mentioned under each of the eight Goals. Minorities were mentioned most often in relation to Goal 2 on access to primary education.[176]

In all cases, very few examples of specific policies for minorities were noted and disaggregated data on progress towards the MDGs was rarely included. The result was that the likelihood of persons belonging to minorities achieving the MDGs (where they had not done so already) remained obscured. This lack

175 UN Doc. E/CN.4/2003/56, 16 January 2003: *Adverse of the illicit movement and dumping of toxic and dangerous products and wastes on the enjoyment of human rights*, report by Ms. Fatma-Zohra Ouhachi-Vesely, Special Rapporteur, in accordance with Commission Resolution 2002/27, p.19.

176 UN doc. A/HRC/4/9/Add.1, 2 March, 2007, p. 39.

of information was not necessarily conclusive of practice on the ground, but it did suggest that ensuring that strategies for the MDGs included attention to minorities was still a low priority for most governments.[177]

There was, she continued, an absence of a comprehensive understanding of the poverty of minorities and its manifestations in the social, economic, cultural and political spheres. In particular, even in those reports where minorities were mentioned, there was a lack of discussion on how and, crucially, why, minorities were experiencing disproportionately high levels of poverty and other serious inequalities. Ignoring the root causes of poverty and low human development only served to weaken the effectiveness of MDG policies and Poverty Reduction Strategy Papers (PRSPs). The issue of discrimination, both direct and indirect, was noticeably absent in the poverty analyses and also in policy responses both direct and indirect, for poverty reduction. Discussion of other rights of minorities was rarely evidenced in the reports she had examined.[178]

Furthermore, women belonging to minority groups remained invisible in poverty reduction efforts. The compound effects of discrimination on the basis of gender and national, ethnic, religious or linguistic identity meant minority women continued to be among the most excluded.[179]

She advanced a number of recommendations to correct these gaps, dealing with data collection, consultative bodies, national action plans, capacity building and MDG country reports. She suggested that all MDG country reports should include consideration of the situation of minorities in relation to each of the Goals. Disaggregated data on the progress of minorities towards the Goals should be included.[180]

IV. CONTRIBUTING TO THE DEVELOPMENT OF STANDARDS FOR THE PROTECTION OF PEOPLE IN NEED

The Representative of the Secretary-General on human rights of internally displaced persons, Walter Kalin, submitted to the Human Rights Council in 2006 a report presenting Operational Guidelines on Human Rights and Natural Disasters.[181] He saw need for preventive and protective actions in situations of natural disasters. If an imminent natural disaster created a serious risk for the life, physical integrity or health of affected individuals and communities, all appropriate measures necessary to protect those in danger, in particular vulnerable groups, should be taken to the maximum extent possible (e.g. emergency

177 Ibid, p. 39.

178 Ibid, p. 39.

179 Ibid, p. 39.

180 Ibid, p. 43.

181 A/HRC/4/38/Add.1, 23 January, 2006.

shelter arrangements). If such measures would be insufficient, endangered persons should be allowed, and assisted to leave the danger zone. To the extent that they could do so on their own, endangered persons should be evacuated from the danger zone by using all available means.[182]

These evacuations should be carried out in a manner that fully respected the rights to life, dignity, liberty and security of those affected. Measures should be taken to safeguard homes and common assets left behind. Evacuated persons should be registered and their evacuation monitored. When the natural disaster had occurred, persons affected by it should be allowed to move to other parts of the country and to settle there. This right may not be subject to any restrictions except those which are provided by law, and are necessary to protect national security, the safety and security of affected populations, public order (*ordre public*), public health or the rights and freedom of others.[183]

Persons, including evacuees, who had been ordered to flee or to leave their homes or places of habitual residence as a result of a natural disaster or its effects, or had left in order to avoid them, and had not crossed an internationally recognized State border should be treated as belonging to the category of internally displaced persons covered by the 1998 Guiding Principles on Internal Displacement. After the emergency phase, persons displaced by the natural disaster should be granted the opportunity to choose freely whether they wanted to return to their homes and places of origin, to remain in the area to which they had been displaced, or to resettle in another part of the country. Their right of choice may not be subjected to any restrictions, except those provided by law, and necessary to protect national security, the safety and security of affected populations, public order (*ordre public*), safety, public health or morals or the rights and freedom of others. In particular, the return of persons displaced by the disaster to their homes and places or origin should only be prohibited if these homes or places of origin were in zones where there were real dangers to the life or physical integrity and health of the affected persons. Restrictions should only last as long as such dangers existed and only be implemented if other, less intrusive, measures of protection were not available or possible.[184]

Furthermore, persons affected by the natural disaster should not, under any circumstances, be forced to return to or resettle in any place where their life, safety, liberty and/or health would be at further risk. Unless it was necessary for the protection of affected persons against very serious and imminent threats to their lives, their physical integrity or health, evacuations against their will, or prohibitions against their return, should not be supported by or-

182 Ibid, p. 7.

183 Ibid, p. 7

184 Ibid, pp. 7-8

ganizations providing protection and assistance to persons affected by natural disasters, even if they have been ordered by the competent authorities. Such organizations should not become involved in involuntary evacuations in any manner.[185]

V. SOUNDING THE ALERT ABOUT PRACTICES AND TRENDS THAT ARE VIOLATIVE OF HUMAN RIGHTS, FOR EXAMPLE, THE GROWTH OF ARBITRARY DETENTION IN THE "WAR AGAINST TERROR"

In its report to the Commission on Human Rights on 20 December 2000 the working group on Arbitrary Detention alerted the Commission to the following:

(a) *Arrest and detention for dissemination of "State secrets"*: The Group recommends that Governments take all necessary measures, of a legislative or other nature, to ensure that any legislation and regulation concerning national or State security should in no case be extended to cover information relating to the protection either of the environment or of human rights standards;

(b) *Detention of conscientious objectors*. The Group recommended that all Governments which had not already done so adopt appropriate legislative or other measures to ensure recognition of the status of conscientious objectors, in accordance with an established procedure, and to see it that, pending the adoption of such measures, the prosecution of conscientious objectors did not give rise to more than one conviction, so as to avoid the judicial system being used/abused to force a conscientious objector to change his conviction;

(c) *Issues relating to extradition*. The Group recommended that Governments lay down in domestic law, the maximum permissible period of detention pending extradition of an individual to a requesting State, after conviction and when imposing sentence on an individual, credit the period of detention served by the said individual pending extradition. [186]

Disappearances

In a Statement by the Chair and Rapporteur of the Working Group on Enforced or Involuntary Disappearances, dated 19 September 2006, on the work of the Working Group to date, Professor Stephen Toope noted that the

185 Ibid, p. 8.

186 UN Doc. E/CN.4/2001/14, 20 December 2000, *Report of the Working Group on Arbitrary Detention*, p.2.

Group had covered four main areas during the previous year:

> First, the Working Group was particularly concerned about reports it had received of the disappearance of children and, in a few cases, of people with physical and mental disabilities. All States have an obligation to protect such vulnerable groups. We will continue to monitor this issue closely, and treat all such cases as particularly serious.
>
> Second, the Working Group was preoccupied with the harassment of and threats to human rights defenders, relatives of disappeared persons, witnesses and legal counsel. States were reminded of their obligation under article 13, paragraph 3, of the Declaration to protect against "ill-treatment, intimidation or reprisal" all persons involved in the investigation of disappearances.
>
> Third, the Working Group was gravely concerned that anti-terrorist activities are being used by an increasing number of States as an excuse for not respecting the obligations of the Declaration. Credible reports point to the repression of opposition groups in many States in the name of the "war on terror". In addition, States have used "extraordinary rendition" to transport terrorist suspects to other States for aggressive interrogation. We continue to receive information concerning the existence of secret detention centres where terrorist suspects are held in complete isolation from the outside world. In all three situations, people disappear. As is well documented, disappearance is often a precursor to torture and even to extrajudicial execution.
>
> Finally, the Working Group noted that in some post-conflict situations, mechanisms of truth and reconciliation are used as one of the ways of moving the affected societies from war to peace and from conflict to post-conflict government. We are concerned that such circumstances can give rise to the enactment of amnesty laws and the implementation of other measures that lead to the same result: impunity.[187]

VI. STUDYING AND ALERTING THE WORLD TO VIOLATIONS OF HUMAN RIGHTS STEMMING FROM MASS POVERTY

In a report that he submitted to the former Commission on Human Rights on 2 March 2006, Arjun Sengupta, Independent Expert on Human Rights and Extreme Poverty argued that:

> The international community must accept the eradication of extreme poverty as a human rights obligation. The definition of poverty will have to

187 Statement of the Chair and Rapporteur of the Working Group on Enforced or Involuntary Disappearances, Professor Stephen J. Toope, to the Human Rights Council, 19 September 2006, paras. 11-15, pp.2-3.

be in accordance with the consensus of the different countries concerned. The predominant consideration would be to choose a small section of the population which is clearly and demonstrably most vulnerable to suffering from all forms of deprivation. Since poverty is defined as the sum total of income poverty, human development poverty and social exclusion, extreme poverty would be regarded as an extreme form of that poverty. That form can be most conveniently defined as an intersection of all three types of poverty. In some countries, however, especially those which are relatively developed and may not have the severe problem of either income poverty or human development poverty, the group suffering from social exclusion may dominate the set of extremely poor people, supplemented by conditions of income and human development poverty to the extent that they exist. The idea is to identify as extremely poor any group whose number is limited so that the society does not find it unmanageable to deal with their problems. Once such a group is identified, the removal of their conditions of extreme poverty must be taken as an obligation corresponding to the fulfilment of human rights norms. Even if the countries concerned may not be able to ensure the realization of all human rights, those rights the denial of which have directly caused poverty, should be subject to immediate fulfilment. The international community and all member States should thus take up the obligations for removing extreme poverty as a core element of their human rights obligations.[188]

VII. SOUNDING THE ALARM ON SPECIFIC SITUATIONS

Special procedures mandate holders are well placed to sound the alarm on specific situations:

- Though their continuous monitoring of human rights situations, special procedures have access to a wealth of information, the analysis of which can help detect potential emergency situations at a relatively early stage;
- in view of their high profile and independent status, special procedures mandate holders can raise publicly sensitive issues at the highest levels of Government and the UN ;
- mandate-holders have developed extensive networks of partnerships with NGOs and civil society, in very broad areas of all civil, cultural, economic , political and social rights;
- under certain circumstances special procedures have access to the Security Council (Arria formula) and can informally brief its members

188 UN Doc. E/CN.4/2006/43, 2 March 2006, p. 20. See T. Pogge, "World Poverty and Human Rights" in *Ethics and International Affairs*, Vol. 19, No.1, Spring 2005.

with respect to strategic and specific country situations in emergencies and crises.

In the past the Commission on Human Rights had acknowledged the key role of relevant special procedures – in particular the Special Rapporteur on extrajudicial, summary or arbitrary executions – as early warning mechanisms, and had urged the Special Rapporteurs to draw the High Commissioner's attention to situations of concern where early action might prevent further deterioration.

More specifically, special procedures can play a role at the following stages:

- Early detection and warning: On the basis of the hundreds of communications processed each year, Special procedures holders can identify trends and patterns of recurrent/emerging situations of concern and observe the evolution of specific situations; mandate holders have increasingly resorted to the issuing of press releases on situations of particular concern, a public awareness function; press releases are used as early warning tools; field visits mostly take place in countries with problems where crises may easily erupt. Such visits can provide a useful insight into potential emergency situations. They also facilitate the identification of root causes and various facets of emerging/persisting phenomena of human rights violations, as well as preventive and remedial measures which can ease tensions.
- Crisis management: In some instances the undertaking of a fact-finding mission could be prompted by a request by the HC or the HRC to the relevant Special procedure mandate holder; During crises, the ongoing monitoring of the situation through the analysis of communications received and sent by Special procedures mandate holders can provide the High Commissioner with elements for an assessment of the situation; SPs can be used to publicly raise concerns and make recommendations through press statements, adding their voice to that of the HC or in particularly sensitive situations, substituting for her.
- Post-conflict support: Through their thematic studies, SPs contribute to clarify the contents and implications of human rights norms and standards, thus providing a normative basis for rights-based programming; visits by mandate holders to post-conflict countries can bring essential elements for support programmes and capacity building. Trends identified through processing communications help identify specific areas in need of reform and strengthened support and can inform technical cooperation needs assessment and programming.

In a report on the situation in Rwanda that he submitted to the then

Commission on Human Rights on 11 August, 1993[189], the Rapporteur on Extrajudicial, summary or arbitrary executions warned of the absence of any system for the protection of ethnic minorities:

> "Despite the terrible lessons to be learned from the country's recent history, no effective system for the prevention of ethnically-motivated massacres has been set up. There are no real police in the over-populated rural areas; at most, there are one or two local officials, who would be incapable of facing up to a rampaging mob. Nor is there any effective warning system within reach of ethnic minorities themselves or their representatives. In fact, everything is left to the diligence of local government officials, who, as has been seen on repeated occasions, are often accomplices in the massacres or even instigate them."[190]

He therefore recommended:

> "A mechanism for the protection of civilian populations against massacres should immediately be set up, in terms of both prevention … and monitoring and intervention in cases of violence."[191]

He further recommended that:

> "… inadequacies should be corrected by setting up a system for sending information rapidly from the place where the violence is occurring directly to the security service responsible for taking action, if possible as soon as the first signs of difficulty appear, for example, by setting up a radio link. To this end, international teams of human rights observers and a civilian police force might be established, particularly in the high-risk areas; with the agreement of the Rwandese authorities, they would be placed under international supervision."[192]

Unfortunately, no action was taken on these recommendations with the resultant genocide in that country.

VIII. URGENT ACTION INTERCESSIONS[193]

The first thematic mechanism established, by the UN Commission on

189 UN document E/CN.4/7/Add.1, 11 August, 1993

190 Ibid, para.55.

191 Ibid, para. 65.

192 Ibid, para. 65.

193 See generally N. Rodley … See, generally, O. de Frouville, *Les Procédures thématiques: Une Contribution efficace des Nations Unies à la protection des droits de l'homme* (Paris, Pedone, 1996), 63-6; N. Rodley, *The Treatment of Prisoners under International Law* (Oxford, Clarendon Press, 2nd edn., 1999), 148, 200-01, 240-41, 275-76; Van Boven, 'Urgent Appeals on Behalf of Torture Victims', in *Mélanges en homage au Doyen Gérard Cohen-Jonathan* (Brussels, Bruylant,

Human Rights, the Working Group on Enforced or Involuntary Disappearances (1980), adopted at its first session, a procedure for dealing with 'urgent reports ... requiring immediate action'. Specifically, where such reports were received between sessions of the Group, its Chairman was authorised to transmit the reports to the government of the country concerned, the latter being invited to respond with 'such information as it might wish'.[194] The reports were cabled or telexed (now they are faxed) directly to the foreign ministry of the country concerned, thus avoiding problems of delay or inaction that could occur in using the usual channel, namely, the country's permanent mission to the UN Office at Geneva, to which copies would nevertheless be sent. The model set by the Working Group was emulated by special procedures established subsequently.

IX. CONTRIBUTING TO THE DEVELOPMENT OF EARLY WARNING SYSTEMS

In a path-breaking report that he wrote at the request of the former Commission on Human Rights, former UN High Commissioner for Refugees, Prince Saddrudin Aga Khan and Special Rapporteur of the Commission on Mass Exoduses, called, among other things, for a programme of preventive action and for the establishment of a corps of humanitarian observers.[195]

Prince Saddrudin advocated the creation of an early-warning system based on regular collection of information from all the relevant and reliable sources. On the basis of this data, the Secretary-General of the United Nations would be provided with reports on the development of situations likely to produce mass displacements. After studying those reports, the Secretary-General would determine whether and what action might be required on the part of the UN system. The Secretary-General might, at an early stage, initiate discussions with the governments most closely concerned as well as with the relevant regional organizations.

In the next stage, an executive designated by the Secretary-General, and acting on his behalf, could bring the situation to the attention of States in a position to take preventive action. Humanitarian agencies would also be alerted, enabling them to respond quickly if mass movements of people did in fact take place. The executive might also be entrusted with the tasks of monitoring and forewarning others about a situation and to carry out functions which other

2004) 1651-66; J. Gutter, *Thematic Procedures of the United Nations Commission on Human Rights and International Law: In Search of a Sense of Community* (Utrecht, School of Human Rights Research, 2006) 253-66.

194 UN doc. E/CN.4/1435, para 30.

195 E/CN.4/1503*

agencies could not assume because of institutional or mandate constraints. The executive might be assisted by small *ad hoc* corps of 'humanitarian observers' who could monitor situations in the field and, through their presence, contribute to the de-escalation of tension.[196] Prince Saddrudin's study led eventually, to the first experimental early warning procedure in the human rights and humanitarian fields.[197]

CONCLUSION

Preventive human rights strategies are still in the early stages of development nationally, regionally, and internationally. As this chapter will have shown, special procedures mandate holders have already put down important building blocks as foundations for the strengthening of preventive strategies in the future.

---

196 See UN doc. E/CN.4/1503*. See also, *Refugees. Dynamics of Displacement. A Report for the Independent Commission on International Humanitarian Issues*. London, Zed Books, 1986, p.137.

197 See on this, B.G. Ramcharan, "Early Warning at the United Nations: The First Experiment" *International Journal of Refugee Law* (1989), 379-386.

Chapter VII

CONTAINMENT AND MITIGATION: THE TRANSMITTAL OF COMPLAINTS TO GOVERNMENTS AND VISITS ON THE SPOT

INTRODUCTION

Special procedures contribute to the containment and mitigation of situations of gross violations of human rights in a variety of ways. In this chapter we discuss two of them, the transmittal of complaints to Governments and Visits on the Spot.[198]

I. THE TRANSMITTAL OF COMPLAINTS TO GOVERNMENTS

On the basis of credible and reliable information received from victims of alleged human rights abuses or from civil society partners, mandate-holders may send communications to Governments requesting clarification on a specific case, application of adequate preventive or remedial measures and respect for international human rights standards. Special procedures mandate-holders can also address in communications concerns they have about draft or existing legislation, which they deem inconsistent with human rights standards.

Communications are addressed to the concerned Government either through an urgent appeal – where the alleged violation is imminent or is ongoing – or a letter of allegation – when a violation has allegedly already occurred. These communications are confidential until the special procedures report publicly on their activities to the Human Rights Council, including all communications sent to, and responses received from, States. The experts follow principles of transparency and consistency in their communications, however, the source of the information in the communication is always kept confidential and is never mentioned to the Government.

The Quick Response Desk (QRD) in the Office of High Commissioner for Human Rights, created in June 2001, ensures a coordinated approach to communications to Governments. The QRD processes information received concerning human rights violations; shares information among different mandates; sends communications to Governments through the thematic database (created in January 2004); and stores and files the relevant information on the

198 I should like to acknowledge in this chapter information provided by the staff of the Office of High Commissioner for Human Rights.

case in the thematic database. The centralization of information through the QRD has reduced processing and reaction time to communications received and has improved coordination among mandates. In 2004, 53 per cent of communications sent were joint communications. At the same time, the thematic database has proved to be a useful tool to monitor communications statistics, trends and patterns.

II. COUNTRY VISITS

Country visits represent an essential feature of the special procedures system. They provide a unique opportunity for direct contacts and dialogue both with Government officials and representatives of the civil society and a possibility to assess concretely the human rights situation in a given country. They help substantiate or reject allegations. They contribute to raise the profile of human rights concerns through opportunities to meet the media and spread better awareness about the legal framework and possible remedies available. They constitute an opportunity to rally the UN family around specific human rights concerns, helping them get more familiar with some analytical aspects and providing an environment conducive to the search of solutions and capacity building. They can provide a record for the future (post-conflict societies in search of truth and reconciliation. Taken together, they constitute a vast source of information and expertise to assess the human rights situation over the world.

Requests for visits are either initiated by the experts or by the Human Rights Council in resolutions. Experts may be requested by the Council to carry out joint visits when human rights problems in a specific situation are multi-dimensional.[199] Otherwise, the expert may respond favourably to an invitation from a Government for him/her to visit the country or to a standing invitation from a Government.[200] The visits are normally organized in coordination with the UN Country Team, led by the UN Resident Coordinator or the UN Information Centres.

During the mission, the experts assess the general human rights situation in a given country as well as the specific, institutional, legal, judicial, administrative and *de facto* situation under their respective mandates, through meetings with authorities; members of the national human rights institutions; parliamentarians; NGOs, CSOs and victims of human rights violations and/or their

---

199 This happened, for example, with regard to East Timor and the former Yugoslavia.

200 A standing invitation is an open invitation to visit a country extended by a Government to all thematic special procedures. Currently, 58 countries have extended standing invitations to thematic procedures. For the list, see <http://www.ohchr.org/english/bodies/chr/special/invitations.htm>.

relatives; the UN and other inter-governmental agencies; the diplomatic community; and the press.

On the basis of their findings, they issue conclusions and make recommendations, through their public reports to the Human Rights Council and to the General Assembly where so mandated. There is a general practice for mandate-holders to hold a press conference at the end of country visits.

Terms of reference for Fact-finding missions by Special Procedures were adopted at the fourth annual meeting of the Special Rapporteurs (E/CN.4/1998/45) and presented to the CHR. These are intended to guide Governments in the conduct of their visit. During the fact-finding mission, special procedures mandate-holders, as well as UN staff accompanying them, should be given the following guarantees and facilities by the Government that invited them to visit its country:

1. Freedom of movement in the whole country, including facilitation of transport, especially to restricted areas;
2. Freedom of inquiry, in particular with regard to:
   a. Access to all prisons, detentions centres and places of interrogation;
   b. Contacts with central and local authorities of all branches of government;
   c. Contacts with representatives of NGOs, other private institutions and the media;
   d. Confidential and unsupervised contact with witnesses and other private persons, including persons deprived of liberty, and considered necessary to fulfil the mandate of the Special Rapporteur; and
   e. Full access to all documentary material relevant to the mandate.
3. Assurance by the government that no persons, official or private individuals who have been in contact with the Special Rapporteur in relation to the mandate will suffer threats, harassment or punishment or be subjected to judicial proceedings;
4. Appropriate security arrangements without restricting the freedom of movement and inquiry.

Interaction with the Media

Special procedures generally interact with the media in the following ways:

Mandate-holders may issue a "press release" prior to undertaking a mission and at the end of a country visit.

- "Press briefings" may be held by mandate-holders at the end of their country visit, during the Commission on Human Rights, and/or at the General Assembly.
- Mandate-holders, whenever they deem it necessary, may issue "statements" individually or jointly to inform the public on particular issues of concern or of positive developments.
- "Press briefings" may be held by mandate-holders in order to commemorate days devoted to a specific issue, such as the United Nations International Day in Support of Victims of Torture.

"Press releases" and "statements" provide facts about a particular situation, the opinion of the mandate-holder on the events in question and his or her comments in that regard. The mandate holders may use the opportunity to publicly underline the relevant international norms to be respected.

Mandate-holders share, as a matter of courtesy, press releases with concerned countries shortly before they are publicly released. Official statements and "press briefings" by mandate-holders should be processed either through the OHCHR Media Unit or the United Nations Information Centres, when on mission.

III. VISITS FROM THE PERSPECTIVES OF PROTECTION

In his report to the sixty-second session of the Commission on Human Rights the Special Rapporteur on the Question of Torture, Manfred Nowak, recapitulated the ground rules for visits to a country.[201] A country visit, he noted, is undertaken upon the invitation of the Government. However, an invitation alone is not sufficient and acceptance by the Special Rapporteur is contingent upon an express agreement by the Government of its commitment and cooperation by assuring full compliance with his terms of reference. According to the Special Rapporteur:

> "The aim of carrying out country visits is to see first-hand what the true practice and situation of torture and ill-treatment is: to identify gaps as well as acknowledge positive measures, to recommend ways to improve the situation, and to initiate a process of sustained constructive cooperation with the Government together with the international community and civil society in order to eradicate torture and ill-treatment. Such visits necessarily entail meetings with authorities most directly concerned with the issues, alleged victims or their families as well as NGOs and relevant international actors." [202]

201 UN Doc. E/CN.4/2006/6, 27 December 2005, *Report of the Special Rapporteur on the Question of Torture*, pp.8-11.

202 UN Doc. E/CN.4/2006/6, 27 December 2005, Report of the Special Rapporteur on the

To ensure that any assessment of the situation of torture and ill-treatment will be honest, credible and objective, the Special Rapporteur considered that a number of basic preconditions must be guaranteed by the Government to ensure that the Special Rapporteur can carry out his work effectively. The Special Rapporteur recalled that these conditions, or terms of reference for fact-finding missions, were adopted at the fourth meeting of independent experts of the Commission on Human Rights in May 1997 (E/CN.4/199845, appendix V). In particular, they included freedom of movement within the country; access to all prisons, detention centres and places of interrogation; confidential and unsupervised interviews; assurance by the Government that no persons who have been in contact with the Special Rapporteur will be subject to reprisals; and assurances that the same guarantees and facilitates extended to the Special Rapporteur will be extended to his United Nations staff. These terms of reference were integral to his methods of work. The Special Rapporteur noted that similar standards for conducting visits to detention facilitates had been recognized in international instruments, such as in the European Convention for the Prevention of Torture and Inhuman or Degrading Treatment of Punishment, article 8, and the Optional Protocol to the Convention against Torture, articles 14 and 15.

The Special Rapporteur deemed it axiomatic that freedom of inquiry in places of detention implied: unimpeded access, with or without prior notice, to any place where persons may be deprived of their liberty (e.g. police lock-up, pretrial, prison, juvenile, administrative, psychiatric or other facilities, as well as detention facilities within military installations); not being subject to arbitrary time limits for carrying out his work (e.g. visiting hours, working hours of daytime prison staff, etc.); free movement within the facility and access to any room in order to gather information, including by use of electronic means, such as photography, having access to any detainee or staff, and the possibility of conducting confidential and private interviews, unsupervised by government officials, in places either chosen by the Special Rapporteur or in cooperation with the detainee; being assisted by independent medical specialists who are qualified to document and assess injuries, in accordance with the Istanbul Protocol, as well as being assisted by independent interpreters; and being provided with copies of relevant information and documentation as requested.

The Special Rapporteur observed that in recent years much concern had been raised by Governments with respect to the above-mentioned terms of reference, particularly with regard to unannounced visits to places of detention. While in some cases he might indicate to the authorities in advance which fa-

---

question of torture, Manfred Nowak, pp.8-10: *Civil and Political Rights, Including the Questions of Torture and Detention. Torture and Other Cruel, Inhuman or degrading treatment*, p.8, para. 21.

cilities he intended to visit, access to all places implied that he would also conduct visits with little or no prior notice. Unannounced visits aimed to ensure, to the greatest extent possible, that the Special Rapporteur could formulate a distortion-free picture of the conditions in a facility. Were he to announce in advance, in every instance, which facilities he wished to see and whom he wished to meet, there might be a risk that existing circumstances could be concealed or changed, or persons might be moved, threatened or prevented from meeting with him. This was an unfortunate reality that the Special Rapporteur faced. In fact, such incidents had even occurred where he had been delayed in entering a facility by as little as 30 minutes.

On occasion, in order to deny the Special Rapporteur the unimpeded access described above, it had been argued that national legislation restricted access to facilities except for a select number of enumerated individuals. However, he pointed out, an official visit of the United Nations Special Rapporteur, undertaken at the express invitation of a Government, was clearly an exceptional event. Therefore, one would expect that the Government would demonstrate its good faith and cooperation by facilitating the work of the Special Rapporteur with letters of authorization signed by the relevant ministries.

In the view of the Special Rapporteur, these terms of reference were fundamental, necessary and common sense considerations. Moreover, by their nature, "common sense" methods for fact-finding could not be subject to negotiation or selective approval by States. Any suggestion to the contrary could only be considered as an attempt to compromise later findings. Likewise, subsequent violations of these conditions would seriously call into question the intentions behind inviting the Special Rapporteur.

The Special Rapporteur reiterated that the conclusion of a visit marked the beginning of a long-term process of cooperation with the Government with the common aim of eradicating torture and ill-treatment.[203]

CONCLUSION

This chapter has shown the painstaking efforts of the special procedures mandate holders to act for the protection of those at risk of serious violations of human rights. If anything comes out from the foregoing discussion, it is a story of striving for protection. And sometimes striving succeeds, even if there are many occasions where it does not. The mission at hand is to help avoid such risks in the future, a long and arduous task that faces the international human rights movement.

203 Un Doc. E/CN.4/2006/6, 27 December 2005, Report of the Special Rapporteur on the question of torture, Manfred Nowak, pp.8-10: *Civil and Political Rights, Including the Questions of Torture and Detention. Torture and Other Cruel, Inhuman or degrading treatment.*

Chapter VIII

FACT-FINDING, RECOMMENDATIONS, AND FOLLOW-UP

INTRODUCTION

The role of the special procedures in conducting fact-finding into human rights problems and publishing reports with their findings and recommendations is among their strongest contributions to the protection of human rights. One cannot assess too highly this pivotal protection function of the special procedures in the human rights movement.

For a start, we should recognize that, to date, there is no UN world global human rights report. In 2006 High Commissioner Louise Arbour announced her intention to prepare and publish such a report but she has so far not followed up on the idea. There are annual reports of NGOs such as Amnesty International and Human Rights Watch and they are helpful but they do not have the authority of the world organization. Annual Reports published by national governments, such as that of the US State Department contain useful information but they are seen as having been prepared through the national lens of the issuing country.

The reports prepared by Special Procedures mandate holders and submitted annually to the Human Rights Council and, in some instances, to the UN General Assembly, represent, together, the United Nations' and the world's annual human rights report. The thematic and country scope of the reports over time is truly global. Every country has, at one time or another, come under scrutiny in a report by a special procedure.

In 2003 mandate holders undertook over 80 fact-finding missions and the information contained in their reports proved to be useful and relevant in supporting the work of UN country teams and in the development of technical cooperation projects.

Since 1999 58 countries have extended standing invitations to the thematic special procedures. In 2003 over 670 urgent appeals were communicated, some 60 percent of which were joint appeals. During the same period some 350 letters of allegations were processed. In 2003 Special Rapporteurs issued both jointly and individually more than 20 press releases on issues of concern in particular countries. In 2007, some 1,000 urgent appeals were made.

The world survey of violence against women, published by the Special Rapporteur on Violence against Women in 2003, was an example of the universal coverage of the special procedures. Another example was the study on the situation of trade and production of torture equipment, a study conducted by the Special Rapporteur against Torture; the development of guiding principles on internally-displaced persons; the encouragement of work on judicial ethics (Bangalore Principles on Judicial Conduct): the study on Islamophobia: the study on political platforms which promote racial discrimination. Special procedures also jointly and publicly raise concerns over human rights issues such as the potential threat to human rights posed by counter-terrorism measures and the need to protect witnesses cooperating with human rights bodies.

The reports of the special procedures mandate holders document facts, make findings, and offer recommendations in respect of particular situations or in respect of broader problems. It is here that that the Special Procedures rise in stature as the world's premier protection actors. Special Procedures contribute to a better understanding of the root causes, factors, and possible ways to combat and prevent phenomenon affecting the enjoyment of human rights.

I. METHODS OF FACT-FINDING

Theodor Van Boven, then Special Rapporteur against Torture, in a report submitted to the Commission on Human Rights in 2002-2003, provided a magisterial illustration of the methods of work of a professional Special Rapporteur.[204] His work as Special Rapporteur, he reported to the Commission, was characterized by the following main types of activity:

a) Seeking and receiving credible and reliable information from Governments, specialized agencies and intergovernmental and non-governmental organizations as well as private individuals;
b) sending urgent appeals to Governments to clarify the situation of individuals whose circumstances give grounds to fear that treatment falling within the Special Rapporteur's mandate might occur or be occurring;
c) Transmitting to Governments information of the sort mentioned in (a) above, indicating that acts falling within his mandate may have occurred or that legal or other measures were needed to prevent the occurrence of such acts:
d) Exploring the possibility of undertaking fact-finding visits to States where information suggested that torture may involve more than isolated and sporadic incidents, with a view to gaining more direct knowledge of the situation and practice relating to matters falling within his mandate and identifying measures to prevent the recurrence of such cases

204 UN doc. E/CN.4/2003/68, 17 December, 2002: *Torture And Other Cruel, Inhuman Or Degrading Treatment, Report Of The Special Rapporteur On The Question Of Torture Submitted In Accordance With Commission Resolution 2002/38.*

and to improve the situation; and

e) Submitting annual reports on his activities and mandate, as well as his conclusions and recommendations, to the Commission on Human Rights and the General Assembly.[205]

He expanded upon his methods of work as follows[206]:

SOURCES OF INFORMATION

With respect to the credibility and reliability of the information that comes before him, the Special Rapporteur takes into account a number of factors, any one of which may be sufficient, through generally more than one will be present. These factors include: (a) the established previous reliability of the source of information; (b) the internal consistency of the information; (c) the precision of the factual details included in the information; (d) the consistency of the information as compared with information on other cases from the country in question that has previously come to his attention; (e) the existence of authoritative reports of torture practices from national sources, such as official commissions of inquiry and national commissions on human rights/ombudsperson's offices; and (f) the findings of other international bodies, such as United Nations country rapporteurs and representatives, human rights treaty-monitoring bodies and regional human rights bodies. The Special Rapporteur may also rely on assessments made by professionals of the Office of the High Commissioner for Human Rights (OHCHR) as well as of other United Nations agencies. With respect to information pertaining to individual cases, it should be noted that a number of basic requirements must be contained in the information submitted to him, such as the identity of the alleged victims, the date and place of the incident, a description of the alleged perpetrators and of the situation, and the identity of the source of information. It should be stressed that the last element will remain confidential.

URGENT APPEALS

With respect to the "urgent appeals" procedure, the Special Rapporteur acknowledged that his work has been considerably facilitated by the creation within OHCHR of a Quick Response Desk which allows information to be processed in a more timely and consistent manner and also facilitated the sending of joint appeals with other special procedures of the Commission.

These appeals served urgent humanitarian purposes in their request for clarification and relief. The urgent appeal procedure was not not per se accusa-

205 Ibid, pp. 3-4.

206 Ibid., UN doc. E/CN.4/2003/68, 17 December, 2002, pp.4-8

tory, but rather essentially preventive in nature and purpose. The Government concerned was requested to look into the matter and to take steps aimed at protecting the right to physical and mental integrity of the person concerned, in accordance with the international human rights standards.

The circumstance that led to urgent appeals were diverse, but they had in common that they indicated, on the basis of information of the sort mentioned above, that any identifiable risk of torture or other cruel, inhuman or degrading treatment or punishment existed. Such circumstances included *incommunicado* detention, prolonged solitary confinement, use of physical constraints in circumstances contrary to international standards, lack of essential medical care and treatment, imminent corporal punishment, and serious risk of extradition or deportation to a State or territory where the person in question would reportedly be in danger of being subjected to torture. The Special Rapporteur might also address the enactment of legislation or other measures that might undermine the prohibition of torture. Owing to the time-sensitive nature of such an appeal, the Special Rapporteur transmitted it directly to the Minister for Foreign Affairs of the country concerned, urging the Government in question to take the necessary measures to ensure the physical and mental integrity of the persons concerned but without drawing any conclusions as to the facts.

Because urgent appeals served immediate humanitarian purposes, the Special Rapporteur might exceptionally decide to send such appeals to entities other than official *de jure* authorities in cases where the entities in question, as well as a channel of communication for reaching them, had been clearly identified. In the past, situations of armed conflicts had provoked such action. The Special Rapporteur recalled that all parties to an armed conflict, be it of an international or an internal character, were bound by the minimum standards of humanitarian law that prohibited violence to life and person, in particular cruel treatment and torture, as well as outrages upon personal dignity, by any party to the conflict at any time and in any place whatsoever. The Special Rapporteur stressed that such urgent humanitarian appeals did not in any way determine the international legal status of such entities.

Allegation Letters

Information alleging torture received by the Special Rapporteur which did not require him to take immediate action was transmitted to Governments in the form of "allegation letters". These letters contained summaries of individual cases of torture and, where applicable, included general references to the phenomenon of torture, such as alleged systematic patterns of practice of torture, patterns relating to a specific group of victims or of perpetrators, or specific legislation deemed not sufficient to guarantee the right to physical and mental integrity. In these letters, the Special Rapporteur would request the Government concerned to clarify the substance of the allegations and urge it to take steps to investigate them, to prosecute and impose appropriate sanctions on any persons guilty of torture regardless of any rank, office or position they may hold, to take effective measures to prevent the recurrence of such acts, and to compensate the victims or their relatives in accordance with the relevant international standards.

Because of the limited staff resources, such communications were usually sent once a year – at the end of the Summer – to Governments which were given some two months to respond. The Special Rapporteur hoped that he would be in a position to send such communications more regularly during the course of the year and would do his utmost to facilitate the processing of these communications by Governments concerned. He noted that it was desirable for Governments to receive relevant information as expeditiously as possible and to have their replies thereto in the same report that contained the summary of the original information transmitted by the Special Rapporteur. Thus, reports of the Special Rapporteur would provide the reader with a balanced perspective on the matter.

Individual cases regarding which no reply had been received were re-sent the following year until a reply was received. The Special Rapporteur noted with concern that a number of Governments had failed to provide any replies on cases originally sent in 1997 and 1998. The Special Rapporteur analysed responses from Governments and transmitted the contents to the sources of the allegations, as appropriate, for comment. This practice mainly concerned cases where the facts appeared to be contradicted. If required, dialogue with the Government was then pursued further.

The Special Rapporteur made it clear that communications regarding individual cases – urgent appeals and allegations – did not constitute any judgment on his part concerning the merits of the cases. In transmitting those communications, the Special Rapporteur did not associate himself with or condone in any way acts or activities of the persons on whose behalf he intervened. No matter how wrongly, dangerously, or even criminally a person might act, every human being is legally and morally entitled to protection on the basis of internationally recognized human rights and fundamental freedoms. This applies *a fortiori* where a non-derogable right, such as the prohibition of torture and other cruel, inhuman or degrading treatment or punishment, was involved.

Fact-Finding Missions

The Special Rapporteur carried out visits to countries on invitation, but also took the initiative of approaching Governments with a view to carrying out visits to countries concerning which he had received information indicating the existence of a significant incidence of torture. Such visits should allow the Special Rapporteur to gain more direct knowledge of situations falling within his mandate, and were intended to enhance the dialogue between the Special Rapporteur and the authorities most directly concerned, as well as with the alleged victims, their families and legal representatives and non-governmental organizations, with a view to making detailed recommendations. When contemplating whether to request an invitation, the Special Rapporteur took into account, first and foremost, the number, quality and gravity/nature of the allegations received and the potential impact that a mission to the country concerned might have on the overall human rights situation. The Special Rapporteur welcomed the decision by an increasing number of States to extend a standing invitation to all thematic special procedures and urged others to seriously consider extending such an invitation.

The Special Rapporteur did not, as a rule, seek to visit a country in respect of which the United Nations had established a country-specific mechanism such as a Special Rapporteur/representative for the country, unless a joint visit seemed to both to be indicated. For countries where the mandates of other thematic mechanisms might also be affected, the Special Rapporteur consulted with the latter with a view to exploring with the Government in question, whether jointly or in parallel, the possibility of a joint visit. Where the Committee against Torture was considering the situation in a country under article 20 of the Convention against torture and Other Cruel, Inhuman or Degrading Treatment or Punishment, especially if that consideration involved a visit or possible visit by the committee to the country in question, the Special Rapporteur did not seek a visit.

In accordance with the terms of reference for fact-finding missions by Special Rapporteurs/representatives of the Commission on Human Rights adopted by the fourth meeting of Special Rapporteurs/representatives, independent experts and chairpersons of working groups of the special procedures of the Commission on Human Rights and of the Advisory Services Programme (E/CN.4/1998/45, annex V), before a fact-finding mission took place, the Government concerned was asked to guarantee the following to the Special Rapporteur and accompanying United Nations staff: freedom of movement throughout the country; freedom of inquiry, especially in terms of access to all detention centres and places of interrogation; free contact with central and local authorities of all branches of Government; free contact with representatives of non-governmental organizations, other private institutions and the media; confidential and unsupervised contacts with witnesses and other private individuals, including persons deprived of their liberty; and full access to all documentary material relevant to the mandate. The Government was also asked for assurance that no persons, be they officials or private individuals, who had been in contact with the Special Rapporteur in connection with the mandate would suffer threats, harassment or punishment on that account or be subjected to judicial proceedings. As stated by the meeting, these terms of reference "are the minimum necessary to ensure the independence, impartiality and safety of visits by the Special Rapporteurs to the field. These terms of reference did not exclude additional safeguards, depending on the mandates or circumstances".

During the mission, the Special Rapporteur met with representatives of the Government, non-governmental organizations and the legal profession, alleged victims of torture and relatives of the victims. He visited places of detention and of interrogation to obtain first-hand knowledge of how the criminal legal process operated, from arrest to enforcement of the sentence. Confidential and unsupervised interviews were conducted with victims of torture, witnesses and other private persons, including those deprived of their liberty. In the mission report, the Special Rapporteur might give an account of individual allegations received. Although the monitoring of conditions of detention was not specifically mentioned in the mandate, they might well be pertinent, especially when they constituted a grave risk to the life or health of detainees.

With regard to countries in which visits had been carried out, the Special Rapporteur periodically reminded the Governments concerned of the observations and recommendations formulated in the respective reports, requesting information on the consideration given to them and the steps take to implement them, or the constraints which might prevent their implementation. The Special Rapporteur also welcomed information from non-governmental organizations and other interested parties regarding measures taken in follow-up to his recommendations. Thus a dialogue on measures that might be undertaken by the concerned authorities could be established.

REPORTS

The Special Rapporteur was mandated by the Commission (now the Human Rights Council) and the General Assembly to report on an annual basis to both organs. Reports to the Commission/Council contained summaries of all communications (urgent appeals and allegation letters) transmitted to Governments and the latter's replies thereto. The Special Rapporteur might also include general observations on specific countries. Nevertheless, no conclusion as to individual cases were drawn. He might also address specific issues of concern and development that had an impact on the fight against torture and usually drew general conclusions and made recommendations. Because of financial constraints and limitations on the length and time of submission of documentation, summaries of communications sent to Governments and replies received by the Special Rapporteur had in recent years not been translated; they appeared in addendum 1 to the main report of the Commission/Council in the original working language of the United Nations Secretariat used to communicate with the respective Governments. Interim reports to the General Assembly outlined overall and recent development of relevance to the Special Rapporteur's mandate.

In the mission reports, which were addenda to the main Commission report, the Special Rapporteur outlined legislation of relevance to the prohibition of torture such as provisions making torture a crime and provisions governing arrest and detention. Special attention was paid to periods of incommunicado detention, disciplinary sanctions, access to qualified legal representation and legal aid, access to family members and medical care, bail provisions, witnesses protection, the admissibility of confessions, the status and independence of medical experts and forensic services, and access of members of civil society to places of detention.

As indicated in his first report to the Commission (E/CN.4/2002/137, para. 6), the Special Rapporteur attached great importance to follow-up activities and considered them to be an essential requirement of his mandate. He therefore intended to seek ways to enhance the quality of such activities, in particular in cooperation with the Quick Response Desk. He also paid particular attention to cooperation with other mechanisms, especially other special procedures mandate-holders, with a view to taking concerted actions and avoiding duplication of work. In that respect, he sought the cooperation of other Special Rapporteurs/representatives when sending communications, be they urgent appeals or allegation letters, regarding information that fell within other special procedures mandates.

II. FACT FINDING IN PRACTICE

In this section we provide glimpses into the fact-gathering and fact-finding role of special procedures mandate-holders based on their reports to the former Commission on Human Rights, and its successor, the Human Rights Council.

A. Problems of Protection Nationally: Attacks on Judges, Prosecutors and Lawyers

The Special Rapporteur on the independence of judges and lawyers, Leandro Despouy, has provided chilling evidence of the problems of protection existing in the judiciaries and legal professions of many countries. He has expressed grave concern that despite the legal guarantees provided by each State and the many international instruments intended to preserve their independence, lawyers, judges, prosecutors and court officers in all regions are frequently subjected to pressures, harassment and threats that may result in their enforced disappearance, assassination or extrajudicial execution, simply because they are doing their job. Also of concern are the wide ranges of situations which undermine the independence of judicial systems throughout the world, and their impact on the rule of law, insofar as the judiciary is one of its main guardians.[207]

In a report submitted to the Human Rights Council in 2007 the Special Rapporteur provided a summary of the issues in this area since the establishment of the mandate in 1994.[208] It was clear, he reported, that throughout the world those who worked in the judicial system faced situations that resulted in violations of their human rights. This included threats, harassment, intimidation, vilification and various forms of interference. The threats may be direct, anonymous, or under cover of a false identity, and may be delivered by telephone, post or e-mail. There might be interference with mail, press campaigns, house raids, or travel bans which can even prevent travel to attend events or training on human rights or public international law. Regrettably there were also instances of physical attacks, threats of abduction or actual abduction, enforced disappearances, arbitrary detention, torture, and even assassinations and summary executions. In such cases, complaints to the Special Rapporteur often alleged inadequate or no effort by the authorities to respond and provide protection, even when reports had been submitted to the police or judicial authorities.

Experience showed, the Special Rapporteur continued, that those who worked in the judicial system were particularly at risk of such attacks if they were prominent defenders of human rights. This included lawyers for victims of enforced disappearances or extrajudicial executions, or those who specialized in sensitive fields, for example, terrorism; organized crime such as people trafficking; land ownership; protection of the environment and natural resources; advocacy for vulnerable groups such as indigenous peoples, or ethnic, linguistic, religious or cultural minorities who were critical of the status quo and asserted their rights; women who were victims of violence or discrimination; and those who opposed war or campaigned for their region's independence. Many judges were also subjected to pressure, intimidation, death threats or actual assassination attempts because of their role in investigating the involvement of politicians or other well-connected figures in assassinations or other serious human rights violations. Confronted with such risks arising from their beliefs

207 A/HRC/4/25, 18 January, 2007, paras. 61-62.

208 A/HRC/4/25

or activities, those who worked in the judicial system were quite often forced to resign, move to another town, or go underground or into exile, and the threats may extend to family members. The authorities did not always provide sufficient protection or a clear condemnation of these criminal activities, which often went unpunished.

These circumstances most commonly affected judges and lawyers, particularly when they became identified with the cases they took on. Governments often regarded judges and lawyers' efforts to defend human rights and fundamental freedoms as political interference. Lawyers were regularly hunted down and arrested because they were identified with their clients, and continued to be harassed by the authorities following their release. This in turn meant that individuals accused of sensitive crimes might have difficulty finding a lawyer who would take their case.

Cases recorded in 2006, the Special Rapporteur continued, showed how regularly such circumstances arose. About 55 per cent of communications, relating to some 148 cases in 54 countries, concerned violations of the human rights of judges, lawyers, prosecutors and court officials. Threats, intimidation and acts of aggression directed against lawyers accounted for 17 per cent of communications issued by the Special Rapporteur, and the corresponding figure for judges and prosecutors was 4 per cent. Arbitrary detention and judicial harassment accounted for 26 per cent of communications concerning lawyers and 4 percent of those concerning judges and prosecutors. Assassinations of lawyers, judges and prosecutors accounted for 4 per cent of the total number of communications. In some countries, the level of violence was especially high. For example, in one Latin American country, the Special Rapporteur had recorded the assassination of 16 employees of the judicial system, 63 cases of threats, 2 abductions and 2 cases of exile between January 2995 and August 2006. In one Asian country no fewer than 15 lawyers and 10 judges had been assassinated with impunity between 2001 and 2006.[209]

B. The Global Scourge of Pervasive Violence against Women

In 2003 the first Special Rapporteur on violence against women, Radhika Coomaraswamy, reported to the then Commission on Human Rights on problems and progress during the previous decade of efforts to protect women from violence. She considered that achievements had been made in awareness-raising and standard-setting. Despite these, however, very little had changed in the lives of most women. A few women had benefited from the changes but, for the vast majority, violence against women remained a taboo issue, invisible

209 Ibid, pp. 7-8.

in society and a shameful fact of life. Statistics continued to show high rates of violence and abuse. Most cases of violence against women resulted in impunity for the perpetrators, which fuelled the perpetuation of this grave violation of human rights. More must be done to provide equal access to effective judical protection and guarantees. States must be assisted in eradicating discrimination in law and practice and monitoring the effectiveness of strategies to end violence against women.[210] The Special Rapporteur's report contained a country -by- country survey of violence against women perpetrated in all parts of the world.[211]

The current Special Rapporteur on violence against women, Yakin Erktuk, reported to the Human Rights Council in January, 2007 that across all regions, culture constituted a primary source of diverse and sometimes contradictory normative systems that provided the rationale for varied patterns of gender roles and identities. At the global level, values commonly shared by the international community had been formalized into international human rights law and other instruments, including declarations and policy frameworks. Even though these standards, which included the principle of equality between women and men as a key value, were universally applicable and legally binding, they were inadequately implemented.[212]. In the period from 1 January through 1 December 2006, the Special Rapporteur had sent 78 communications bringing alleged human rights violations to the attention of Governments. Thirty-one of these communications had been joint appeals, 44 had been joint letters of allegation and 3 had been letters of allegation sent by her mandate alone. As of l December 2006, only 36 Government replies to these communications had been received.[213]

C. Shocking Violations of the Rights of Children World-Wide: Sale of Children, Child Prostitution and Child Pornography

The scale and dimensions of human rights abuses of children is truly numbing. In his first report on this topic to the Commission on Human Rights, submitted in January, 1991, the Special Rapporteur, Mr Vitit Muntarbhorn, alerted the Commission that the sale of children was a universal phenomenon, even if the extent varied from country to country. The phenomenon of child labour was vast and an insidious issue to appear on the international scene in recent years had been the question of organ transplants affecting children. Child pros-

210 E/CN.4/2003/75, 27 February, 2003, pp. 19-21.

211 Ibid : International, regional and national developments in the area of violence against women, 1994-2003.

212 A/HRC/4/34, 17 January, 2007, para. 18.

213 A/HRC/4/34, 17 January, 2007, para. 12

titution was a global phenomenon and child pornography was rampant.[214]

The current Special Rapporteur on this topic considers the phenomenon of child abduction to be of particular concern, as these disappearances and abductions often constituted the first step in abuses against children that could lead to sexual exploitation of the victims. The number of States having set up organized and effective systems to respond to children abductions was very limited, which resulted that when such a situation occurred, the first hours and days which were key for finding a missing child were being lost. Therefore, a coordinated, comprehensive, and global approach was required, where the different State institutions as well as NGOs and private business had a role to play. Among this, outreach on prevention and on fast and effective responses was essential. Rapid response programmes and initiatives taken by international and regional organizations were to be encouraged. States that had already elaborated legislative and administrative measures to tackle this issue were commended for their efforts and their successes in finding abducted children. These rapid response programmes were not only tools to respond to abducted and missing children, but also allowed considerable improvement between the different organizations for prevention of violence against children.[215]

D. Extrajudicial, Summary, or Arbitrary Executions

The first Special Rapporteur on this topic, Amos Wako, reported to the Commission on Human Rights in 1983 that from the information he had received, summary and arbitrary executions occurred on a wide-scale throughout the world. In the previous decade and a half it had been practiced in many countries and in a number of them in a consistent pattern. Conservative estimates had put the known victims of summary or arbitrary executions to at least two million persons. The number could be even higher and more widespread given the fact that not all cases were reported or known.[216] His report presented information on arbitrary and summary executions in thirty nine countries. He wrote:

> "Summary or arbitrary executions have occurred in all social, economic and ideological systems in nearly all parts of the globe. All classes of people, rich and poor, peasants, urban workers, professional classes, religious groups and ethnic minorities and majorities, have been affected. The old, the young and women have not escaped it. A factor common to all these victims is that they were in opposition or were perceived or imagined to have been in opposition either to those who wielded political or economic

214 E/CN.4/1991/51, 28 January, 1991.

215 A/HRC/4/31, 26 December, 2006, para. 81.

216 E/CN.4/1983/16, pp.40-41.

power in the state or government or were perceived to be in opposition to certain aspects of their political and economic policies.

...

"Governments have been extremely reluctant to investigate cases and where found guilty to punish those law enforcement officers or civilians who have acted with their authority, complicity or acquiescence who are guilty of summarily or arbitrarily executing persons. In fact in some cases laws have been passed granting such persons immunities from the acts they commit in 'good faith.' "[217]

The problem has not abated. The current Special Rapporteur, Philip Alston reported to the Human Rights Council that in 2007-2007 135 communications had been sent to 51 countries and 2 other actors (including 44 urgent appeals and 75 letters of allegations and 16 communications following up on previous correspondence) concerning more than 1, 531 individuals. More than 145 persons had been killed for exercising their freedom of opinion or expression, 4 had been killed in the name of honour, 4 had been killed for their sexual orientation and 19 of those killed had been suspected terrorists.[218]

E. Torture

The first Special Rapporteur on this topic, Professor, later Judge Peter Kooijmans, advised the Commission on Human Rights in February, 1986 that torture had been deemed "the plague of the second half of the twentieth century." Torture was widespread and there were situations in which torture easily occurred, such as in situations of civil war and civil strife. As Special Rapporteur he had received an alarming amount of information about alleged torture. Torture often took place during interrogation in isolation and in secret places. There was a considerable number of techniques of torture which left no traceable marks on the body. All of his successors as Special Rapporteurs reported a similar situation. Torture had therefore not slackened in the world.

The current Special Rapporteur, Professor Manfred Novak, reported that during the period 16 December 2005-15 December, 2006, he had sent 79 letters of allegations of torture to 35 Governments and 157 urgent appeals to 60 Governments on behalf of persons who might be at risk of torture or other forms of ill-treatment.[219]

---

217 Ibid.

218 A/HRC/4/20, 29 January, 2007, para.8.

219 A/HRC/4/33, 15 January, 2007, para.5.

F. Arbitrary Detention

In its annual report to the Human Rights Council dated 9 January, 2007[220], the Working Group on Arbitrary Detention reported on an increase in the number of people being detained around the world, particularly in developed countries, the majority of the detainees being in pre-trial detention. The Working Group recommended that this recent growth be studied and debated with a view to developing measures favouring respect of the rights of the detainees.[221]

With regard to the international transfer of detainees, particularly in the context of countering terrorism, the Working Group recommended: (a) Governments removing persons in their custody from their territory and into the custody of another Government should do so within proceedings that offered adequate safeguards, in particular to argue before an independent body offering judicial guarantees that removal would expose those persons to extrajudicial killing, torture, or other cruel, inhuman or degrading treatment of punishment, or arbitrary detention and denial of fair trial; (b) Governments should not engage in so-called arbitrary detention and denial of a fair trial; (c) Governments should refuse to give assurances that they will deprive of their freedoms persons transferred to their territory, unless such assurances can be given in accordance with both the domestic legislation and the Government's international human rights obligations.[222]

A joint report by several mandate-holders on persons detained by the US authorities for several years in Guantanamo in the aftermath of the conflict in Afghanistan provides a good example of the special procedures at work on this issue.

G. Guantánamo

In a joint report regarding detainees at Guantánamo Bay, Cuba, by five holders of mandates of special procedures of the former Commission on Human Rights, (now the Human Rights Council) submitted to the sixty second session of the Commission on 27 February 2006, the mandate holders concluded, as follows:

> 83. International human rights law is applicable to the analysis of the situation of detainees in Guantánamo Bay. Indeed, human rights law applies at all times, even during situations of emergency and armed conflicts. The war on terror, as such, does not constitute an armed conflict for the purposes of the applicability of international humanitarian law. The

220 A/HRC/4/40, 9 January, 2007.

221 Ibid, p. 27.

222 Ibid, pp. 27-28.

United States of America has not notified to the Secretary-General of the United Nations or other States parties to the treaties any official derogation from the International Covenant on Civil and Political Rights or any other international human rights treaty to which it is a party.

84. The persons held at Guantánamo Bay are entitled to challenge the legality of their detention before a judicial body in accordance with article 9 of ICCPR, and to obtain release if detention is found to lack a proper legal basis. The right is currently being violated, and the continuing detention of all persons held at Guantánamo Bay amounts to arbitrary detention in violation of article 9 of ICCPR.
85. The executive branch of the United States Government operates as judge, prosecutor and defence counsel of the Guantánamo Bay detainees: this constitutes serious violations of various guarantees of the right to a fair trial before an independent tribunal as provided for by article 14 of the ICCPR.
86. Attempts by the United States Administration to redefine "torture" in the framework of the struggle against terrorism in order to allow certain interrogation techniques that would not be permitted under the internationally accepted definition of torture are of the utmost concern. The confusion with regard to authorized and unauthorized interrogation techniques over the last years is particularly alarming.
87. The interrogation techniques authorized by the Department of Defense, particularly if used simultaneously, amount to degrading treatment in violation of article 17 of ICCPR and article 16 of the Convention against Torture. If in individual cases, which were described in interviews, the victim experienced severe pain or suffering, these acts amounted to torture as defined in article 1 of the Convention. Furthermore, the general conditions of detention, in particular the uncertainty about the length of detention and prolonged solitary confinement, amount to inhuman treatment and to a violation of the right to health as well as a violation of the right of detainees under article 10, paragraph 1, of ICCPR to be treated with humanity and with respect for the inherent dignity of the human person.
89. The excessive violence used in many cases during transportation, in operations by Initial Reaction Forces, and force-feeding of detainees on hunger strike must be assessed as amounting to torture as defined in article 1 of the Convention against Torture.
90. The practice of rendition of persons to countries where there is a substantial risk of torture, such as in the case of Mr. Al Qadasi, amounts to a violation of the principle of non-refoulement and is contrary to article 3 of the Convention against Torture and article 7 of the ICCPR.

91. The lack of any impartial investigation into allegations of torture and ill-treatment and resulting impunity of the perpetrators amount to a violation of articles 12 and 13 of the Convention against Torture.
92. There are reliable indications that, in different circumstances, persons detained in Guantanámo Bay detention facilities have been victims of violations of the right to freedom of religion or belief, contrary to article 18 of ICCPR and the 1981 Declaration. It is of particular concern that some of these violations have even been authorized by the authorities. In addition, some interrogation techniques are based on religious discrimination and are aimed at offending the religious feelings of detainees.
93. The totality of the conditions of their confinement at Guantanámo Bay constitute a right-to-health violation because they derive from a breach of duty and have resulted in profound deterioration of the mental health of many detainees.
94. There are also serious concerns about the alleged violations of ethical standards by health professionals at Guantánamo Bay and the effect that such violations have on the quality of health care, including mental health care, the detainees are receiving.
95. The treatment of the detainees and the conditions of their confinement have led to prolonged hunger strikes. The force feeding of competent detainees violates the right to health as well as the ethical duties of any health professional who may be involved.

In light of these findings the mandate holders recommended the following:

95. Terrorism suspects should be detained in accordance with criminal procedure that respects the safeguards enshrined in relevant international law. Accordingly, the Government of the United States of America should either expeditiously bring all Guantánamo Bay detainees to trial, in compliance with articles 9, paragraph 3, and 14 of ICCPR, or release them without further delay. Consideration should also be given to trying suspected terrorists before a competent international tribunal.
96. The Government of the United States should close the Guantánamo Bay detention facilities without further delay. Until the closure, and possible transfer of detainees to pre-trial detention facilities on United States territory, the Government should refrain from any practice amounting to torture or cruel, inhuman or degrading treatment or punishment, discrimination on the basis of religion, and violations of the rights to health and freedom of religion. In particular, all special interrogation techniques authorized by the Department of Defense should immediately be revoked.
97. The Government of the United States should refrain from expelling,

returning, extraditing or rendering Guantánamo Bay detainees to States where there are substantial grounds for believing they would be in danger of being tortured.

98. The Government of the United States should ensure that every detainee has the right to make a complaint regarding his treatment and to have it dealt with promptly and, if requested, confidentially. If necessary, complaints may be lodged on behalf of the detainee or by his legal representative or family.
99. The Government of the United States should ensure that all allegations of torture or cruel, inhuman or degrading treatment of punishment are thoroughly investigated by an independent authority, and that all persons found to have perpetrated, ordered, tolerated or condoned such practices, up to the highest level of military and political command, are brought to justice.
100. The Government of the United States should ensure that all victims of torture or cruel, inhuman or degrading treatment or punishment are provided with fair and adequate compensation, in accordance with article 14 of the Convention against Torture, including the means for as full a rehabilitation as possible.
101. The Government of the United States should provide the personnel of detention facilities with adequate training, in order to ensure that they know that it is their duty to respect international human rights standards for the treatment of persons in detention, including the right to freedom of religion, and to enhance their sensitivity of cultural issues.
102. The Government of the United States should revise the United States Department of Defense Medical Program Principles to be consistent with the United Nations Principle of Medical Ethics.
103. The Government of the United States should ensure that the authorities in Guantánamo Bay do not force-feed any detainee who is capable of forming a rational judgement and is aware of the consequences of refusing food. The United States Government should invite independent health professionals to monitor hunger strikers, in a manner consistent with international ethical standards, throughout the hunger strike.
104. All five mandate holders should be granted full and unrestricted access to the Guantánamo Bay facilities, including private interviews with detainees.[223]

---

223 UN doc. E/CN.4/2006/120, 27 February 2006, pp.24-26: *Situtaion of Detainees at Guantánamo Bay, Report of the Chairperson-Rapporteur of the Working Group on Arbitray Detention, Leila Zerrougi; the Special Rapporteur on the Indpendence of Judges and Lawyers, Leandro Despouy; the Special Rapporteur on Torture and other Cruel, Inhuman or Degrading Treatment of Punishment, Manfred Nowak; the Special Rapporteur on Freedom of Religion or*

H. Racism, Racial Discrimination, Xenophobia and Related Intolerance

In the view of the Special Rapporteur on this topic, Mr Doudou Diene, efforts to combat racism, racial discrimination, xenophobia and related intolerance encounter a number of serious major challenges manifested by the following worrying trends: the resurgence of racism, racial discrimination and xenophobia, demonstrated by the spread of racist and xenophobic political platforms and by their implementation through alliances with Governments, which enabled the political parties responsible for these platforms to invest them with legal and democratic legitimacy; the criminalization of, and the exclusively security-based approach to, immigration, asylum and the status of foreigners and national minorities; the general increase in the defamation of religions and racial and religious hatred, in particular anti-Semitism and Christianophobia, and more particularly, Islamophobia; the ideological and intellectual acceptance of racist and xenophobic speech and rhetoric, which favoured an ethnic or racial interpretation of social, economic and political problems and their legal instrumentalization, as demonstrated by the tendency to establish a dogmatic, ideological and political hierarchy of the freedoms guaranteed by the International Covenant on Civil and Political Rights, such as freedom of expression, to the detriment of other freedoms and restrictions and limitations contained in the Covenant; the increasing importance in identity constructs of a rejection of diversity and resistance to the process of multiculturalism of societies, and the increase in violent manifestations of racism in sport, in particular, football.[224]

The Special Rapporteur had invited the Human Rights Council to draw the attention of the member States to the alarming signs of regression in efforts to combat racism, racial discrimination and xenophobia, particularly the upsurge in racist violence, and to remind them of the crucial importance of political will in the refusal to trivialize racism, xenophobia and intolerance, the rejection of their use in politics and electoral campaigns and the systematic combating of racist and xenophobic political platforms.[225]

I. Human Rights of Indigenous Peoples

The Special Rapporteur on this topic, Rodolfo Stavenhagen, has reported that while there had been progress in the adoption of standards that recognize the rights of indigenous people, the gap when it comes to implementing those

---

Belief, Asma Jahangir; and the Special Rapporteur on the Right of Everyone to the Enjoyment of the Highest Attainable Standard of Physical and Mental Health, Paul Hunt.

224 A/HRC/4/18, 5 February, 2007, Summary, p. 2.

225 Ibid, para. 54.

standards still remained. To give greater visibility to their needs and rights, indigenous peoples had resorted to various forms of social organization and mobilization that often proved the only way to make their claims heard. However, it was all too often the case that social protest was criminalized, giving rise to new and sometimes grave human rights violations.

The Special Rapporteur found that the continuing trend was towards a decline in the resources of indigenous people, reduction of their land and territorial base, and progressive and accelerated loss of control over their natural resources, in particular their forests. Particularly affected were indigenous peoples living in isolation, above all in the Amazon basin. The existence of pastoral peoples in arid and semi-arid regions was also endangered.[226]

J. Minority Issues

The Independent Expert on this topic, Ms Gay McDougall, has reported that in every region of the world there were minorities who were the poorest of the poor, often having faced long-standing discrimination, exclusion, denial of their basic rights, and sometimes violence. Minorities faced high and disproportionate levels of poverty and the dynamics of that poverty were often more complex in nature for minority groups and defied the rationale of common denominator policies of poverty alleviation. Often minorities were neglected or excluded from efforts to achieve the Millennium Development Goals (MDGs). Recognizing the urgent need to address the situations of minorities more fully in international and national efforts to alleviate poverty and achieve the Goals, the Independent Expert decided to target this issue for particular attention.[227]

K. The Human Rights of Migrants

The first Special Rapporteur on the human rights of migrants, Ms Gabriela Rodriguez Pizarro, in her first report submitted to the Commission on Human Rights on 6 January, 2000, provided extensive evidence of serious violations of the human rights of migrants, including discrimination and intolerance, violence against women migrant workers, discrimination against migrant children, the vulnerability of migrants, and severe obstacles to the protection of the human rights of migrants. One of the basic institutional obstacles was the absence or non-acceptance in domestic legislation of universal standards explicitly recognizing the human rights of migrants. Another institutional obstacle was the failure to achieve widespread ratification of international instruments dealing with migrants' rights.[228]

---

226 A/HRC/4/32, Summary, p. 2.

227 A/HRC/4/9, 2 February, 2007, p. 2, Summary.

228 E/CN.4/2000, 6 January, 2000.

In its resolution 2005/47 the then Commission on Human Rights requested the current Special Rapporteur, Mr J. Bustamante, to include in annual reports a chapter on the impact of legislation and the measures adopted by some States that restricted the human rights and fundamental freedoms of migrants. By note verbale sent on 8 and 9 September, 2006, the Special Rapporteur submitted a questionnaire to all United Nations Member States, which addressed questions relating to five main themes: border control and measures to reduce/address irregular migration; expulsion; conditions for admission/stay; rights of migrants and the protection of migrants. To date the Special Rapporteur has received 26 responses to the questionnaire. The Rapporteur recommends that Member States should take concrete measures to include a human dimension when formulating migration policies, such as providing both documented and undocumented migrants access to the enjoyment of basic economic, social and cultural rights, including access to health care, education and basic services. Member States should demonstrate their commitment towards improving the rights of migrants by ratifying the International Convention on the Protection of All Migrant Workers and Members of Their Families.[229]

L. Internally-displaced persons

In his first report to the then Commission on Human Rights, submitted on 21 January, 1993, the Special Representative of the Secretary-General on internally displaced persons, Francis Deng, noted that 24 million people, largely women and children, were estimated to be displaced. This had been the figure presented in an analytical report of the Secretary-General on internally displaced persons which had identified six causes of displacement: armed conflict and internal strife, forced relocation, communal violence, natural disasters, ecological disasters, and the systematic violations of human rights. Information reaching him as special representative had confirmed this. Among the serious violations of human rights that occurred were deliberate starvation of the civilian population, forced labour, forcible conscription into governmental or rebel armies, and killings by high-intensity weapons and land mines.[230]

Unfortunately, these problems persist and the current representative on this topic, Walter Kalin, has advised the Human Rights Council that responding to the protection needs of internally displaced persons (IDPs) was one of the main challenges of the world today. Much still remained to be done in order to respond effectively, comprehensively and in a timely manner to the needs of IDPs world-wide.[231]

---

229 A/HRC/4/24, 14 February, 2007, paras.7-9 and 140.

230 E/CN.4/1993/33, 21 January, 1993.

231 A/HRC/4/38, 3 January, 2007, para.82.

M. Trafficking in Persons

The Special Rapporteur on this topic, Ms Sigma Huda, in her first report to the Commission on Human Rights, dated 22 December, 2004, advised the Commission that the majority of victims of trafficking were women and girls trafficked for commercial sexual exploitation. However, significant numbers of human beings were trafficked for labour exploitation and children were also trafficked for the purpose of international adoption. Trafficking, she continued, represented the denial of virtually all human rights.

In recent times, she continued, there had been reports of marketing of women and children via the Internet or in the guise of marriage brokering services and pen pal clubs. There was also trafficking of persons for domestic servitude. Despite its overwhelming human rights dimension, trafficking was often perceived as a 'law and order problem' and was primarily located within the crime prevention framework. In addition to violations suffered at the hands of traffickers, victims often suffered from re-victimization. Victims of cross-border trafficking were criminalized and prosecuted as illegal aliens, undocumented workers, or irregular migrants, rather than as victims of a crime. Women and young girls trafficked into the sex industry were penalized on charges of prostitution instead of receiving assistance. Often, when detained they were denied basic judicial guarantees: they were not informed of their rights and how to exercise them, and they were not given access to lawyers or interpreters. Often, victims of trafficking were not protected against violations of the right not to be returned to a country where they would face serious human rights abuses.[232]

N. Protection of Human Rights While Countering Terrorism

The Special Rapporteur on this topic, Martin Scheinin, has found that terrorist-profiling practices that are based on 'race' are incompatible with human rights. To the extent that States are obliged to rely on counter-terrorism efforts based on profiling, the Special Rapporteur recommended they be based on individual conduct, that is behaviour rather than ethnic or religious characteristics. The Special Rapporteur recommended that States establish clear and strict standards as to what factors law-enforcement agents may or may not employ for their search efforts in the counter-terrorism context. These guidelines should make clear that criteria such as ethnicity, national origin and religion may only be used in very limited circumstances: namely, for *descriptive* profiles or where there is specific intelligence suggesting that someone fulfiling these characteristics is preparing a terrorist act. Furthermore, these standards should make clear that any terrorist-profiling practices that involved interference with

232 E/CN.4/2005/71, 22 December, 2004.

the freedom of movement, the right to liberty or the right to privacy – regardless of the criteria on which they are based – must strictly comply with the principle of proportionality.[233]

O. Freedom of Opinion and Expression

The Special Rapporteur on this topic, A. Ligabo, has found that regrettably, repressive machineries are speedily adapting to new technologies, which are often used as tools for political propaganda and a conduit for racial discrimination and hate speech. Together with a constant trend towards the polarization of ideas and ethnic tension, the systematic oppression of the most active supporters of the free circulation of information and opinions – journalists, trade unionists, social workers, students and teachers, writers and artists – continued to remain an issue of concern throughout the world.

Furthermore, the form and the extent of repression can differ considerably, depending, *inter alia*, on the existence of the rule of law and its implementation in a given society. Unfortunately, the range of violations still included killings, enforced disappearances, arbitrary arrest and detention, mistreatment, threats and harassment, unfair trial, and various types of judicial and administrative measures. More than ever, the safety and security of media professionals remained essential for the progress of freedom of expression.[234]

P. Freedom of Religion or Belief

In recent reports to the Human Rights Council and the UN General Assembly, the current Special Rapporteur on freedom of religion or belief provided a summary of the problems that had been of concern to her mandate over the twenty one years of its existence. These included worrying situations where the freedom to adopt, change or renounce a religion or belief had been infringed, for example when State agents tried to convert, reconvert or prevent the conversion of persons. Many believers belonging to religious communities were not allowed to worship or conduct any religious activities without State approval or prior registration. Women, persons deprived of their liberty, refugees, children, minorities and migrant workers could be identified as particularly vulnerable groups with regard to their freedom of religion of belief. The right to life and the right to liberty were also frequently infringed, as evidenced by numerous cases of killings or arbitrary detention for reasons of religion or belief.[235]

The number and seriousness of mandate-related allegations received by the

233 A/HRC/4/26, 29 January, 2007, para. 86.

234 A/HRC/4/27, 2 January, 2007, paras. 64-65.

235 UN doc. A/62/280, pp. 10 – 11.

Special Rapporteur's predecessor had led him to the conclusion that the protection of freedom of religion or belief and the implementation of the 1981 Declaration on the Elimination of all Forms of Intolerance and Discrimination Based on Religion or Belief were far from being a reality. Governments should redouble their efforts to uphold the provisions in their everyday work and non-governmental organizations may continue to exercise their role as public watchdogs and also inform on national best practices. Numerous differing approaches in various countries could be noted and there still was a huge gap between rhetoric and practice in many instances.[236]

During the period from 1 December 2005 to 30 November, 2006, a total of 64 communications were transmitted to 34 different countries. The communications sent during the period were made up of 27 urgent appeals and 37 allegation letters. 21 of the urgent appeals and 18 of the allegation letters were sent jointly with other special procedures.[237] During the period from 1 July 2006 to 30 June 2007, the Special Rapporteur had sent 53 communications concerning reported cases in 29 countries.[238]

Q. Human Rights Defenders

The Special Representative on human rights defenders, in her first report to the Commission on Human Rights, submitted on 26 January, 2001, expressed deep concern at the considerable number of communications she had already received alleging serious violations targeting human rights defenders throughout the world. In particular, the Special Representative was concerned that a variety of repressive trends, measures and practices persisted which threatened the freedom of action of human rights defenders. No region was free of those trends. The failure of States to offer effective guarantees against the violation of fundamental rights had given a more critical dimension to issues of human security. Disparities in economic, social and political empowerment emphasized the need for groups and individuals who strove to facilitate the exercise of rights by others. It was an unfortunate reality that the role of human rights defenders was not recognized or accepted by Governments in many parts of the world. State apparatus, oppressive laws and other tools of repression continued to be used against defenders in attempts to deter them from the valuable work they contributed to the promotion of human rights.[239]

The Special Representative, reported to the Human Rights Council in 2007 that since the establishment of her mandate, she had sent at least 368 com-

236 A/HRC/4/21, 26 December,2006, para.48.

237 Ibid, paras.8 and 10.

238 A/62/280, p.5.

239 E/CN.4/2001/94, 26 January, 2001.

munications to Governments concerning human rights defenders promoting economic, social and cultural rights. Defenders and their families had been threatened verbally, in writing and through the use of symbolic acts, such as deliveries of funeral wreaths to their families. Defenders had been attacked in demonstrations, meetings, and other kinds of assemblies. Both defenders and members of their families had been physically attacked, kidnapped, tortured and even killed. These violations had allegedly been perpetrated both by the State or its agencies, and non-State entities.[240]

III. FOLLOW-UP

The biggest challenge facing the special procedures' system remains the follow up to its recommendations and communications. This is crucial to guarantee a concrete impact in the protection and promotion of human rights. Ensuring better follow-up to special procedures' recommendations and communications has been identified as a priority by OHCHR, mandate-holders and their partners.

"Follow-up" is generally understood to mean the variety of measures taken to encourage, facilitate and monitor the implementation of recommendations of the special procedures. The special procedures mandate-holders hold dialogues with Governments and other partners on their findings and recommendations. This dialogue may be an effective means of implementing the recommendations of the experts when the Government addresses the concerns raised in a serious manner. The system of special procedures is effective only where there is adequate follow-up to the experts' communications, conclusions and recommendations.

Follow-up may be divided into two types – follow-up to communications and follow-up to missions. Both require certain specific actions on the part of the State(s) concerned, mandate-holders and other relevant actors. The type of follow-up required for these may be distinguished by the need, in the case of communications, to address a particular set of facts allegedly amounting to a violation or likely to result in a violation of human rights which may require the provision of individual remedies and the need, in the case of mission follow-up, to address more systemic causes for violations or situations likely to entail violations of fundamental rights which might involve progressive dialogue, technical cooperation and developmental assistance.[241]

240 A/HRC/4/37, 24 January, 2007, para. 37.

241 For example, after the visit of the Special Rapporteur on Indigenous Peoples to Guatemala and Mexico, a pilot project of technical cooperation was designed jointly by OHCHR Headquarters, indigenous representatives and OHCHR field offices in both countries. The project was designed by indigenous representatives based on suggestions of the

Some mandate-holders have developed a matrix compiling the recommendations contained in their reports, which are routinely transmitted to Government(s) and other partners, requesting them to provide comments and indicate the measures they have taken or intend to take, to implement, even progressively, the recommendations. The responses from Governments are included in the reports submitted to the Commission.

In 2005 and 2006, the Special Procedures Branch (SPB), now the Special Procedures Division (SPD) of the office of High Commissioner for Human Rights strengthened its expertise in analyzing and presenting the work of special procedures by producing and improving a number of tools, which illustrate the work of special procedures in a more friendly manner and pave the way to follow up initiatives.

Quantitative analysis of communications is undertaken on a monthly basis with a bulletin on special procedures communications. The bulletin gives information on the amount of communications, be they joint or individual; the number of individual situations addressed, disaggregated by sex, regions and countries; the mandates involved; the rate of governments' replies; follow up on cases; and further information received from the sources.

The Special Procedures Division (SPD) also provides qualitative analysis on communications in 3 areas: country-based, thematic, and on positive outcomes documented as follow up to communications. Some three dozen country analyses on the main trends emerging from communications had been prepared so far. Country trends on communications are prepared upon request of OHCHR staff, both within and outside SPB, and mandate-holders, and are used as background information to prepare and follow up on country engagement activities of the Office.

Thematic analysis of communications has been prepared on women, children (i.e. how special procedures have been addressing the situation of women and children in their communications), and counter-terrorism.

"Good news stories" on follow-up to communications have been compiled since April 2005. They document positive developments that followed one or more communications of mandate-holders. Information on positive developments may come from different sources, governments' replies, further information submitted by the source, initiatives undertaken by the UN Country Team, media reporting on a human rights situation, and the information provided by rights-holders themselves in their direct contacts with mandate-holders or staff assisting them. The compilation of "good news stories" demonstrates the positive impact of communications in improving the human rights situation of individuals covered by this mechanism.

Special Rapporteur during his official and non-official contacts in both countries.

These information tools are made available regularly to mandate-holders and within OHCHR. A compilation of all country-related recommendations by the special procedures, arranged thematically for each concerned country, was posted on the OHCHR's web site: www.ohchr.org/english/bodies/chr/special/docs/compilation2005.doc).

OHCHR publishes a *Bulletin on special procedures* issued three times a year. It summarizes, in a media-friendly language and format, the Special procedures' main activities. The OHCHR communications database, established in January 2004, allows the retrieval of all existing information on a specific case. This may facilitate better follow-up as cases can be tracked and monitored. There have been more regular meetings and exchange of information between mandate-holders and States and regional groups on an *ad hoc* basis or during the annual meeting of special procedures, the CHR, or mandate-holders' induction sessions. This facilitates dialogue and leads to better cooperation in the follow-up phase.

During the interactive dialogue, Special Rapporteurs may comment on efforts by Governments to implement recommendations and receive on-the-spot updates by the concerned State(s). A number of mandate-holders have included an addendum to the annual report devoted to follow-up to country visits' recommendations. This involves requesting all States visited by the mandate-holder to submit information on measures taken for each recommendation, as well as obstacles encountered. The information is complemented by submissions from non-governmental, UN and other sources. Basic guidelines for submitting information for this report have been developed and disseminated widely. The report simply consists of the list of the Special Rapporteurs recommendations showing for each of them the information received. The guidelines are annexed to the addendum together with a table of document references of all country visit reports and past information on follow-up.[242]

Certain mandate-holders have requested information from both States and NGOs on progress in implementing the recommendations from official visits, and have published a summary of the responses received from Governments and NGOs on the recommendations made. Others have included a new section in their general report on follow-up to country visits undertaken.

CONCLUSION

The work of the special procedures of the Human Rights Council represent, each year, a veritable global report on human rights issues and problems and violations of human rights in different parts of the world. Unfortunately, to

242 See UN Doc. E/CN.4/2005/62/Add.2.

date, the United Nations has not yet succeeded in presenting and communicating the essence of this work as such. This is one of the challenges for the future development of the system. It is an important issue, for at heart are issues of justice for the victims, a topic we discuss in the next chapter.

Chapter IX

REMEDIES

INTRODUCTION

In this chapter we look at the role of special procedures in facilitating or providing remedies to victims. We shall submit that in one instance, that of the Working Group on Arbitrary Detention, it operates as a quasi-judicial body and does serve as a forum of redress. It has earned respect for the work it does. Beyond this, special procedures mandate-holders do endeavour generally to make the case for remedies and reparations for victims and their families and there are numerous instances in their reports where they have called for redress. To begin with, we look at the general principles of remedies based on a United Nations declaration of 2006 on the subject.

I. THE UN BASIC PRINCIPLES AND GUIDELINES

The former Commission on Human Rights adopted, in 2005, after years of study by independent experts and governmental comments, a set of Basic Principles and Guidelines on the right to a remedy and reparation f or victims of gross violations of international human rights law and serious violations of international humanitarian law.[243] The document was subsequently endorsed by the ECOSOC and adopted by the United Nations General Assembly.[244]

The Basic Principles and Guidelines (BPG), as eventually adopted by the General Assembly, underlined that in cases of gross violations of international human rights law and serious violations of international humanitarian law constituting crimes under international law, states have the duty to investigate and, if there is sufficient evidence, the duty to submit to prosecution the person allegedly responsible for the violations and, if found guilty, the duty to punish her or him. Moreover, in these cases, states should, in accordance with international law, cooperate with one another and assist international judicial organs competent in the investigation and prosecution of these violations.

The BPG defines victims as persons who individually or collectively suffered harm, including physical or mental injury, emotional suffering, economic loss or substantial impairment of their fundamental rights, through acts or omissions that constitute gross violations of international human rights law, or

243 Commission resolution 2000/35, adopted by 40 votes to none with 13 abstentions.

244 GA resolution 60/147.

serious violations of international humanitarian law. Where appropriate, and in accordance with domestic law, the term "victim" also includes the immediate family or dependants of the direct victim and persons who have suffered harm in intervening to assist victims in distress or to prevent victimization. A person shall be considered a victim regardless of whether the perpetrator of the violation is identified, apprehended, prosecuted, or convicted and regardless of the familial relationship between the perpetrator and the victim.

The BPG registers that a victim of a gross violation of international human rights law or of a serious violation of international humanitarian law shall have equal access to an effective judicial remedy as provided for under international law. Other remedies available to the victim include access to administrative and other bodies, as well as mechanisms, modalities and proceedings conducted in accordance with domestic law. In addition to individual access to justice, states should endeavour to develop procedures to allow groups of victims to present claims for reparation and to receive reparation, as appropriate. An adequate, effective and prompt remedy for gross violations of international human rights law or serious violations of international humanitarian law should include all available and appropriate international processes in which a person may have legal standing and should be without prejudice to any other domestic remedies.

The BPG stipulates that adequate, effective and prompt reparation is intended to promote justice by redressing gross violations of international human rights law or serious violations of international humanitarian law. Reparation should be proportional to the gravity of the violations and the harm suffered. In accordance with its domestic laws and international legal obligations, a state shall provide reparation to victims for acts or omissions which can be attributed to the state and constitute gross violations of international human rights law or serious violations of international humanitarian law. In cases where a person, a legal person, or other entity is found liable for reparation to a victim, such party should provide reparation to the victim or compensate the state if the state has already provided reparation to the victim.

States should endeavour to establish national programs for reparation and other assistance to victims in the event that the party liable for the harm suffered is unable or unwilling to meet their obligations. States shall, with respect to claims by victims, enforce domestic judgments for reparation against individuals or entities liable for the harm suffered and endeavour to enforce valid foreign legal judgments for reparation in accordance with domestic law and international legal obligations. To that end, states should provide under their domestic laws effective mechanisms for the enforcement of reparation judgments.

In accordance with domestic law and international law, and taking account of individual circumstances, victims of gross violations of international human rights law and serious violations of international humanitarian law should, as appropriate and proportional to the gravity of the violation and the circumstances of each case, be provided with full and effective reparation, as laid out in principles 19 to 23, which include the following forms: restitution, compensation, rehabilitation, satisfaction and guarantees of non-repetition.

Restitution should, whenever possible, restore the victim to the original situation before the gross violations of international human rights law or serious violations of international humanitarian law occurred. Restitution includes, as appropriate: restoration of liberty, enjoyment of human rights, identity, family life and citizenship, return to one's place of residence, restoration of employment and return of property.

Compensation should be provided for any economically assessable damage, as appropriate and proportional to the gravity of the violation and the circumstances of each case, resulting from gross violations of international human rights law and serious violations of international humanitarian law, such as: physical or mental harm; lost opportunities, including employment, education and social benefits; material damages and loss of earnings, including loss of earning potential; moral damage; costs required for legal or expert assistance, medicine and medical services, and psychological and social services.

Rehabilitation should include medical and psychological care as well as legal and social services.

II. THE WORKING GROUP ON ARBITRARY DETENTION

The Working Group on Arbitrary Detention was established by the former Commission on Human Rights in its resolution 1991/42 and entrusted with investigating instances of alleged arbitrary deprivation of liberty, according to the standards set forth in the Universal Declaration of Human Rights and the relevant international instruments accepted by the States concerned. The mandate of the Working Group was clarified and extended by the Commission in resolution 1997/50 to cover the issue of administrative custody of asylum-seekers and immigrants. The mandate was confirmed by Commission resolution 2003/31 and taken forward by the Human Rights Council in its decisions 2/102.

During the sixth session of the Human Rights Council on 25 September 2007, the Council decided to extend the mandate of the Working Group for a further period of three years. In doing so, it recalled the mandate of the Working Group, which were outlined earlier in resolutions 1991/42 and 1997/50 of the Commission on Human Rights:

b) To investigate cases of deprivation of liberty imposed arbitrarily or otherwise inconsistently with the relevant international standards set forth in the Universal Declaration of Human Rights or in the relevant international legal instruments accepted by the States concerned;

c) To seek and receive information from Governments and intergovernmental and non-governmental organizations, and receive information from the individuals concerned, their families or their representatives;
d) To act on information submitted to its attention regarding alleged cases of arbitrary detention by sending urgent appeals and communications to concerned Governments to clarify and to bring to their attention these cases;
e) To conduct field mission upon the invitation of Government, in order to understand better the situations prevailing in countries, as well as the underlying reasons for instances of arbitrary deprivation of liberty; [and]
f) To formulate deliberations on matters of a general nature involving a position of principle in order to develop a consistent set of precedents and assist States, for purposes of prevention, to guard against the practice of arbitrary deprivation of liberty;...[245]

The Working Group consists of five independent experts. It considers deprivation of liberty to be arbitrary if a case falls into one of the following categories:

a) When it is clearly impossible to invoke any legal basis justifying the deprivation of liberty as when a person is kept in detention after the completion of his or her sentence or despite an amnesty law applicable to him or her. (category I)
b) When the deprivation of liberty results from the exercise of the rights or freedom guaranteed by articles 7, 13, 14, 18, 19, 20 and 21 of the Universal Declaration of Human Rights, by articles 12, 18, 19, 21, 22,25, 26 and 27 of the International Covenant on Civil and Political Rights (category II)
c) When the total or partial non-observance of the international norms relating to the right to a fair trial, spelled out in the Universal Declaration of Human Rights and in the relevant international instruments accepted by the States concerned, is of such gravity as to give the deprivation of liberty an arbitrary character (category III).[246]

The Working Group has procedures for dealing with the investigation of

245 UN Doc. A/HRC/6/L.30, 25 September 2007, p 2.: *Promotion and Protection of All Human Rights, Civil, Political, Economic, Social and Cultural Rights, Including the Right to Development, 6/...Arbitrary Detention.*

246 See Human Rights Fact Sheet No 26 published by the Office of High Commissioner for Human Rights, May, 2000: The Working Group on Arbitrary Detention, p. 6

individual cases, a 'deliberations' procedure, an urgent action procedure, and for the conduct of field missions.[247]

A. Individual cases

The Group's involvement is generally triggered by communications sent by the individuals directly concerned, their families, their representatives or non-governmental organizations for the protection of human rights, although it may receive communications from Governments and intergovernmental organizations. The Working Group has prepared a model questionnaire to facilitate the task of those submitting communications. Since 1993 the then Commission on Human Rights authorized the Working Group to take up cases on its own initiative when its attention has been drawn to sufficiently substantiated allegations of arbitrary deprivation of liberty.

According to Fact Sheet No. 26 issued by the Office of High Commissioner for Human Rights, 'the Group attaches great importance to the adversarial character of its procedure'.[248] Communications received are forwarded to the Government concerned with an invitation to submit to the Working Group within 90 days its comments and observations on the case, both as regards the facts and the applicable legislation as well as concerning the progress and outcome of any investigations that mayhave been ordered. If the Government desires an extension of this time it needs to inform the Group of the reasons for this and the Group may decide to grant a further period of up to two months.

A reply sent by the Government is transmitted to the petitioner for comments. If the Government has not submitted a reply the Group may decide on the case without it and on the basis of the information available to it. The Working Group adopts one of the following measures in private session: (i)If the person has been released following the submission of the case to the Working Group, the case is filed. The Group, however, reserves the right to render an opinion whether or or not the deprivation of liberty was arbitrary, notwithstanding the release of the person concerned. (ii) If the group considers that the case is not one of the arbitrary deprivation of liberty, it provides an opinion to this effect. (iii) If the Group considers that further information is required from the Government or the petitioner, it may keep the case pending until the information is received. (iv) If the Group considers that it is unable to obtain sufficient information on the case, it may file the case provisionally or definitively. (v) If the Group decides that the arbitrary nature of the deprivation of liberty has been established, it renders an opinion to that effect and makes recommendations to the Government. The opinion is sent to the Government

247 The description of these procedures is taken from Fact Sheet No. 26, op.cit.

248 Fact Sheet No. 26, supra, p.7.

together with the recommendations. Three weeks after this the opinion is conveyed to the petitioner. The opinions are published in an annex to the annual report of the Working Group to the Human Rights Council.[249]

In the year 2006 the Working Group adopted 47 Opinions concerning 104 cases in 23 countries During the period from 9 November, 2005 to 8 November, 2006, the Working Group transmitted 156 urgent appeals to 58 Governments covering 1,615 individuals (1,394 men, 151 women, and 70 minors). In conformity with paragraphs 22 to 24 of its methods of work, the Working Group, without prejudging whether the detention was arbitrary, drew the attention of each of the Governments concerned to the specific case as reported, and appealed to them to take the necessary measures to ensure that the detained persons' rights to life and physical integrity were respected.[250]

B. The 'Deliberations' procedure

The Working Group has developed a procedure according to which it may formulate 'deliberations' on matters of a general nature involving a position of principle in order to develop a consistent set of procedures and assist States, for purposes of prevention, to guard against the practice of arbitrary detention of liberty. The Group has already adopted various such 'deliberations', specifically in the areas of house arrest and deprivation of freedom for purposes of rehabilitation through labour. By means of these 'deliberations' it defines the criteria on the basis of which deprivations of freedom linked with such situations may become arbitrary.[251]

During the first fifteen years of the exercise of its mandate the Working Group has adopted numerous Opinions on individual cases of detention and has also formulated the following Deliberations and Legal Opinions in order to develop a set of guidelines and support States in their efforts to prevent arbitrary deprivation of liberty:

- Restricted residence or house arrest (Deliberation No.1)
- Rehabilitation through labour (Deliberation No. 4)
- Guarantees concerning detention of immigrants and asylum seekers (Deliberation No. 5)
- Legal Analysis of allegations against the International Criminal Tribunal for the Former Yugoslavia (Deliberation No. 6)
- Issues related to psychiatric detention (Deliberation No. 7)
- Deprivation of liberty linked to/resulting from the use of the Internet

---

249 Ibid, pp. 8-9.

250 Ibid, p.6

251 See Ibid, p. 9

(Deliberation No. 8)[252]

Deliberations Nos. 2 and 3 were adopted in response to specific questions which had been put forward by a Government concerning the Working Group's criteria and methods of work. Furthermore, the Working Group adopted a Legal Opinion on Allegations of detention ordered by the International Criminal Tribunal for Rwanda and on the Deprivation of liberty of persons detained in the naval base of Guantanamo Bay.

The issues analysed over the years in the Working Group's reports included the following:

- Applicability of provisions of conventions on human rights to States that are not party to them
- Interpretation of the term 'detention'
- Excesses of military justice
- Abuses of states of emergency
- Protection of human rights defenders
- Detention prior to extradition and extradition not followed by trial
- Detention of conscientious objectors
- Arrest and detention for dissemination of State secrets
- Protective custody and detention as a means of protecting victims
- Imprisonment related to insolvency
- Failure to take pre-trial detention into account
- Detention motivated by sexual orientation
- Deprivation of liberty of vulnerable persons
- Discrimination in detention
- Impact of inadequate conditions of detention on the right to defence
- Deprivation of liberty as a measure to countering terrorism
- Hostage-taking and arbitrary detention
- Secret prisons
- Over-incarceration.[253]

In a Legal Opinion adopted in 2006 the Working Group concluded that the transfer of detainees without procedural safeguards was in conflict with international law. Governments, it urged, should stop all forms of rendition and return to the legal proceedings of extradition, deportation and expulsion. Furthermore, the practice of diplomatic assurances was acceptable only if the very stringent conditions mentioned in the Legal Opinion were met.

252 See the report of the Working Group on Arbitrary Detention to the Human Rights Council, UN. Doc. A/HRC/4//40, p.4

253 Ibid, p.5

C. Urgent action procedure

The Working Group has developed an urgent action procedure for cases in which there are sufficiently reliable allegations that a person is being detained arbitrarily and that the continuation of the detention may constitute a serious danger to that person's health or life. The urgent action procedure may also be resorted to in other circumstances, when the Working Group deems that the situation warrants such an appeal. In such a case, an urgent appeal is sent, by the most rapid channel of communications, to the Minister for Foreign Affairs of the State concerned, requesting that his Government take appropriate measures to ensure that the detained person's right to life and to physical and mental integrity are respected. In addressing such communications, the Working Group emphasizes that its urgent appeals are of a purely humanitarian character and in no way prejudges the Group's final assessment of whether the deprivation of liberty is arbitrary or not.[254]

D. Field Missions

Visits to countries provide an opportunity for the Working Group, through a direct dialogue with the Government concerned, as well as with representatives of civil society, to understand better the situation prevailing in the country, as well as the underlying reasons for instances of arbitrary deprivation of liberty. During such visits discussions take place with the judicial, penitentiary and other officials, as well as with detainees, thereby enabling the members of the Working Group to understand better the state and the evolution of national legislation from the perspective of international human rights norms, taking into account the social, political and historical context in each country. Such visits take place on the basis of an invitation from the Government. Normally the Working Group does not visit countries in respect of which there is a Special Rapporteur of the Human Rights Council unless the Special Rapporteur requests or agrees to this.[255]

During its first fifteen years the Working Group visited the following twenty one countries: Argentina, Australia, Bahrain, Belarus, Bhutan, Canada, China, Ecuador, Honduras, Indonesia, Iran, Latvia, Mexico, Nepal, Nicaragua, Peru, Romania, South Africa, Turkey, UK, and Vietnam.[256]

Exhaustion of local remedies

In a report to the sixty-second session of the Commission on Human Rights, dated 12 December 2005, the Chairperson of the Working Group on Arbitrary

254 Ibid, p.9.
255 Ibid, p. 10.
256 Ibid, p.6

Detention dealt with the issue of exhaustion of local remedies as follows:

> "The permanent representative of the United States of America, by letter dated 6 September 2005, considered that it was disappointing that the Working Group had issued its Opinion No. 19/2005 (United States of America) despite the fact the matter was under active judicial review and pending appeal in the United States at the time. Under the customary international law doctrine of exhaustion of local remedies, ongoing, available and timely domestic proceedings must be respected and allowed to run their course prior to international adjudication. States should have the opportunity to redress allegations of human rights violations by their own means within the framework of its own domestic legal system. According to the Government, international tribunals and mechanisms were not intended to replace national adjudication. The Working Group concurs with the Government of the United States of America in its restatement of the doctrine in customary international law. It observes, however, that while this principle applies to communications to United Nations treaty bodies, it does not find application in the practice of the Commission's special procedures. On the contrary, as far as the Working Group is concerned, Commission resolution 1997/50 establishes that, as a rule, the Working Group shall deal with cases in which the national judiciary has not yet spoken its final word; paragraph 15 of that resolution "decides to renew … the mandate of the Working Group … entrusted with the task of investigating cases of deprivation of liberty imposed arbitrarily, provided that no final decision has been taken in such cases by domestic courts."… The resolution then proceeds to qualify this principle: the Working Group shall be competent in cases in which the domestic courts have rendered a final decision insofar as that decision is contrary to relevant international standards.
>
> It is thus clear that the Commission on Human Rights never intended the doctrine of exhaustion of domestic remedies to apply to the activity of the Working Group as a criterion for the admissibility of communications. This will not, however, preclude the Working Group from keeping in mind the rationale underlying the doctrine, i.e. that the State where a human rights violation has allegedly occurred should have the opportunity to redress the alleged violation by its own means within the domestic framework. In the spirit of this doctrine, the Working Group often postpones adopting an opinion on a communication when the submissions of the Government and the source credibly suggest that the alleged victim's release might be near.
>
> To sum up, while the doctrine of exhaustion of remedies does not apply as an admissibility criterion in the Working Group's communications proce-

dure, the Working Group does not ignore the idea and concerns underlying it. The case in question, which was matter of Opinion No. 19/2005 (United States of America), was considered during several Working Group sessions, precisely because the Working Group was waiting for the resolution of the appeal by the Court of Atlanta, which, in the end, considered in its resolution arguments similar to those retained by the Working Group.

Finally, the Working Group recalls that the doctrine of exhaustion of domestic remedies cannot be applied to cases it raises with Governments in its urgent appeal procedure, as that procedure is premised on a serious risk to the life or physical integrity of the alleged victim."[257]

III. CALLS FOR REDRESS

In the reports that they submit to the Human Rights Council documenting gross violations of human rights, special procedures mandate holders regularly call on the governments concerned to provide redress for the victims.

CONCLUSION

In the nature of things, special procedures are able to draw attention to problems, strive where they can to head off new problems, and serve as advocates for remedies and justice. In only a few instances are they themselves the providers of remedies. The Working Group on Arbitrary Detention is a distinguished exception to this and has done foundation work in pioneering the development of human rights remedies at the United Nations.

In the final chapter of this work we look at the role of special procedures as advocates for protection.

---

257 UN Doc. E/CN.4/2006/7, 12 December 2005, pp.8-9: Civil and Political Rights, Including the Question of Torture and Detention, Report of the Working Group on Arbitrary Detention, by Leila Zerrougui.

Chapter X

ADVOCACY FOR PROTECTION

INTRODUCTION

Special procedures mandate holders invariably engage in advocacy for the protection of human rights, economic, social and cultural and civil and political. In this chapter we present some glimpses of this advocacy role.

I. AWARENESS RAISING

Special procedures mandate holders consider that awareness raising is an important element in the performance of the tasks of most Special Procedures, but the precise nature of measures taken varies from one mandate to another. All mandate-holders have a web-page on the OHCHR website that provides information about the mandate as well as links to their reports and other relevant documents.[258] Special procedures contribute immeasurably to the development of knowledge about severe human rights violations. The global campaigns of special procedures help raise public consciousness about the need for protective measures. Later in this chapter we give several examples of this process at work.

II. NORMATIVE WORK

As we saw in an earlier chapter, some special procedures mandate holders have helped develop authoritative norms and standards in their areas of work. The Representative of the Secretary-General on internally displaced persons steered the development of the Guiding Principles for the protection of the internally displaced. The Working Group on Arbitrary Detention, in its Deliberation No. 5, adopted in December 1999, established criteria to govern cases of arbitrary detention of asylum seekers.[259]

The normative recommendations of special procedures mandate holders contain numerous suggestions for the development of legal standards nationally, regionally, and internationally. A good example of this is the Special Rapporteur on the right to adequate housing who, in a report submitted to the

258 Manual, para. 79.

259 Questions and Answers, pp. 10-11.

then Commission on Human Rights in 2005[260] called for legislative and regulatory action as follows:

> "*Legislation and regulation:*
>
> National and regional legislation should reflect people's rights to information and participation. These provisions need to be supported with effective implementation;
>
> States should work to provide legal recognition of the collective/community-based property rights of indigenous and other local communities in order to minimize insecurity of land ownership and protect against forced displacement;
>
> Legislation to check the activities and growth of land and housing speculators needs to be brought into effect in order to curtail escalating property prices. This includes the development of legal and regulatory frameworks that place ceilings on both rural and urban land ownership, and political commitment to implement land and agrarian reform programmes designed to redistribute land to the landless;
>
> If not already in place, Governments should develop legislation prohibiting forced evictions and displacement of people. Provisions for adequate and timely rehabilitation must be an integral component of such legislation;
>
> Domestic violence legislation must incorporate women's rights to adequate housing and their right to be free from violent offenders;

III. PLEAS FOR INTERNATIONAL SOLIDARITY

The Human Rights Council's independent expert on this topic has advised the Council that the world has become more globalized and the interaction between international actors is more rapid, so there are new challenges to be faced. The benefits and burdens of this global world are not evenly distributed and, without wishing to say that globalization has a detrimental impact on the world, it does produce some negative effects. The world needs a fairer distribution of the benefits of globalization. Furthermore, globalization has also rendered the interaction between international actors more and more interdependent, and has engendered a more humane approach, including that of upholding the rights of people in the light of human rights.[261]

---

260 UN Doc. E/CN.4/2005/48, 3 March 2005, pp. 19-21: *Report of the Special Rapporteur on Adequate Housing as a Component of the Right to an Adequate Standard of Living.*

261 A/HRC/4/8, 7 February, 2007, para. 47.

IV. EXTREME POVERTY

The Independent Expert of the Human Rights Council has submitted to the Council that the international community must accept the eradication of extreme poverty as a human rights obligation. The definition of poverty will have to be in accordance with the consensus of the different countries concerned. The predominant consideration would be to choose a small section of the population which was clearly and demonstrably most vulnerable to suffering from all forms of deprivation. Since poverty was defined as the sum total of income poverty, human development poverty and social exclusion, extreme poverty would be regarded as an extreme form of that poverty. That form could be most conveniently defined as an intersection of all three types of poverty. In some countries however, especially those which were relatively developed and might not have the severe problem of either income poverty or human development poverty, the group suffering from social exclusion might dominate the set of extremely poor people, supplemented by conditions of income and human development poverty to the extent that they existed. The idea was to identify as extremely poor any group whose number was limited so that the society did not find it unmanageable to deal with their problems. Once such a group was identified, the removal of their conditions of extreme poverty must be taken as an obligation corresponding to the fulfilment of human rights norms. Even if the countries concerned might not be able to ensure the realization of all human rights, those rights the denial of which had directly caused extreme poverty, should be subject to immediate fulfilment. The international community and all member States should thus take up the obligations for removing extreme poverty as a core element of their human rights obligations.[262]

V. THE RIGHT TO FOOD

The Human Rights Council's Special Rapporteur on the Right to Food has warned that the eradication of hunger and violations of the human right to food was the most urgent priority facing Governments today. In a world richer than ever before, it was unacceptable to allow children, women and men to suffer from hunger and famine. Hunger and people's lack of access to sufficient productive resources to be able to feed themselves would continue to create conflicts and force children out of school into forced labour, including recruitment into armed forces. Hunger would also continue to force people to flee their own countries. The answer was not a criminalization of those who suffered from hunger. The answer was to take immediate action to respect, protect

262 Human Rights and Extreme Poverty. Report of the independent expert, Arjun Sengupta, UN document E/CN.4/2006/43, 2 March, 2006, p. 20.

and fulfil the right of every human being.[263]

Without adequate food and nutrition during their first five years, children suffered from physical stunting and limited intellectual development, condemning them to early death or a marginal existence for the rest of their lives. Without respect for their right to food, children became involved in forced labour to help feed themselves and their families, including recruitment as child soldiers. Thousands of children made decisions to enlist in armed groups as a result of hunger, malnutrition and food insecurity, yet this was rarely discussed. Children's right to food must be the priority in efforts to combat hunger and guarantee peace.[264]

This was a superb example of advocacy for protection. The Special Rapporteur continued his efforts in the report dated 16 March 2006, submitted to the then Commission on Human Rights. The Special Rapporteur emphasized that the right to food was a human right that entailed Governments' obligations to guarantee the food security of their populations. In a world richer than ever before, he noted, it was unacceptable that people can be left to die of starvation. Nor should anyone be condemned to the misery of stunted mental and physical development that resulted from chronic hunger and malnutrition. All human beings had a right to live in dignity, free from hunger.

All Governments, the Special Rapporteur continued, had a responsibility to prevent starvation and hunger. The primary responsibility always rested with national Governments. However, all other Governments had a responsibility to refrain from taking action that caused food insecurity and to respond to requests for emergency assistance, to the extent that their resources permitted. In a context of globalization, when national Governments no longer enjoyed a full monopoly on power, it was also essential to extend human rights obligations to other powerful actors, such as international organizations and private transnational corporations.[265]

Although the primary responsibility to ensure human rights always rested with the national Government, he continued, it was not always able to protect its citizens from the impact of decisions taken in other countries, given the current context of globalization and strong international interdependence. All countries should therefore ensure that their policies did not contribute to human rights violations in other countries.[266]

263 A/HRC/4/30, 19 January, 2007, para. 68. Jean Ziegler, Special Rapporteur.

264 Ibid, Summary, p. 2.

265 UN document E/CN.4/2006/44, 16 March, 2006, paras. 17-18.

266 Ibid, para. 28.

VI . THE RIGHT TO HEALTH

The Human Rights Council's Special Rapporteur on the Right to Health has advanced the position that the right to the highest attainable standard of health should be understood as a right to an effective and integrated health system, encompassing health care and the underlying determinants of health, which is responsive to national and local priorities, and accessible to all. More specifically, however, when looking at a health system from the right-to-health perspective, what are the key components that need to be present? For example, from a human rights perspective a health system would have to include an adequate system for the collection of health data; otherwise it will be impossible for the State, or any other interested party, to monitor the progressive realization of the right to health. Moreover, the data must be disaggregated on certain grounds, such as sex, age and urban/rural, otherwise it will be impossible to monitor the progressive realization of the right to health in relation to vulnerable populations, such as women, children and those living in remote rural communities.[267]

In a report submitted to the Commission on Human Rights on 3 March 2006, Paul Hunt, Special Rapporteur on the right of everyone to the enjoyment of the highest attainable standard of physical and mental health, called on the international community to rally around the right to health, which he spelled out as follows:

The right to health could be understood as a right to an effective and integrated health system, encompassing health care and the underlying determinants of health, which was responsive to national and local priorities, and accessible to all. The health system must encompass both health care and the underlying determinants of health, such as adequate sanitation, safe drinking water and health education.

It must be accessible to all, not just the wealthy, but also those living in poverty; not just majority ethnic groups, but minorities and indigenous peoples, too; not just those living in urban areas, but also remote villagers; not just men, but also women. The health system had to be accessible to all disadvantaged individuals and communities.

Further, it must also be responsive to both national and local priorities. Properly trained community health workers such as village health teams knew their communities' health priorities. Also, inclusive participation could help ensure that the health system was responsive to the particular health needs of women, children, adolescents, the elderly and other disadvantaged groups. Inclusive, informed and active community participation was a vital element of the right to health.

267 A/HRC/4/28, 17 January, 2007, para. 91. Paul Hunt, Special Rapporteur.

The health system must also be effective and integrated; it should be more than a bundle of loosely coordinated vertical interventions for different diseases. A health system could not simply be understood in terms of an individual's access to doctors, medicines, safe drinking water and adequate sanitation. The social and economic conditions of the population served by a health system had a dramatic impact upon the population's health. Known as the social determinants of health, these were conditions, such as poverty and unemployment, which might make people ill in the first place. When the Special Rapporteur talked about the underlying determinants of health, he was referring not only to determinants such as safe drinking water and adequate sanitation, but also to the social determinants of health. Those determinants were at the time the focus of the WHO Commission on Social Determinants of Health.

Fundamentally, this was what the right to health was all about: an effective, integrated, responsive health system, encompassing health care and the underlying determinants of health, accessible to all. [268]

VII. RIGHT TO EDUCATION

The first Special Rapporteur on the Right to Education, Katarina Tomasevski approached the implementation of governments' obligations in respect of the right to education through the perspectives of availability, accessibility, acceptability, and adaptability. As to availability, she considered that the obligation of the State to make schooling available constituted a pillar of the individual right to education, and the failure of the State to sustain available schooling constituted an apparent violation of the right to education. She noted that the African Commission on Human and Peoples' Rights had found that a two-year long closure of universities and secondary schools in the then Zaire constituted a violation of article 17 of the African Charter on Human and Peoples' Rights, which guaranteed the right to education.[269]

As to accessibility, she noted that where schools and teachers were available, access to schooling could be impeded by a variety obstacles, such as the payment of school fees. She noted in this regard that the international human rights treaties required primary education to be compulsory and free of charge. The requirement upon Governments to make primary education free implied, in her view, that Governments should eliminate financial obstacles in order to enable all children – no matter how poor- to complete primary schooling. [270]

On the issue of acceptability the Special Rapporteur gave particular atten-

268 E/CN.4/2006/48, 3 March 2006, p.5 : *Report of the Special Rapporteur on the Right of Everyone to the Engjoyment of teh Highest Attainable Standard of Physical and Mental Health.*

269 UN document E/CN.4/2000/6, 1 February, 2000, p. 13.

270 Ibid, p. 16.

tion to girls' access to school and their continuation in schools. She studied issues such as pregnancy, which often led to the expulsion of pregnant girls from school, thereby excluding them from continuing education. She noted that the views of parents, teachers and community leaders tended to support the expulsion of pregnant girls from school. However, she pointed to a decision of the Supreme Court of Colombia, which had established an important precedent by demanding that school regulations which provided for the penalization of pregnancy by suspending pregnant girls from schooling and rerouting them into tutorials be altered and the pregnant girls to whom they were applied should be returned to normal schooling.[271]

On adaptability, the Special Rapporteur studied linkages between schooling and working. She advocated international standards in support of a minimum age before children could legally work. Where children were required to work, educational opportunities should still be available to them: 'learn and earn'. She noted that the Supreme Court of India had accepted the 'learn and earn' approach for non-hazardous employment of children below the age of fourteen years, mandating a reduction of working hours to six, coupled with at least two hours of education at the expense of the employer. For hazardous work, the Court had recalled that child labour could not be eliminated without tackling underlying poverty and suggested ensuring work for an adult member of the family in lieu of the child or, if this was impossible within the limits of the economic capacity of the State, the provision of a minimum income to the family in order to enable them to send the child to school payable as long as the child was attending school.[272]

VIII. ADEQUATE HOUSING

In a report submitted to the Commission on Human Rights on 3 March 2005[273] Miloon Kothari, Special Rapporteur on the right to adequate housing as a component of the right to an adequate standard of living, called upon the international community to rally around the right to adequate housing. Responses to the causes and consequences of homelessness needed, he pointed out, to draw upon key principles of international human rights law and practice: indivisibility of rights, gender equality and non-discrimination. The right to adequate housing had to be recognized as linked to and congruent with the right to security of the person, the right to security of the home, the right to participation, the right to privacy, the right to freedom of movement, the right

271 Ibid, p. 21.

272 Ibid, p. 22.

273 UN Doc. E/CN.4/2005/48, 3 March 2005, pp. 19-21: *Report of the Special Rapporteur on Adequate Housing as a Component of the Right to an Adequate Standard of Living.*

to information, the right to be free from inhumane and degrading treatment, and the right not to be arbitrarily detained.

He continued that the widespread discrimination that women faced in all aspects of housing, land and property matters, including homelessness in the context of domestic violence, called for the specific recognition of women's right to adequate housing and their rights to security of home and person. Gender-sensitive housing policies and legislation needed also to take into account that some groups of women were even more vulnerable to homelessness and other housing rights violations – victims of domestic violence, widows, women-headed households, women victims of forced evictions and indigenous women.

The principle of non-discrimination, he emphasized, must guide all aspects of programme design and implementation in a range of policy areas connected to the right to adequate housing. Worldwide, individuals and communities were facing discrimination in terms of access to essential civic services such as transportation, which in turn affected the ability to access employment, education, health services and child care. Such occurrences of discrimination drove physical and social segregation and 'ghettoization'. When members of identifiable groups, including women and minority populations, faced barriers to the enjoyment of the right to adequate housing and other rights, international human rights law required the development and implementation of positive measures to overcome such barriers. Governments must turn their attention to the needs of vulnerable populations as a matter of urgency as part of their development of effective and comprehensive responses to homelessness.

The state of sheer homelessness in the world today, along with the immense crisis faced by millions living in inadequate and insecure housing and living conditions, called, he continued, for the combination of a humanitarian and a human rights approach. With these and the foregoing considerations in mind, the Special Rapporteur recommended the legislative measures cited at the beginning of this chapter and made the following recommendations:

Programme design and financing:

Strong social housing programmes are required in both rural and urban areas. Governments are encouraged to explore the range of policy options available to them in financing these initiatives, including the reallocation of existing budgetary resources as well as negotiated cuts in external debt financing;

State health programmes must take into account the special housing needs of disadvantaged groups, including people living with mental and other disabilities;

State-run shelters, in particular for women and children, should be set up close to sources of livelihood in urban centres, with the aim of reintegrating people into the community;

Government are encouraged to collaborate with development agencies and donors to create integrated rural development strategies, including schemes for employment generation in rural areas to minimize forced migration to cities;

The Special Rapporteur recommends that Governments work more closely with NGOs and local communities in developing city master plans and urban development schemes and projects. The special concerns of women and their housing needs must be reflected in master plans for urban and rural development;

Enforcement, protection and monitoring:

i. State-sponsored violence and police brutality against the homeless must be urgently checked and those responsible for offences must be brought to justice;
ii. Laws criminalizing homelessness need to be repealed and replaced with laws and policies that recognize the right to adequate housing for the homeless.[274]

The Special Rapporteur has pointed out that the need for the elaboration of an operational framework for the realization of the right to adequate housing, including indicators and methods of monitoring, has become more pertinent with the emergence of the Millennium Development Goals (MDGs). Developing rights-based indicators and monitoring tools could contribute to more effective implementation of the MDGs and the realization of relevant human rights.[275]

IX. THE EFFECT OF ECONOMIC REFORM POLICIES AND FOREIGN DEBT

The Special Rapporteur of the Human Rights Council on this topic has pointed out that World Bank statistics indicated that the overall debt stock of low-income countries currently stands at about US $426 billion. The annual debt service arising from this stock was estimated at US $32.6 billion. The debt stock figures were considerably higher for middle-income countries that have accumulated a debt stock of about US $2.3 trillion and annual debt service obligations of US$ 415 billion.[276]

274 UN Doc. E/CN.4/2005/48, 3 March 2005, pp. 19-21: *Report of the Special Rapporteur on Adequate Housing as a Component of the Right to an Adequate Standard of Living.*

275 A/HRC/4/18, 5 February, 2007, para.3.

276 A/HRC/4/10, 3 January, 2007, para.8.

Trade reform, he continued, could be a powerful tool for improving availability and access to goods and services essential to the realization of basic human rights. In order to fulfil this function, trade liberalization must be based on sound economic and social impact assessments, allowing for a careful design and scheduling of reform steps. Adequate transition periods with temporary or permanent exclusion of strategic products or sub sectors from liberalization should be defined with a view to maximizing human rights and development benefits. Human rights-inspired safeguard clauses in trade agreements should also be considered. Trade liberalization in poor developing countries should not be conducted without putting in place adequate safety nets for the most vulnerable population. It should always be combined with measures to improve the productive capacity of such country's economy and to strengthen its competitiveness on the global market. This required not only an adequate policy by the concerned countries but also improved donor aid in all trade related areas.[277]

CONCLUSION

Advocacy for protection is one of the great roles of the special procedures mandate-holders of the Human Rights Council, as we have seen in this chapter. It shows the special procedures calling the world to conscience and to action to vindicate the basic human rights proclaimed in the Universal Declaration of Human Rights of 1948.

277 Ibid, para. 76.

CONCLUSION

At the end of this examination of the different facets of the protection roles of UN human rights special procedures the question arises how might one assess what the special procedures are doing for the protection of human rights?

The first point that may be made is that the special procedures are providing a historical record of the violations of our times. Some 40 special procedures produce on average two reports per year amounting cumulatively to some 3000 pages annually on different aspects of the state of human rights in the world. Where they document violations of human rights in particular countries the materials and the evidence they have gathered and published is available for future generations to call to justice the violators of today.

We have seen this before. Fact finding into human rights violations in Chile and Argentina in the 1970s and the 1980s would be used in criminal prosecutions of violators in those countries. Likewise materials gathered at the United Nations in the late 1970s on violations of human rights by the Pol Pot regime in Cambodia is now available to be used in the Special Cambodian Court established to try the leaders of the Pol Pot regime. True enough, to those who have died from gross violations of human rights documentation for history and subsequent trials long after they are dead is of little use to them, but at least their families and their relatives will have some comfort from the fact that justice has been rendered to their violators.

Second, the urgent action mechanisms of the special procedures do save lives on occasions. The numbers involved may not be spectacular but if the procedures help spare a single life they are worthwhile. It is estimated that in 2007 some 1000 urgent action initiatives were undertaken by the special procedures. This is indeed a drop in the ocean but it is meaningful nevertheless.

Third, mobilization initiatives by the special procedures on particular situations or issues can have a mitigating effect. The Special Rapporteur against racism, for example, has drawn attention to the rise of racist platforms of political parties in a number of countries. By placing the spotlight on an issue such as this the Special Rapporteur is hopefully spurring on corrective and preventive actions.

Fourth, the visits that special procedure mandate holders make to countries can help in the attenuation of violations. Governments are put on notice that the international community is watching and the dialogue with governments can help them deal with problems whose existence or dimensions they might not have been aware of.

Fifth, to the extent that special procedure mandate holders come up with policies and normative recommendations that are acted upon they help to bring about an environment that is more conducive to protection.

Sixth, special procedure mandate holders help identify undetected or emerging problems requiring attention on the part of the international community. The work of the special procedures on the rights of indigenous populations and on minorities are examples of this.

The foregoing positive contributions of special procedures needs to be balanced with an assessment of the difficulties that are being encountered by the mandate holders. Addressing the Human Rights Council on 19 September 2006, the Special Rapporteur on extrajudicial, summary or arbitrary executions identified a number of "key challenges" affecting the special procedure system as he saw them. First, he considered that the system of country visits was close to crisis. Requests for an invitation to visit were all too seldom granted. Second, the rate of meaningful responses to communications was "far too low". For the previous two years, it had been around 50 per cent, which meant that every second communication sent was basically ignored. Third, recommendations had not been adequately reflected in the work of the former Commission on Human Rights. The Human Rights Council therefore needed to ensure that effective action was taken on the flow of recommendations directed to it. Fourth, "effective follow-up to reports has too often been absent. It is indispensable if the system is to be meaningful and productive. Outreach and constructive engagement in public debate should be a crucial part of the role of the Special Procedures."[278]

The Special Rapporteur on freedom of religion or belief, Ms Asma Jahangir, in her report to the General Assembly on 20 August, 2007, informed the Assembly that since the beginning of the mandate in 1986, the Special Rapporteur had sent a total of 1,085 communications, which came to about one letter of allegation or urgent appeal every week. However, the response rate needed to improve. Out of a total of 130 countries which had received communications from the mandate since the inception of the communication procedure, 20 countries had not replied. Throughout the years, the response rates had fluctuated significantly. She provided a chart of these fluctuations.[279]

Having regard to these difficulties how might one assess the contribution of the special procedures to protection on a scale of one to ten? On preventive protection perhaps it would be fair to say two, represented by the urgent action mechanisms and by the deterrent effect of the work of the special procedures cumulatively. On mitigatory protection, perhaps one might say three out of

278 Philip Alston, Special Rapporteur on Extrajudicial, Summary or Arbitrary Executions, Statement to the Human Rights Council, 19 September 2006.

279 UN doc. A/52/280, p.5.

ten, due to the fact-finding, publication of reports, visits on the spot and public statements. On remedial protection one might say one out of ten because the work of the special procedures to date has seen little follow up in dealing with the perpetrators of gross violations of human rights.

Special procedures strive for protection. For that, the international community owes them a huge debt of gratitude. They give of their time generously without recompense and they bring great heart to their work. They are often unjustly vilified. But they persist nevertheless, often in the face of many adversities, give voice to the victims, engage in the diplomacy of human rights protection, and provide a historical record of today's violations of human rights for the justice tribunals of tomorrow.

At the end of this book we may ask whether there is any major gap in protection not covered by a Special Rapporteur. We think there is: the area of democracy and human rights. In so many instances, gross violations of human rights are the direct result of unrepresentative or oppressive governments. The designation of a Special Rapporteur for the promotion and protection of democracy would help place the spotlight on tyrants for whom the will of the people is not the basis of the authority of governments. We end this book with a call for the designation of a rapporteur in this area of fundamental importance.

BIBLIOGRAPHY

BOOKS AND ARTICLES

Bossuyt, M, The Development of Special Procedures of the United Nations Commission of Human Rights. 6 Human Rights Law Journal, No. 2 – 4, 1985, pp. 179-210.

De Frouville, Orville, *Les Procédures thématiques: Une Contribution efficace des Nations Unies à la protection des droits de l'homme* (Paris, Pedone, 1996)

Gutter, Jeroen, Thematic Procedures of the United Nations Commission on Human Rights and International Law: In Search of a Sense of Community. 2006, Intersentia, Antwerp and Oxford.

Kamminga, M., The Thematic Procedures of the UN Commission on Human Rights, XXXIV Netherlands International Law Review 1987, pp. 299-323.

Kooijmans, Peter H. "The Role and Action of the UN Special Rapporteur on Torture," in A. Cassesse, Antonio (ed.). *The International Fight Against Torture.* Publications of the European University Institute. Baden-Baden: Nomos Verlagsgesellschaft, 1991.

Lempinen, M, Challenges Facing the System of Special procedures of the United Nations Commission on Human Rights. Turku/Abo: Institute for Human Rights, Abo Akademi University, 2001.

Nifosi, Ingrid. The UN Special Procedures in the Field of Human Rights. Antwerp: Intersentia, 2005.

Ramcharan, B.G. (Ed.), The International Law and Practice of Fact-Finding in the Field of Human Rights. Martinus Nijhoff, 19..

Rodley, Nigel S. "United Nations Action Procedures against Disappearances, Summary or Arbitrary Executions and Torture," *Human Rights Quarterly* 8, no. 4 (Nov., 1986): 700-730.

Rodley, Nigel S. and David Weissbrodt. "United Nations Non-Treaty Procedures for Dealing with Human Rights Violations," in Hannum,

Hurst (ed.). *Guide to International Human Rights Practice,* 3rd ed. Ardsley NY : Transnational publ., 1999.

Rodley, Nigel S. "United Nations Human Rights Treaty Bodies and Special Procedures of the Commission on Human Rights – Complementarity or Competition?" *Human Rights Quarterly* 25, no. 4 (2003): 882-908.

Tomasevski, K. Responding to Human Rights Violations, 1946-1999. Martinus Nijhoff, 2000.

Weiner, Michael, "The Mandate of the Special Rapporteur on Freedom of Religion or Belief – International, Procedural and Substantive Legal Issues", II Religion and Human Rights, 2007, pp. 3-17.

Weissbrodt, David. "The Three 'Theme' Special Rapporteurs of the UN Commission on Human Rights," *The American Journal of International Law* 80, no. 3 (Jul. 1986): 685-689.

ON LINE SOURCES AND WEBSITES

Amnesty International, www.amnesty.org.

Human Rights Watch, www.hrw.org

United Nations High Commissioner on Human Rights, www.ohchr.org.

World Organization against Torture (OMCT), www.omct.org.

INDEX

D

E

www.ingramcontent.com/pod-product-compliance
Lightning Source LLC
Chambersburg PA
CBHW061209240926
51846CB00006B/1158